Adrian Searle is a native of the Isle of Wight and a member of a long-established Island family. He was born in Ryde, where he currently lives, and has worked as a journalist and writer for more than thirty years. Passionate about the Island, and the maintenance of it's distinctive 'offshore' character, he has written extensively on the rich, colourful Wight heritage in newspapers, magazines and books. He has also published, with the Dovecote Press, *Isle of Wight Folklore*.

'one of the most exciting local interest books out this year'
Isle of Wight County Press

'...will bring back a mindful of memories to those who lived through the war on the Isle of Wight, yet its accuracy and 140 illustrations make it a necessary read for those who didn't.'
Isle of Wight Weekly Post

Frontispiece
The 6th Battalion, The Black Watch, training on the Island in the summer of 1940

ISLE OF WIGHT
AT WAR
1939 – 1945

Adrian Searle

THE DOVECOTE PRESS

This book is dedicated to all the people of the Isle of Wight - men, women and children - who lost their lives during the Second World War.

This new paperback edition first published in 2000
First published in 1989 by The Dovecote Press Ltd
Stanbridge, Wimborne, Dorset BH21 4JD

ISBN 1 874336 73 3

© Adrian Searle 1989, 2000

Photoset in Palatino by Robert Antony Ltd, Ringwood, Hampshire
Origination by Aero Offset Ltd, Bournemouth, Dorset
Printed and bound by Biddles Ltd, Guildford and King's Lynn

3 5 7 9 8 6 4 2

Contents

Foreword

BY CAPTAIN THE LORD MOTTISTONE, CBE, ROYAL NAVY

This is, indeed, a splendid detailed account of the "Isle of Wight at War" in the second of the two World Wars in this century. Though I spent most of that war at sea escorting Atlantic convoys, I happened to be on leave at Mottistone throughout August 1940 and witnessed from the ground, in lovely clear weather, many of the dog fights that were part of the Battle of Britain, when, as we now know, the Island was probably most under threat from the enemy.

The Isle of Wight has always been a potential invasion target for enemies based in France. Indeed, in the Middle Ages, French forces sometimes made landings, albeit only briefly successful. However, it was not till the Second World War that the war and the possibility of death from armed conflict threatened all the Island's inhabitants. This account records in faithful detail the effect of total war on the Island community and brings to life the cheerful attitude and sense of dogged common purpose to resist a detested aggressor, which pervaded all those involved. It also shows the detail of organisation, which was so skilfully developed before and during the war, to harness the efforts of the whole community to tackle a variety of threats, many of which happily did not occur.

To add a couple of family footnotes. On Sunday 11th August 1940, I helped my father, the first Lord Mottistone, then Lord Lieutenant of Hampshire and the Isle of Wight, to succour Squadron Leader Peel, when he crashed 300 yards south of Mottistone Manor as recorded in the text of Chapter 3. When we had freed him from his aircraft and were plying him with a Sunday forenoon drink, he revealed that he was due to make a broadcast that afternoon, at the behest of Lord Beaverbrook (then the Minister for Information) to tell the country how well the air battle was going! Transport communications to London from Mottistone in 1940 were much as they are now and certainly not as fast as a Hurricane fighter, so Lord Beaverbrook to his chagrin had to be told personally by my father that his star RAF broadcaster would not be able to keep his assignment that day! On a more serious note, at the end of the War, the Island beaches were heavily encumbered with a mixture of defences. The Isle of Wight County Council were aware that these must be removed as soon as practicable if the Island's tourist trade was to be resuscitated and the peacetime economy reactivated. They were, however, having much difficulty with the Army, who were pleading other more pressing duties than clearing Isle of Wight beaches. Mr. Baines, the Clerk to the County Council, then appealed to my father, as the Lord Lieutenant. The result was magical. Administrative objections disappeared and the beach defences were removed in record time. Perhaps it helped that earlier in life the first Lord Mottistone had been both a Secretary of State for War and a General in the field in World War I!

In conclusion, I should like to congratulate Mr. Adrian Searle and his publisher for creating such a splendid wartime account of a small self-contained civilian and military community in the "front line" of our Island nation. I trust that it will find many readers.

MOTTISTONE
Lord Lieutenant of the Isle of Wight
October 1989

Introduction

That the Isle of Wight would have a good story to tell of the Second World War was never in doubt. Its geographical location and the strategic potential it offered both sides in the conflict was sufficient guarantee of that — as were the oft-repeated tales of wartime incident and drama on Britain's 'front line' island.

Many Islanders recall, or have had described to them, the action-packed, tension-filled Battle of Britain summer of 1940: the dogfights in the sky . . . the dive-bombing attacks on Ventnor . . . the Messerschmitt which ended its days down a long-lost Island well. Most will know of the constant air raid alerts and the attacks which sometimes followed — particularly the devastating 1942 blitz on Cowes — and few will not be aware, either through first-hand experience or from the graphic accounts of others, of the incredible build-up of shipping in Spithead and the Solent prior to the D-Day invasion in 1944. That the Island contributed significantly to the nation's wartime production of ships and planes is also widely appreciated.

The 50th anniversary year of the outbreak of hostilities in 1939 seemed the appropriate occasion to attempt, for the first time, a comprehensive account of the Isle of Wight's war. Within a short period from beginning work on the book, it became apparent just how good a potential story this was. It quickly became clear that the Island had been affected by just about every aspect of the Second World War.

It had provided an early, if somewhat questionable, place of refuge for evacuated mainland children; served as a vital link in the nation's coastal radar defences against the Luftwaffe (and housed secret installations which hardly anyone knew anything about); been a temporary home to men of some of the most famous infantry regiments in the British Army; and trained countless soldiers (and men of the

fledgling commando units) for both the ill-fated assault on Dieppe in 1942 and the triumphant return of the Allied armies to occupied Europe in 1944. Had the Germans invaded the Island (a plan very much in Hitler's mind at one stage), they would have encountered opposition from a fully trained band of resistance fighters — drawn mostly from the Island's farming community.

The war tested the resolve of Islanders to the full. While they escaped the awesome destruction brought about by the raids on mainland cities such as Portsmouth and Southampton, just the other side of the Solent, the relatively small population of the Isle of Wight suffered considerably at the hands of the Luftwaffe, who gave them hardly a moment's peace before the tables turned in favour of the Allies. Even after D-Day, Islanders were exposed to a renewed threat from the sky — in the shape of Hitler's V1 flying bombs.

While several aspects of the Island's eventful war have been documented (notably by A.J. 'Jock' Leal, whose exhaustive research on the air war has proved invaluable, and in the scholarly works on Island defences by members of The Redoubt Consultancy), it is, perhaps, surprising that no previous attempt has been made to tie all angles of the Island's eventful war together within the pages of a single book. In *Isle of Wight at War 1939-1945* I have endeavoured to do just that. I hope the reader will conclude that, despite the necessary sifting of the mass of information received, nothing of material significance has been omitted. I believe that much of the information contained in the book has never been previously published — that certainly applies to a great many of the illustrations.

The Second World War was very much the people's war. Life on the Home Front was, at times, every bit as hazardous as that on the battlefields. This was certainly true of the Isle of

Wight, and, wherever possible, I have tried to convey — often through their own words, and with frequent reference to the wartime diaries kept by Islanders Mary Watson and Fred Kerridge — the true feelings and emotions of those who lived through those never-to-be-forgotten six years. The humour, comradeship and resiliance — the essential qualties that kept them smiling through — are all there.

ADRIAN SEARLE
St Helens, 1989

Acknowledgements

Overwhelming is the only word to describe the response of Islanders — past and present — when I set out to establish for the first time a comprehensive account of the Isle of Wight's war between 1939 and 1945. So many people offered information, help, encouragement and advice. Their contributions, large and small, were sincerely appreciated — as was the generous hospitality extended to me when I visited their homes.

I hope none of them will feel offended if I single out a few people for special mention. Firstly, this book would have been much the poorer without the considerable help offered, and subsequently given, by Island historian Roy Brinton, curator of the museum at Carisbrooke Castle, who made available a substantial amount of wartime material, and permitted the use of many fine photographs in the ownership of the museum's trustees. These are individually credited (CCM) in the book.

Special thanks go to Robin Freeman (Managing Director), Peter Hurst (Editor) and the staff at the *Isle of Wight County Press* — particularly Caroline Butt — for their invaluable help and co-operation during my research for the book. I am grateful, too, for the assistance given by the Editors of *The News* (Portsmouth) and the *Southern Evening Echo* in publicising my appeal for information — and for the help extended in the same context by the late Reg Orlandini. Editor of *The Islander* magazine.

I acknowledge the co-operation of the publishers of *Battle in the Skies over the Isle of Wight* (IW County Press), *Dunkirk* (Faber & Faber), *War on the Line* (Middleton Press), *Uffa Fox: A Personal Biography* (Angus & Robertson), and *Portsmouth at War* (Portsmouth WEA Local History Group) for permitting me to quote extracts from their books, and the Editor of *Fly Past* magazine, for the same reason.

Many hours of research were spent in the Isle of Wight County Record Office at Newport — mostly with the wartime log books of the Island's ARP organisation, an invaluable aid — and I am indebted to the staff there (particularly Jim O'Donnell) for their guidance. Illustrations from the County Council's collection appearing in the book are individually credited (IWCC).

The help of staff at Tangmere's Military Aviation Museum, the RAF Museum in Hendon and the Imperial War Museum is gratefully acknowledged. The several photographs from the Imperial War Museum archives reproduced in the book are credited (IWM).

Some of the most enjoyable hours of research were spent in the company of that grand old man of Ryde, Ernie Jolliffe, Ryde's Deputy ARP Officer in the war. Sadly, as the production of this book reached its final stages, I read in the *County Press* of Ernie's death. I feel privileged to have been given the opportunity of hearing at first hand his colourful recollections of the war years. Ernie Jolliffe was a true *character* to the end.

I am indebted to both my son, Matthew, for

9

his help in locating surviving wartime relics on the Island, and my late father, Rodney, for his diligent pursuit of the split-infinitives, and other grammatical gremlins, in the draft manuscript, before his own untimely death a month before publication. His deep knowledge, and impeccable use, of the English language, a constant source of inspiration to me, will, I am sure, enhance the reader's enjoyment of the book.

Incidentally, lest the reader should think there is an over-preponderence of my relatives in the pages of this book, the only one of the Searles mentioned with a family connection is Joan, my mother. It was a great pleasure meeting for the first time Geoff and Noreen Searle, of Bembridge, both of whom have made important contributions.

My thanks go to them, and to all the many other people, from both sides of the Solent, who have contributed their wartime memories and anecdotes (by letter, on tape or verbally), allowed me to inspect, or offered the loan of, valuable photographs, documents and other memorabilia, or simply pointed me in the right direction. In alphabetical order, they are: Colonel The Hon W.D. Arbuthnott MBE, Secretary, Black Watch Association; Mr Gary Batchelor, Managing Director, Southern Vectis Bus Company (and Mr Martin Mullins); Mrs Kathleen Blayney, of East Cowes; Mr Frank Botham, of Binstead; Mrs Vera Brown, of Cowes; Mr Roger Bunney, of Romsey; Mr Eddie Cooke, of Binstead; Mr and Mrs D. Corney, of Ryde; Mr Jimmy Croft, of Eastbourne; Mr Reg Davies, of Newport; Mrs D. Dwyer, of Cowes; Mrs Mabel Emms, of Brentwood; Mr Ted Findon, of Sandown; Mr John Fisher, of East Cowes; Leslie and Eileen Foss, of Chale Green; Mr John Gibson, of Cowes; Mrs E. Harvey, of Ryde; Mr Jack Harvey, of Newport; Mr T.R. Hiett, of Southampton; Mr Charles Holbrook, of Atherfield Green; Mr Ron Holland, of Upton; Mr T.C. Hudson, of Cowes; Mrs Teresa King, of Apse Heath; Captain Fred Janes, of Chandlers Ford; Sheila Mabb, of East Cowes; Mr Eddie Mosling, of Christchurch; Mr William E.J. Parker, of Gosport; Mr Theo Pearson, of Cosham; Mrs Agnes Phillips, of Apse Heath; Mrs Christine Pitman, of Waterlooville; Mr A.T. Rodway, of Bursledon; Mr Andy Saunders, of Hastings; Mr Vernon Scambell, of Ryde; Mr Edwin Sheppard, of Ryde; Mrs Minnie Spencer, of Cowes; Mr Raymond Tarrant, of Cowes; Mr T. Thornycroft, of Bembridge; Mr R.R. Trodd, of Chandlers Ford; Mr Hedley Vinall, of Shanklin; Mr Graham Ward, of Marks Corner; Mrs Una Warren, of Totland; Miss Eileen Weeks, of Wootton; Mr Raymond Weeks, of Ryde; Mr and Mrs A.M. Western, of Newport; Mrs Margaret Whitaker, of Brading; Mr Henry Williamson, of Binstead; and Mrs H.E. Wilson, of Ryde.

I am greatly indebted to Lord Mottistone, Lord Lieutenant of the Island, for generously consenting to write the Foreword to the book.

Finally, my sincere thanks go to publisher David Burnett (The Dovecote Press) for entrusting me with this assignment and subsequently guiding it to eventual fruition.

PART I

WAR DIARY

The Island's coastal gun batteries were continuously manned from 25 August 1939. This picture shows a lookout on guard beside a 9.2-inch gun at New Needles Battery. (IWM)

ONE

The Horrible Necessity

" . . . in order that Hitlerism and all its pagan policies should be banished from the earth and the blessings of perpetual peace firmly established."
Isle of Wight County Press

Comfortably shepherded by its close relation, mainland Hampshire, to the north, yet exposed on all other sides to the potentially threatening expanse of the English Channel, the Isle of Wight is both an integral part of England and a distinctly separate land of its own.

Serving as a bastion of defence for the major sea ports on the other side of the Solent, its geographical position has also given it obvious strategic potential as a stepping-stone for any would-be aggressor of Great Britain, particularly one setting out from the coast of northern France — a truism which has cost the Island dear in earlier centuries.

While logic demanded that the Isle of Wight's capture by a foreign invader had always to be regarded as a possibility, it was, of course, entirely unthinkable. Thus, the relationship of the Island to the rest of England was often (and still is) the analogy used by the British to illustrate the effect of strategic land tresspass elsewhere in the world. It was certainly so in the tension-filled weeks before Neville Chamberlain's infamous piece of paper calmed the nerves of the British people with its false promise of peace in September 1938. Referring to the vexed question of the German occupation of the Sudetan area of Czechoslovakia, one member of the Cabinet described it as "almost as direct an attack upon us as an attack on the Isle of Wight."

It is unlikely that anyone at that meeting of the Cabinet gave much thought to the possibility that, within two years, Hitler and his Nazi henchmen might actually be contemplating an invasion of the South Coast holiday isle.

Ryde Carnival, 1937 . . . and a display of wishful thinking on the tableau of the town's Rotary Club. Exactly two years later, in September 1939, the Carnival would prove the last major event on the Isle of Wight before the outbreak of war. (M. Zink)

Yet, as Britain and France decided to tell the beleagured Czech Government they should give up the Sudetan German areas to the Reich, "in the interests of Czechoslovakia herself and the European peace," the Isle of Wight was on red alert. Air raid precautions were tested in the form of an exercise, and the Island's 'own' territorial gunners (recently given the somewhat cumbersome title of 530 Coast Regiment Royal Artillery — Princess Beatrice's Isle of Wight Rifles) had been called out to man the Island's western coastal batteries, part of the outer defences of Portsmouth and Southampton. They remained there for eight or nine days,

The Island's first direct involvement in the European crisis was the October 1938 mobilisation of ten ex-servicemen to join the volunteer British Legion force which was to police the plebiscite areas of Czechoslovakia. The men are pictured with Major-General Sir Frederick Maurice, their National President, at Olympia, London. Although they set sail from Tilbury, the 1,200-strong force was quickly ordered back — the new boundaries of the Czech state were to be decided by other means. (E.M. Weeks)

until Chamberlain returned on 30 September from appeasement's last stand at Munich, waving his piece of paper and promising "peace with honour . . . peace in our time."

In Britain and France, the *Phoney Peace* broke out. Just how phoney became increasingly apparent during the spring of 1939, when Hitler's troops finally marched into Czechoslovakia.

A Dress Rehearsal

While the pitiful dismemberment of the Czech state was taking place on the Continent, the people of the Isle of Wight were being rehearsed in the possible horrors to come in England. The eerie sound that was to dominate their lives between 1940 and 1944, the rising and falling note of the air raid warning siren, was heard repeatedly during the first week of March in preparation for the most comprehensive war drill yet held on the Island.

Indeed, the Air Raid Precautions (ARP) Exercise in the Ryde and Bembridge area on the night of Saturday 11 March was one of the most spectacular yet staged on the South Coast. ARP had been in operation since 1935, but the March exercise was the first combined test on the Island of the effectiveness of its various constituents. It came a month after a special meeting of the IW County Council had decided to appoint a full-time county ARP Officer.

The Borough of Ryde's notice to the public pointed out that no official black-out would be imposed, but it was hoped "that shopkeepers with exterior illuminated signs or illuminated windows will assist by seeing that they are extinquished during these hours. The public are requested to see that as little light as possible is visible from the outside of their houses." Islanders living in the appointed area, which stretched from Wootton Bridge, in the west, to Yaverland Point, in the east, were warned of minor explosions, "to represent bombs," and car drivers were asked to stay off the road if possible.

This recognition of the Island's proximity to the prime wartime targets of Portsmouth and Southampton was at odds with the Government's contention that no large-scale building of air raid shelters and trenches would be undertaken in the Isle of Wight "because it is not considered a vulnerable area." Repeatedly, the Home Office was told by the Island that it had totally misjudged the situation. To those who made the representations, it seemed startlingly obvious that the Isle of Wight, or at least parts of it, was horribly vulnerable in the context of modern aerial warfare, and should, therefore, have qualified for the entitlement to Government-supplied shelters for its whole population. The argument fell on deaf ears.

There were, therefore, no public air raid shelters on the Island in March 1939 (and for many months to follow), nor were there any plans to build any, although the Island's state of civil defence efficiency and readiness was apparently acknowledged by London to compare favourably with many other parts of the country. It was widely-held locally that this splendid response was behind the decision of ARP's Inspector-General to witness the whole organisation in action. With the experience gained from the September 1938 exercise, a full dress-rehearsal was organised, involving the (gas) decontamination squads, the full-time fire brigade, auxiliary firemen, the police and special constabulary, the first-aid and ambulance services, the Royal IW County Hospital at Ryde, and numerous subsidiary officers.

The 'Take Cover' and 'All Clear' sirens were sounded, and the wardens liaised from their various sectors with the district's report centre, then housed at Puckpool Park (before the

Preparing for war. Carisbrooke's civil defence volunteers undergo anti-gas training in August 1937 at Albany Barracks, Newport. (CCM)

former battery was taken over by the Fleet Air Arm). Red flares deputised for incendiary bombs, 'trapped' people were rescued from supposedly wrecked buildings, mock casualties were treated at first-aid centres − or taken to the hospital − and the decontamination squads searched for gas bombs and set about cleansing the streets. With the notable exception of the anti-gas measures, it was all to become frighteningly real in 1940.

The headlong plunge into war had now begun. With annexed Austria and Czechoslovakia under its belt, the acquisitive Reich now threatened Poland's borders, forcing Neville Chamberlain to make his noble gesture of personal assurance − that both Britain and France would come immediately to the aid of the Poles if the threat of attack became reality.

On the Isle of Wight, early in August, Cowes Week was not quite the social extravaganza of previous years, but the yachting itself lived up to expectations. Tommy Sopwith and Howard Vanderbilt were, as expected, involved in "some great duels" for 12-metre International Class supremecy. The Bank Holiday weekend was blessed with sunshine, and the Island was swarming with the holidaymakers upon whom its economy so largely depended. Ryde was delightedly reporting record crowds in the sunshine − but the storm clouds of war were fast gathering.

In fact, the international situation was now so plainly serious that, on Friday 25 August, Sir Godfrey Baring, long-serving Chairman of the Isle of Wight County Council, recalled all officials then on leave. The district councils did the same. From the regional Civil Defence headquarters in Reading came a mass of instructions and advice on just about every aspect of preparation for total war. On the same day, 530 Coast Regiment, the Isle of Wight Rifles of old − having been called out on the morning of the 22nd, then stood down the same night − were dispatched again to their respective gun sites. Other artillery and searchlight units also took up their pre-determined positions.

Friday 1 September

One week later, at 4.17 on the morning of Friday 1 September, with help from Hitler's Wehrmacht, the Free City of Danzig began its "return to the Greater German Reich." Nazi forces were soon across the Polish frontier. The Second World War became inevitable.

The same day, the IW County Council's Emergency Committee for Civil Defence had at last been able to authorise the construction of shelters for children at their schools, together with public shelters designed to accommodate ten per cent of the population − the percentage estimated as likely to be caught in the streets, away from their homes, during an air raid. Councillors had no powers at that time to increase the shelter provision; individual households would have to make their own arrangements for air raid safety. In round figures, the county authority was bracing itself for an £80,000 bill, but the construction programme was to be carried out "with a strict regard for economy," and it was hoped this figure could be "somewhat reduced."

On that fateful Friday thousands of young children in a mixture of moods − some of them excited, others sad, several frightened, many of them irritable and most of them confused − were assembled at the main line railway stations of Britain's great cities. With each group was a smaller number of mothers. They were ready to be transported to areas of the country considered 'safe' by the authorities. For some, however, the journey to supposed safety was by sea, rather than rail.

It was, of course, entirely consistent with the official view on the Isle of Wight's vulnerability − or lack of it − that it should have been chosen as a reception area for evacuated schoolchildren, despite being a mere 4½ miles, just a 30-minute ferry trip, from the clearly 'unsafe' city of Portsmouth, the originating point for the majority of the evacuee intake. The chances of the Island remaining a safe haven in a modern air war were pretty remote − even if, for most of the time, enemy bombers were not going to be specifically aiming for it.

In fact, the Island itself contained a number of the so-called legitimate targets of warfare, with its important shipbuilding and aircraft production industries − principally at Cowes − and its

vital link in the home radar chain on St Boniface Down at Ventnor. All things being relative, it was still a safer bet than Portsmouth or Southampton, but the Government seemed once more to be demonstrating a degree of muddled thinking with its decision to send the young evacuees across the Solent.

Perhaps the people of Portsmouth and neighbouring Gosport also felt the move was somewhat illogical. Although the first steamer from the mainland contained its expected boat-load of evacuees, the remainder that day all made the crossing less than half-full, owing, it was said, to "Portsmouth parents witholding their children." Of the 8,600 expected at Ryde that day, only 4,040 actually made the trip. Three further crossings were then organised for hospital cases.

It was expected that those children who had missed their scheduled appointment with the Island on day one would arrive instead with the following day's complement. They did nothing of the sort. Organisers suffered a further disappointment when only 1,070 of the 5,700 booked to cross on day two itself actually turned up at Ryde. Arrangements had been made by the local authorities, in conjunction with the Women's Voluntary Service, to billet between 15,000 and 20,000.

The temper and condition of the children was said to be "very good" by the Islanders charged with their initial welfare. "The only difficulty (was that) certain schools had been told at Portsmouth that they were destined for certain places in the Island, but it was not possible to

Three weeks before war . . . and the scene at a crowded Ryde Pier Head as the SR Paddle Steamer Whippingham *calls from Portsmouth on Saturday 12 August 1939. A record number of visitors had been reported in Ryde during the Bank Holiday week just ended.* (Author)

Two days before war . . . and a new ferrying role for the SR steamers. Evacuated mainland schoolchildren join the Ryde-bound ship at Southsea on Friday 1 September. (CCM)

ensure this. It appears necessary at a later stage to redistribute children in accordance with educational and other considerations." This initial confusion caused considerable stress among the perplexed city children. Indeed, the whole evacuation episode on the Island – as in many places on the mainland – was fraught with profound difficulties for evacuees and hosts alike. Some of their experiences are recounted in Part 4.

At War with Germany

Abroad, courageously battling alone against the Nazis, Poland desperately awaited the promised declarations of war by Britain and France. Finally, the Allies made their move. At 9am on Sunday 3 September Britain's Ambassador in Berlin, Sir Neville Henderson, delivered his country's ultimatum for German troop withdrawal. By 11am, the expiry time set by Neville Chamberlain's Government, no response had been received. Fifteen minutes later, a despondent Chamberlain relayed to the British public, via their wireless sets, the news that the country was now at war with Germany.

On the Isle of Wight the *Isle of Wight County Press* reported that, "like the rest of the country, the Island received the announcement on Sunday that a state of war exists between England and Germany with a certain sense of relief, having now fully realised that, if a horrible necessity, it was still a necessity." The country's oldest carnival — at Ryde — had just come to the end of its week-long programme. "In view of the unprecedented conditions, a commendably brave show . . ." commented the *County Press*. The people of Ryde had turned out in large numbers for what was to prove the last major peacetime event on the Island for six years.

Run from a control centre in the heavily sandbagged ground floor rooms of County Hall at Newport, the Island's ARP organisation was slipping into gear. Materials for the protection of vital points, gas decontamination and demolition, and for the conveyance and treatment of casualties, had been dispatched to all parts of the Island. The sandbags were everywhere, and the spectacle in the last days of peace of the pen-pushers of the Inland Revenue office in Newport, jackets off, shirt sleeves rolled up, filling bags from a large pile of sand in the street at Nodehill had been a sight to behold — and well worth reporting in the local press!

There was an encouraging response to the Island's appeal for auxiliary firemen to augment the existing force, while the night-time strength of the ARP service had been considerably increased. Keen-eyed wardens now scanned their neighbourhoods at night, and risked a slump in personal popularity, to ensure everyone was correctly observing the total black-out regulations — yet to be sensibly amended to permit at least a suggestion of light from car headlamps and torches etc. It seemed on 4 September that the people in the north of the Island were failing miserably in their black-out tasks. Wardens from over the water, at Bursledon, claimed that "lights are showing prominently at Cowes." A quick investigation revealed, however, that the real culprits were "moonlight reflections on roofs."

A lot of time and effort was being spent painting central white lines on all the Island's 'A' roads (as well as those 'B' roads which ran through the towns) as an aid to motoring safety in the black-out. By 5 September, just over ten miles of roadway had been so treated in the east of the Island, and almost twice that amount in the west. The buses of the Southern Vectis company were soon operating fewer trips as its wartime service came quickly into operation, and passengers found their last bus at night left a good deal earlier than before.

A staged procedure had been adopted for warnings of air raids, culminating in the red alert which would lead to the sirens being set in motion. On 6 September there was a useful rehearsal for things to come when a 'yellow message' at 6.42 in the morning was acted upon with commendable speed by at least one of the six local report centres at Newport, Cowes, Ryde, Shanklin, Ventnor and West Wight (Freshwater). Newport reported that "all warden's posts were fully manned . . . decontamination, casualty and transport services also warned." Like all the other scares in this period, it came to nothing. A 'white message,' indicating the danger was over, was received and acted upon at 9.07.

Contamination by gas was a major fear, one that was certainly equal in those early days of war to the perceived threat posed by high-explosive bombing raids. This pre-occupation — which, in the event, proved completely unwarranted — was illustrated on 9 September when the ARP Officer at Cowes revealed that the smell of mustard gas had been reported at both Cambridge Road, East Cowes, and near The Rectory at Whippingham. Gas detection equipment, quickly dispatched to East Cowes, soon established that the dreaded gas was not the cause of the obnoxious smell after all. It was probably garlic!

The first bomb scare on the Island followed

By the outbreak of war sandbags had appeared at important buildings in all parts of the Island as protection against enemy attack. Those pictured here protected fuel pumps at the Southern Vectis bus depot in Nelson Road, Newport. (Reg Davies)

mass aerial attacks which had been prophesied in some quarters — the ARP wardens continued to busy themselves with diligent checking for breaches in the black-out regulations. Someone in Ryde transgressed on 16 September and found that someone in Portsmouth had reported the misdeed; the offending light was quickly obscured. Three days later the Southern Railway was taken to task for daring to show a "bright signal light" on the Ventnor West branch line between Whitwell Station and Dean Level Crossing.

The sound of heavy guns near Ryde promised a bit more in the way of excitement on the evening of 2 October. Minutes later, the head warden at Bembridge reported that a shell, seen to ricochet twice on the sea, had then "carried away the roof of a house." No-one was hurt in what was the first incident of note in the Island's war. The offending shell was presumed to have come either from the mainland or from one of the sea forts in Spithead. It certainly hadn't come from the enemy, who had proved conspicuous by his total absence.

And that was about the sum of the Isle of Wight's war in 1939. On 17 October the Luftwaffe chose another offshore island, Hoy, in the Orkneys, to drop its first bomb on British soil, but, by that time, compilers of the Isle of Wight's ARP log book had given up recording even black-out transgressions as page after page carried the one-line entry: "Situation report — nil." In common with the rest of the country, those Islanders not on active service of one kind or another filled in countless forms and documents, trudged, groped and bumped miserably through cheerless unlit streets at night — complete with the ubiquitous gas mask — and quickly grew fed up with the whole thing.

just after 4pm on 13 September, when Ventnor's police station reported "a small unexploded aerial bomb" on the beach at Rocken End, west of St Catherine's Point. This caused a fair bit of excitement at County Control, and a certain amount of buck-passing between the locally-stationed armed forces, before a flight-sergeant at RAF Ventnor, the radar station on St Boniface Down, safely disposed of the offending 'bomb' — almost certainly a practice shell — at 7pm.

The *Phoney War*

As the first month of war progressed, and nothing much happened — certainly not the

The *Phoney War* was at its irksome height.

TWO

From Fairyland to Fortress

In common with the rest of England, the Isle of Wight was already in the vice-like grip of one enemy when 1940 arrived. The bitter cold appeared at least as menacing to many as the faraway situation on the European continent. Unusually, it had snowed in the Island on the penultimate day of the old year. As the *Phoney War* continued, it was the weather that was fuelling much of the local conversation, with January bringing more snowfalls, heavy frosts, gales and cheerless fog.

On 6 January fog and low cloud again shrouded the Island – with tragic consequences. At midday an Avro Anson aircraft of Thorney Island's 48 Squadron crashed into St Catherine's Down, near The Hermitage, northwest of Whitwell, while on coastal patrol. Ventnor's ARP Officer reported a local warden's assistance in freeing the wireless operator from the wreckage of aircraft K6246 and providing on-the-spot first aid. Badly hurt, Aircraftman Cecil Ritter was taken to hospital at Ryde following the arrival on the crash scene of police and doctors. He had fared better than his three colleagues in the Anson. The pilot, Flying Officer Pearson, and the remaining crew members, Flight Sergeant Fennell and Aircraftman Rook, were all killed.

The same area, between the villages of Niton and Whitwell, in the south of the Island, witnessed another drama ten days later – happily without the tragic results of the earlier incident. At 4pm an RAF plane was reported to have force-landed there, but this time without either damage to the aircraft – unidentified in contemporary records – or injury to the crew, who were billeted overnight in Whitwell.

Mine-dropping exercises in Spithead, off Ryde, claimed a victim on 24 February when a Blackburn Botha from the Fleet Air Arm station at Gosport hit the sea – although the crew

escaped in their rubber dinghy. Four days later an 'unexploded bomb' was reported on the beach at Woodside, Wootton. Special Constables mounted a guard pending the arrival of a mainland RAF bomb disposal team from Calshot. Out at sea, the first German aerial attack on shipping in the Channel saw the liner *Domala* bombed off the Island's coast on 2 March by a single aircraft. It was set on fire and seriously damaged, with heavy loss of life.

Gas attacks were constantly feared. On 7 March the Island's ARP authorities were warned of "balloons, resembling toy balloons, being strewn by the enemy. They contain gas which is highly dangerous and explodes on touch. They should only be handled by line attached . . ." In fact, a suspect balloon had been found in Seagrove Bay, east of Ryde, a fortnight earlier. But this particular scare was quickly defused. Just hours after the warning was issued – and after all ARP personnel had been notified – Regional Control at Reading circulated the following: "Statements of rumours that (the) enemy is dropping small balloons containing dangerous gas are without foundation, and are based on (the) finding of a meteorological balloon . . ."

March of the Wehrmacht

Abroad, Hitler's war machine rolled mercilessly across Europe. On Wednesday 10 April, the entry in an Isle of Wight housewife's diary was full of poignant contrasts. "The almond blossom and primroses are here again, making the Island so beautiful," wrote Mary Watson from her home at Lower Gills Cliff Road in the west of Ventnor. But the war news was bad. "Germany invaded Denmark and Norway yesterday and a big naval battle is raging," her diary recorded. A month later, on 10 May, Hitler made his first moves in the West, breaking non-aggression promises to the peoples of the neutral Low Countries. In London, Winston Churchill succeeded a disillusioned Chamberlain as Prime Minister and named his wartime coalition Cabinet. On the same day it was announced that arrangements for the reception of foreign refugees in the Isle of Wight had been completed.

Five days later, on 15 May, Mary Watson was moved to write that "the Island is like fairyland just now . . . all kinds of blossom, camelia and tulip . . . the trees are beautiful." In the land of the tulip it was anything but fairyland. "Holland invaded and forced to surrender," wrote Mary Watson. "Their Queen is in England."

The Germans, by-passing the supposedly impregnable Maginot Line by smashing through the Ardennes, were meeting with little worthwhile resistance. Queen Wilhelmena's Holland had fallen after just five days' fighting, and, by the end of the month, Belgium had also been added to the apparently unstoppable conquests of *Blitzkrieg*. With Rommel through the last French defences, the withdrawal of the British Expeditionary Force had begun on 16 May.

Two days earlier, people on the Isle of Wight had listened to the broadcast appeal by War Minister Anthony Eden for British subjects, aged between 17 and 65, to register for the new Local Defence Volunteer Corps, "against enemy landing by parachute or otherwise." The Island's police force was soon fully occupied processing some 4,500 application forms from would-be recruits for the LDV, which, at Churchill's behest, would be re-styled the Home Guard a couple of months later. Questions were asked about "aliens in the civil defence services." There was only one on the Island — a 41-year-old Swiss Army Reservist serving as an ARP warden at Ventnor. Instructions followed for the demobilisation of private cars at night, or whenever the vehicles were not being used, and a warning was issued that recently-captured British uniforms could be worn by an invading force. Code words were now to be used between ARP report centres and the warden posts.

The German panzers were hot on the heels of the retreating BEF and French First Army, with the Channel ports of France now the focus of attention in an increasingly nervous England.

Bitter fighting only prolonged the fall of Boulogne and Calais to the enemy. Then, on 26 May, the evacuation of the beleagured and encircled British and French troops from Dunkirk began. King George VI decreed it a day of national prayer; the Isle of Wight was on tenterhooks.

It was natural that the Island, with its obvious dependence on shipping links, and its relative proximity to the coastline of northern France, should have a significant role to play at Dunkirk. It was an obvious place to look for vessels to augment the evacuation fleet, and many local craft were pressed, or went voluntarily, into service. The story of the contribution they made, and the sacrifices, is told in Chapter Eighteen.

A Tragic Preliminary

As the desperate escape of the British and French troops from Dunkirk entered its closing stages, confusion reigned in the clear skies above the Isle of Wight on the dramatic Sunday night of 2/3 June. At 12.50am Fred Kerridge made the first entry at Ryde in his private log of Island air raids — a meticulously kept handwritten record — with the following note: "Very intense gunfire. No siren. One raider came down at Appley. One raider shot down at Bembridge." Mr Kerridge added a question mark to his unofficial observation. He couldn't be sure what had happened — but the first official communication on the incident from Ryde's ARP report centre seemed to back up much of his interpretation. "Enemy plane brought down off Seaview. Enemy pilot has been captured and is now outside report centre," the wardens told County Control at Newport. East of Ryde, and within its then borough boundaries, Appley and Seaview are only a mile or so apart.

Twenty-five minutes later, however, the wardens had a significantly different story to report. The Fleet Air Arm at shore-based HMS *Medina*, the former Puckpool Battery (and, since 1929, public park) between Appley and Seaview, had confirmed a plane crash "half a mile away" — but it was a *British* aircraft. The pilot was reported to be "safe" and the crew were "being looked after." This amended information was

The 6th Black Watch arrived on the Island in June 1940 as part of the new garrison force. This classic official photograph shows men breaking off from training at Coppidhall Farm, Havenstreet, in response to an alarm. Note the Southern Vectis bus – the battalion's hastily requisitioned transport – on the left.(IWM)

followed immediately by the news, again substantially confirming Fred Kerridge's account, that a German plane had been brought down on Ashey Down, south-west of Ryde.

Much later in the day came the tragic confirmation. No German plane had crashed – at Appley, Seaview or on either Ashey or Bembridge Downs. The one aircraft shot down, mistakenly, was, indeed, British – a Fairey Battle light bomber of 12 Operational Training Unit, based at Andover in Hampshire. Pilot Officer A.G. McIntyre, the pilot, was injured. His crew, Sergeant G.H. Hudson and Aircraftman 1st Class D.L. Leonard, were both killed. What had given rise to reports of a crash on the Downs was almost certainly the descent of a stray anti-aircraft shell, discovered – unexploded – in chalk pits on Brading Down late on the Monday afternoon. It was disposed of by a team of Royal Engineers from Freshwater.

The anti-aircraft barrage had been savage. Islanders still clearly recall the sight of P/O McIntyre illuminated in the searchlight beams from either side of the Solent as he parachuted from his stricken plane that night, having desperately, and unsuccessfully, attempted to signal his non-aggressive intentions with navigation and landing lights. It was understandably assumed that the Island had claimed its first enemy scalp. Any elation over that turned to deflation when the truth spread round Ryde at daylight.

In the Front Line

The real thing was not long in coming. Operation *Dynamo*, the great Allied evacuation from Dunkirk, preventing a numbing military defeat turning into an irrevocable disaster, was completed on 4 June. Would the Germans follow the exhaused BEF across the Channel? Islanders, only too aware of the enemy's proximity to their own coastline, awaited Hitler's next move with much trepidation.

Gunfire and air raid sirens were heard in tandem on several occasions in the early hours of the next few days, and there were reports of enemy aircraft directly above the Isle of Wight on 6 June. The Island was undoubtedly in the front line of the nation's defence, a situation emphasised on 9 June with the arrival of its new garrison force – provided by the 12th Infantry Brigade of the Army's 4th Division, just re-formed after its retreat from Dunkirk. The appearance of the soldiers came the day before

The enemy in waiting . . . the much-feared Junkers Ju 87 Stuka dive-bombers were poised to create havoc in the Island sky. (IWM)

Mussolini decided Italy was ready for its own declaration of war on Britain and France – and four days before the British Ministry of Home Security's instructions that church bells should henceforth be used only to give warnings of enemy parachute or aircraft landings.

The Nazi forces triumphantly entered Paris on 14 June. Two nights later the first high-explosive German bombs to fall on the Isle of Wight were reported to have exploded at the Chale golf links on St Catherine's Hill, courtesy of a solitary enemy raider on a probing mission. Telephone wires were destroyed and windows were broken in houses between 100 and 200 yards away – but there were no casualties. A bomb crater six feet across and some five feet deep was reported. Total war had begun on the Isle of Wight.

German bombers were back three nights later with more unwelcome presents for Islanders. Heading north, the enemy planes discarded their lethal cargo over several parts of the Island; mercifully, most fell in open country. Among the areas hit was Carpenters, at St Helens, where eight bombs were dropped in two equal salvoes some 30 yards apart. Some had failed to explode, reported the local ARP and LDV groups; the problem was locating them in the marshy ground. There were also unexploded

bombs at Alverstone Nurseries while, at Lynn Farm, Havenstreet, a solitary bomb had exploded in a field. Again, no serious damage and no casualties were reported.

Cowes entered the war that night, too. Three high-explosive bombs were dropped in the Rew Street area of Gurnard, to the west of the town, causing slight damage to the windows of a nearby bungalow. With one of the bombs having failed to explode, Cowes police mounted a guard while the military experts were called to the scene – in a field 200 yards from Hillis Corner.

"Lend us the courage our souls need, that we go forward unafraid," wrote Mary Watson in her diary that day. "France has ceased hostilities, so now Britain stands alone . . . everybody's nerves (are) on edge, but Mr Churchill bids us be brave and face up to it. Our navy and air force are strong."

A Catalogue of Bombs

As 20 June progressed, reports of still further bombs were flooding the Island's ARP Control Centre. One had fallen on Brading Down; another three at nearby Kern Farm, where craters 30 feet wide and 12 feet deep were recorded. Broken windows were reported at Wootton following the fall of a bomb in a field near the Woodman's Arms pub – and a second bomb was to explode in the same locality two

A view of the anti-invasion barrier at Shanklin. The picture was taken from Hope Hill, looking along Hope Beach. (Hedley Vinall)

days later. In the West Wight an anti-aircraft shell had fallen overnight on the 19th at Apes Farm, the subsequent explosion partially blocking the Newport-Calbourne road by uprooting two trees. Workmen from Sir John Simeon's nearby Swainston Estate had the road cleared by mid-morning on the 20th. It had been a sleepless night for Mary Watson at Ventnor. "Kept up for four hours with the raiders . . . I suppose they will come every night now," she wrote in her diary.

On the evening of Friday 21 June two more unexploded bombs were discovered, 100 yards apart, south of the Pallance Lane-Pallance Road junction at Cowes. A 250lb bomb had made a clean 30-inch tunnel 20 feet into the ground. Most notable of those which fell on the Island over the next fortnight, during further night-time visits by German raiders, were the four which descended on Godshill's Park Farm during the night of 26/27 June, causing blast damage to property.

At Ryde that Wednesday night, Fred Kerridge recorded the siren's warning of the Luftwaffe's arrival at 12.15am, and entered his summary of the aerial activity off the Island's north coast: "Heavy gunfire. One raider reported shot down before siren, 12 midnight. Another raider held by searchlights and engaged by AA guns. Shot down later by Spitfire . . ."

Five bombs were dropped at Alverstone during this period and, nearby, two fell at Princelett Farm, Newchurch. Unexploded shells or bombs were located at Grove Farm, Adgestone; London Heath, near Newtown; Barnsley Farm, near Ryde Airport; on the Great Budbridge Farm-Moor Farm footpath at Godshill; and in a garden at Wroxall. "The Island is like a fortress now," wrote Mary Watson. "Pill boxes and guns (are) all over, and thousands of soldiers. Last Saturday we went to Freshwater, but it is quite military there now, with a pill box on the beach."

An Island Defended

All along its beaches *Fortress Wight* was rapidly becoming encircled with a variety of anti-invasion obstacles, installed by the soldiers of 12th Brigade to hamper the progress ashore of the enemy's troops and tanks. Gaps were appearing in the necks of the seaside pleasure piers dotted along the eastern coastline to make them less attractive to the would-be invaders. There were pill boxes on the beaches; ditches on the downs. If Islanders needed confirmation of the neccessity for all this, it came on 30 June. To the south, the Nazis had occupied the Channel Islands. From the sky, however, despite the almost nightly catalogue of air raids, the Isle of Wight had yet to suffer any serious bomb

23

Sections were removed in 1940 from piers on the Island's east coast as part of the local anti-invasion measures. This post card view, taken shortly after the war, shows the gap in Ventnor Pier. (Roger Bunney)

damage or casualties.

But the Luftwaffe strategy was about to change. The first daylight visit to the Isle of Wight by enemy bombers came on 2 July — they were chased ignominiously back out to sea by a trio of British fighter planes — and the second week of the month was to prove the most dramatic of the Island's war so far, mirroring the situation elsewhere in the South of England. The spectacle of a Dornier bomber, returning from a German reconnaissance mission, crossing Newport on Monday 8 July — evading the anti-aircraft guns below its flight path — was followed three days later by the real start of the enemy's daylight onslaught against the South. The Battle of Britain had begun.

Part of the Yar Line defences in the West Wight. The pill box on the Causeway at Freshwater was built in 1940/41 and is the best-preserved of the several which survive today in the area.

THREE

The Battle of Britain

What became known as the preliminary phase of the Battle of Britain was decreed by historians to have started on Wednesday 10 July 1940, when British shipping in the Channel was heavily bombed by the Luftwaffe. So far as the Isle of Wight was concerned, the opening exchanges of battle came one day later, on Thursday 11 July.

There had been considerable activity in the sky south and west of the Island that day, and the Hurricane fighters of 601 Squadron, based at Tangmere in Sussex, were in the forefront of the defensive action. They were scrambled again in the evening after the Island's radar station at Ventnor reported an approaching force of enemy aircraft in the Channel. A dozen or more Heinkel He 111 bombers from 1./KG55 at Dreux were headed for Portsmouth, with their Messerschmitt Bf 109 fighter escort. As the German force reached the coast, the Hurricanes intercepted.

At the controls of Hurricane P3681 was Flight Sergeant A.W. Wooley. Off Selsey Bill, to the east of the Island, he attacked one of the Heinkel raiders. The Hurricane, hit by anti-aircraft gunfire in the fuel tank, burst into flames. F/S Wooley, badly burned, baled out and landed safely at Thorness Bay, on the Island's north-west coast. His stricken plane nose-dived into the ground a little further west, at Cranmore, near Yarmouth. Its burnt-out remains lay there for 42 years until a 'dig' on 24 April 1982 retrieved the wreckage from the mud. Remarkably preserved, the Rolls Royce Merlin III engine of P3681 can today be seen at the Military Aviation Museum which opened in 1982 at the former Tangmere airfield — from where the ill-fated plane had taken off.

On 12 July the Germans launched another offensive against the Portsmouth area. A dog-fight above the Island between a returning Junkers Ju 88 and a Hurricane from 145 Squadron at Westhampnett, RAF Tangmere's satellite landing ground, culminated in the German raider escaping through the clouds with one engine on fire — only to ditch in the Channel when some 20 miles from the safety of the French coast.

Bombs continued to fall on the Island in the succeeding days as enemy planes, often thwarted in their original mission further north, unloaded their cargo *en route* for home. At 1.50pm on 18 July Fred Kerridge recorded Ryde's 25th air raid warning since the beginning of June. "Some near gunfire; raider overhead," he wrote, adding: "One raider attacked French destroyer, but was shot down by it. Another raider shot down off Whitecliff (Bembridge)."

Hitler Plots Invasion

When the possibility of invading England — as opposed to an all-out trade blockade or an attempt at forcing submission by indiscriminate terror bombing raids — was first mooted in May 1940 by Grand Admiral Erich Raeder, the German Naval Commander, it had been ruled out by Hitler as an impossible objective. By the end of June he had changed his mind; service chiefs were ordered to prepare plans for just such a contingency. Hitler's decision to proceed with Operation *Sea Lion* soon followed.

He proposed that "the landing will be in the form of a surprise crossing on a wide front from about Ramsgate to the area west of the Isle of Wight." He added that "the possible advantages of a limited operation before the general crossing (e.g. the occupation of the Isle of Wight or of the County of Cornwall) are to be considered from the point of view of each branch of the Armed Forces . . ." To the consternation of

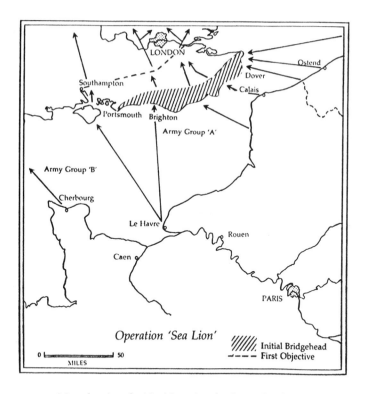

Operation 'Sea Lion'

//// Initial Bridgehead
---- First Objective

0 ————————— 50
MILES

Map showing the Nazi invasion for Operation Sea Lion, *as envisaged in July 1940. A landing was proposed in the Sandown Bay area of the Island.*

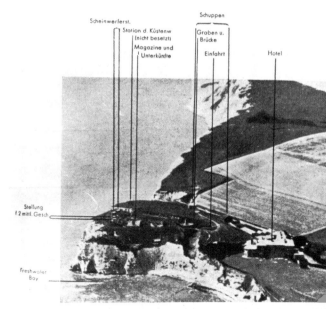

Fort Freshwater, von Osten.

Extract from a briefing book issued to German troops for the planned invasion of England in 1940. It an aerial reconnaissance photograph of Freshwater Bay. (IWCC/CCM)

Another page from the German briefing book . . . the coastal profile of the Island's western tip. (IWCC)

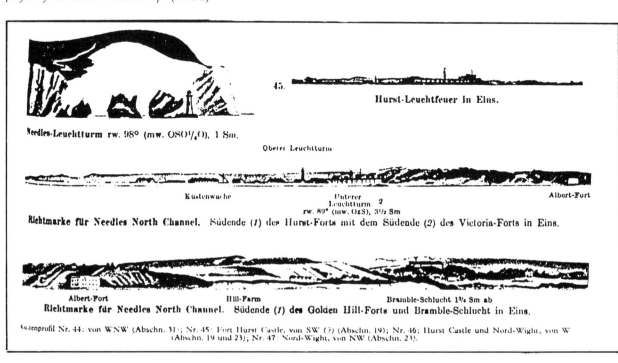

those charged with the planning of the invasion, Hitler ordered that "preparations for the entire operation must be completed by the middle of August."

When the German Army's proposals for initial landings with 13 divisions (the eight landing sites included one at Sandown Bay, on the Isle of Wight's east coast), followed by a further 27-division force, were made known to the Navy, Admiral Raeder and his colleagues quickly recognised the impossibility of such a scheme. Their alternative was to land on a considerably narrower front, between Deal and Beachy Head. The two extremes of thought were eventually married with a compromise plan which envisaged four separate landings between Folkestone and Selsey Bill, although disagreement between the two services over the method of carrrying out the plan was to continue throughout August.

The Isle of Wight was thus excluded from the plans for the enemy's initial thrust — although Selsey, in Sussex, was perilously close to the Island.

As July progressed, ARP wardens in the West Wight reported four bombs at Yarmouth on 22 July and a further two — one unexploded — at Blakes Hill, Brighstone, the following day. The 25th was notable for a dive-bombing attack by six Junkers Ju 87s, the dreaded Stukas, on a derelict tanker (beached four days earlier after an earlier attack out at sea) off the Island's southernmost tip at St Catherine's Point. Some miles inland, the raid was observed by fascinated Army staff at 12th Brigade's Billingham headquarters. The official war diaries reveal how officers "watched this dive-bombing with great interest, fondly believing that the bombers were English, demonstrating dive-bombing one day earlier that had been expected." An unidentified aircraft — almost certainly one of the raiders — was lost in the sea during the attack.

August opened tragically when a Vickers Vildebest (K6408 of Gosport-based 22 Squadron) crashed off Ryde Pier while on torpedo-dropping exercises, killing its pilot, Pilot Officer A. Bailey, and injuring the plane's other occupant, Aircraftman 2nd Class R.S. Budd. On the morning of Sunday 4 August Fred Kerridge's account at Ryde of air raid alert number 40 recorded "sharp gunfire — about twelve guns — before Hurricanes appear. Raiders brought

down. Esplanade machine-gunned." Four days later he was logging details of a much larger engagement, a "great Channel battle," the drama and tragedy of Convoy CW 9 — code-named *Peewit*.

CW 9: A Convoy Fiaso

The fact that Britain was still shipping convoys through the Channel in August — within easy range of the Luftwaffe's French bases — has been the subject of much debate and criticism ever since. It was risky in the extreme, overland alternatives were available and it tied up a disproportionate amount of the country's then limited air resources. All this was finally recognised in mid-August — too late to save the many lives lost in the Convoy CW 9 fiasco.

Peewit assembled in the Medway on Wednesday 7 August, setting out under the cover of darkness that evening for Dorset with a cargo of coal. The twenty merchant ships had been provided with a Naval escort of nine vessels. Disaster was not long in coming. The new German radar installation at Cap Gris-Nez, west of Calais, located the convoy as it entered the Dover Strait at dawn on 8 August. Torpedo boats set off in pursuit, and three merchant ships were sunk, with several others damaged. The Luftwaffe took over the assault as *Peewit* steamed on towards the Isle of Wight's southeast coast. The real battle was about to commence.

A massive aerial force had been despatched by the Germans. 'Jock' Leal puts it at 57 Stuka dive-bombers and 20 Bf 110 fighter-bombers, with a fighter escort of some 30 Bf 109s. The RAF scrambled 41 Squadron at Tangmere and Westhampnett's 145 Squadron, while reports emerged from Ventnor observers of more losses in the convoy as it approached St Catherine's Point. Another four merchant ships had been sunk before CW 9 was able to re-group early in the afternoon and set course hopefully for the Dorset coast.

Just after 3pm Ventnor Radar plotted another substantial force of aircraft moving across the Channel — this time the Bf 109 fighters were escorting 90 Ju 87s and 70 Bf 110s. The beleaguered convoy was attacked all along the coast off the *Back of the Wight*, between St

Catherine's and The Needles. As the Bf 109s engaged the heavily outnumbered RAF fighters, the 110s aimed for the convoy's balloon barrage and the Stukas dived to create further havoc with their bombs. The anti-aircraft guns from the ships added to the incredible noise. So much was happening that it was impossible for the shore-based watchers to keep up with the action. "The sky is black with planes," wrote Mary Watson in her diary. "Bombs are dropping . . . the water (is) shooting up as high as houses."

At 4.40pm the local ARP team was reporting "heavy and continuous bombing in the vicinity of Ventnor — believed to be mostly out at sea. One plane, unidentified, reported shot down on cliffs near Royal National Hospital; one Hurricane reported down near Whitwell . . ." Twenty minutes later an update from the same source reported that another plane, marked with a 'cockerel,' had come down at The Shute, St Lawrence. Of the crew, one was dead and the other was in military custody.

This aircraft was to prove the only enemy

The first German plane to crash-land on the Island. Caen-based Junkers Ju 87b S2+LM from 4./StG77, shot down by Pilot Officer P.L. Parrott on 8 August 1940, was photographed at The Shute, St Lawrence, before its dismantling by the RAF personnel pictured with it. (Andy Saunders)

plane of the 19 lost in the attacks on the convoy to crash-land on the Island, rather than in the sea around it. Indeed, it was the first to do so since the outbreak of war. A 4./StG77 Junkers Ju 87b from the dive-bomber base at Caen, its two-man crew on that fateful day were Unteroffizier (Uffz) Fritz Pittroff and Uffz Rudolph Schubert. The beginning of the end for their Stuka had come with the scrambling of 145 Squadron's Hurricanes from Westhampnett at 4.15pm.

Flying Hurricane P3896 was Pilot Officer P.L. Parrott, who was ordered initially to the Dorset coast, off Swanage. Later, in his official combat report, he wrote:

I was flying as No 2 in Yellow Section when, over The Needles, a large number of enemy aircraft were seen dive-bombing a convoy. Yellow 1 led the section to attack two Me (Bf) 109s. I broke away and found a Ju 87 pulling out of its dive after bombing. I attacked (the) enemy aircraft from the beam and he immediately turned tail and headed north. I continued to attack from astern and the enemy aircraft finally crash-landed in a field on the edge of the sea about two miles west of St Catherine's. The pilot appeared to be all right and the enemy aircraft, which struck a tree at the end of the landing run, did not appear to be badly damaged.

Many years later the now Wing Commander Parrott DFC (Retd) recalled further details of the

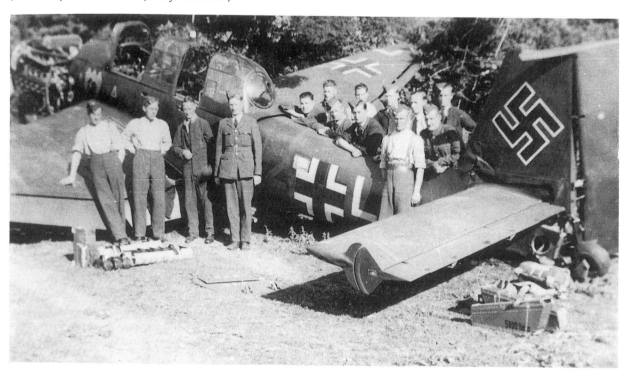

28

incident at the request of Tangmere's Military Aviation Museum:

The 109 top cover made it unwise, to say the least, for me to try to attack the Ju 87s before they started their dive, so the best tactic seemed to be to go down with them and try to get them in the dive or as they pulled out at the bottom, and this is what I did. We were very close to the sea, possibly less than 100 feet, while I followed the aircraft towards the Isle of Wight. His only evasive action, apart from flying low, was gentle turns each way. As we approached the Island it seemed that he intended to land, so I ceased fire and shadowed him until he touched down. That flight was my third that day, flying in protection of the convoy. Each time we went out, there were fewer ships to protect.

Of the two-man Stuka crew, Uffz Schubert was killed and Uffz Pittroff was taken prisoner-of-war. Their descent had been witnessed by many horrified observers in the Ventnor area. In her diary, Mary Watson recorded:

People were sitting all around the Winter Gardens when (the plane) came right at them, machine-gunning all the way. They flew for their lives. Then it

Flight Lieutenant D.E. Turner . . . his Hurricane (P3823 from Middle Wallop) was shot down during the CW 9 convoy battle above the Isle of Wight on 8 August 1940. The plane plunged into the sea south-west of the Island, killing the pilot. (Andy Saunders)

came up here; men on the Whitwell road dropped in the gutters. A plane of ours followed it, machine-gunning it and killing the pilot. Then it careered down the Undercliff and crashed in a field near the hospital. When some of the staff from the hospital ran down to it, the man who was alive put up a fight and Mr Francis pinned his arms down; the other boy was just breathing.

Its bombs intact, the aircraft was the first Stuka to land in good condition on English soil; it was later dismantled at St Lawrence by the RAF. But what of the Hurricane reported to have crashed near Whitwell? At 5.15 Ventnor's ARP Officer reported that the aircraft had come down at Ford Farm, Whitwell "due to engine trouble." The pilot was said to be unhurt. He was Pilot Officer H.C. Upton, of Tangmere's 43 Squadron – the only one of the RAF's ten Hurricane casualties that day in the vicinity of the Isle of Wight to have come down on the Island itself, and the first British fighter plane to have made a crash-landing on Island soil since the start of the war.

The single most important statistic, however, was the number of ships in the convoy arriving at their destination undamaged: precisely four.

The next couple of days were relatively quiet on, and above, the Island, due no doubt to the thundery weather over the South of England. There were the occasional forays by Bf 109s, but nothing remotely to approach the drama of 8 August. On the 9th, evacuations from homes were needed following the discovery of an unexploded shell or bomb at the rear of Woodlands Vale Cottage in Springvale, near Seaview, on the Island's north-east coast. On the 10th, four bombs went off in The Wilderness, between Rookley and the Army-occupied Billingham Manor; windows were damaged at nearby Cridmore Farm. These two days proved the lull before a veritable storm which was to see the Luftwaffe launch its attempt to eliminate once and for all the outnumbered RAF Fighter Command – and gain the essential invasion prerequisite of superiority in the air.

An Able and Courageous Man

Just before 10am on Sunday 11 August, Ventnor Radar picked up the approach of the largest aerial force yet sent by the Germans across the

Channel. Some 170 planes, with formidable fighter escort, were heading for the Royal Navy base at Portland, Dorset. The RAF scrambled nearly 70 Hurrricanes and Spitfires, and a spectacular dogfight soon ensued.

On the Island Vernon Scambell and a school-friend had taken a morning cycle ride from their homes in Shanklin to the golf course on The Fairway at nearby Sandown. It was to be a trip they would never forget. Vernon recalls:

We had just begun to retrace our way back . . . when we heard the sound of aeroplane engines. Having learnt by now that aircraft could be unfriendly (to say the least!), we looked upward to see two low-flying planes approaching from the south-west . . . on a line which would take them across Sandown and Culver Point to the mainland, and probably Tangmere aerodrome. Of the two aircraft, both Hurricane fighters, the lower one was trailing smoke from just below the cockpit . . . but no flames were visible. As the aircraft came to our front, the damaged plane turned to port in our direction; the other continued on course.

The damaged plane continued to descend and lowered its undercarriage to make a three-point landing on the football field. It was a well-controlled approach, with the aircraft in level flight and the engine throttled back. If the pilot had been wounded, he must have been a most able and courageous man to hold the plane in this manner. The approach had taken the aircraft on a broadside line to the football field perimeter hedge, which may, from the air, have looked like a low privet surround. Unfortunately, the hedge contained a raised level of earthwork, as many old boundaries did in those days. Since the under-carriage was down, the aircraft impacted against the earthwork, pulling down the nose and spinning the plane violently to starboard. In a great cloud of dust and debris the Hurricane came to rest about 20 feet inside the football ground; no movement was seen from the cockpit.

Having taken cover in a ditch during the approach, we had hoped to assist the pilot in clearing his aircraft, and had come to within 30 feet of the downed plane. Suddenly, the port wing burst into flames. With hindsight, very little fuel could have been in the tank, as it exploded with a dull thump; a full or half-full tank would have exploded with considerably more violence. The flames, nonetheless, spread rapidly from wing to engine and very shortly engulfed the whole aircraft. Horrified, we realised there was nothing we could do to assist. Again, with hindsight, I doubt if we could have been strong enough to lift the pilot, though we would have tried had the fire not become so intense.

Pilot Officer J.A.J. Davey, pictured shortly before his tragic crash-landing in the Island on 11 August 1940. (Andy Saunders)

We withdrew from the burning plane by crawling back across the field, since ammunition had begun to explode and random bullets, including tracer, were adding to the destruction. Although young, we were not to forget that young pilot and the way of his passing, though, hopefully, it was mercifully quick.

Pilot Officer J.A.J. Davey lies buried in San-down Cemetery, a short distance from the site of his tragic crash-landing in 1 Squadron's P3172. His gravestone records that he was just 20 years of age. More fortunate was Squadron Leader J. Peel, who suffered only slight injuries when his Hurricane (145 Squadron's P3164) crash-landed at Mottistone, in the West Wight. The sea around the Island's south-western coast also claimed victims — both RAF and Luftwaffe — on a day of heavy losses for both sides.

Attack on the Pylons — 1

Thunder storms again intervened, temporarily halting the aerial onslaught from across the Channel. By dawn on 12 August, however, the

Pilot Officer Davey's gravestone at Sandown . . . a short distance from the site of his crash in Hurricane P3172. He is the only Battle of Britain pilot buried on the Island. (Ben Houfton)

weather had improved sufficiently to permit its savage resumption, and, for the first time, an Isle of Wight target was on the Luftwaffe hit-list.

The radar station at Ventnor was one of four within the RAF's 11-Group earmarked for attack that day by an enemy which had begun to learn the hard way about the effectiveness of British radar. Shortly before midday the sirens wailed on the Island to herald the raiders' approach. The radar station itself had plotted a large force of Ju 88s (from KG51), escorted by 120 Bf 110s (from ZG2 and ZG76) and 25 Bf 109s (JG53) — more than 200 aircraft in total — over the Cherbourg Peninsular, beginning their ominous advance across the Channel.

The bulk of this impressive formation was making for mainland targets, but, as the planes approached Spithead, a detachment of Ju 88s did an about-turn and flew over the Island to attack the radar installation on St Boniface

Down. Just as they began their dive on the station from a height of about 10,000 feet, fighter planes from Warmwell's 152 and 609 Squadrons intercepted, the former reaching some of the Ju 88s before they could release their bombs, while the latter engaged the Messerschmitt fighter escort.

At 12.08 Ventnor's ARP Officer succinctly summed up the situation with the following message to County Control: "Ventnor being heavily bombarded." At Ryde, his opposite number was soon reporting "one English plane down on Bembridge Marsh; one German plane down at Ashey," and at Newport the town's police recorded an enemy aircraft's crash-landing at Godshill. "Four occupants. One burned to death; three captured and in custody of military," they told the ARP authorities.

It was nearly 2pm before the damage at Ventnor could be properly assessed by the town's ARPO. The attack had been delivered by 18 planes, each of them dropping four high-explosive bombs and adding to the chaos with the use of machine-guns. The radar station had been heavily and accurately bombed. Despite the considerable efforts of local firemen — hampered by the lack of available water on the site — most of the service buildings had been destroyed. Mercifully, the only injuries were sustained by a soldier on station defence duties.

On the Bonchurch side of Ventnor itself, two houses — White House in Leeson Road and Hollymount in Trinity Road — were badly damaged in the attack. In addition, there was widespread damage elsewhere, mainly to ceilings and windows, including those at Ventnor's Holy Trinity Church (an incident worthy of a front page mention in the national press the next day) and at the ARP report centre. Two women were reported to have been injured.

Details of unexploded, or delayed action, bombs were coming in thick and fast. Several were located near the radar pylons, leading to the total evacuation of the site and significantly delaying the start of repair work. Others were found in Ventnor and its neighbouring towns and villages, and some lay dangerously close to the Ryde-Ventnor railway between Shanklin and Wroxall stations. Bombs which did explode were also posing problems for the Southern Railway in this area. One fell so near the permanent way, it caused a partial collapse of

Smoke rising from the radar pylons on St Boniface Down, Ventnor, following the first attack by the Luftwaffe on 12 August 1940. The photograph was taken from St Lawrence. (Andy Saunders)

the embankment. There were a number of kinks in the track itself and a large crater had undermined several sleepers. Train services south of Shanklin were suspended.

A simultaneous 20-minute raid on the docks, harbour and city centre of Portsmouth spread the aerial activity above the Island. There were reports of damage from anti-aircraft shells or bomb blast in Ryde and Cowes. By 5.45, the ARP report centres at Ryde (which also had responsibility for Bembridge) and Shanklin (whose area included Godshill) were finally able to confirm two of the earlier reports of plane crashes on the Island. Forced down at Bembridge Aerodrome — which was closed throughout the war — had been Spitfire N3175, of Wittering's 226 Squadron. Pilot Officer W.S. Williams escaped unhurt from the aircraft before it burst into flames. Several other Spitfires and Hurricanes from Tangmere, Warmwell, Northolt and Wittering had come down in the sea off the Island coastline.

That was also the fate of five Luftwaffe planes. A sixth German casualty, the subject of the Godshill crash-landing, was piloted by Oberst Dr Fisser, Kommodore of Orly-based KG51 and destined to be the highest-ranking Luftwaffe officer shot down on the Island during the war. The victim of a 213 Squadron Hurricane, Dr Fisser's Junkers Ju 88a, of Stab/

KG51 (the headquarters flight), came down at Bridgecourt Farm, south of Godshill village, bursting into flames on impact. While his three crew members (Oblt Luderitz, Lt Schad and Sdfhr Northelfer) emerged safely — into military custody — Dr Fisser cleared the burning cockpit with his clothes on fire, fell into a nearby hedge and, despite the attempts of a British Army colonel and his driver to save him, died soon afterwards.

Thus, the people of Ventnor and its surrounds were the first on the Isle of Wight to experience the horror of aerial warfare. Summing up 12 August in her diary the next day, Mary Watson wrote:

It was dreadful; we shall never forget it . . . quite suddenly bombs were dropping. We sat in the hall, then I said: 'Let's get under the bed.' There we lay with our hands pushed over our ears through the most terrifying experience. It was a glorious day; all the doors and windows were wide open. We left them, so that the blast could get through, but it all sounded louder by so doing . . . we thought every bomb would be our turn. The planes came in just over here, flying at a great height, swooping down with ear-splitting screams and releasing their bombs, which went whistling through the air to their objectives. Then came the crash of the bombs and other formations of planes arriving and repeating the process until it was all going on at the same time, just as if Hell had opened and let the screaming mass through.

The Shooting of Bindorfer

Three days later, on Thursday 15 August, the day which was to see the heaviest fighting of the entire Battle of Britain, the Luftwaffe took advantage of an unexpected improvement in the weather — having earlier accepted that conditions would be unsatisfactory for the planned assault — and attacked on a wide front. Airfields and radar installations around the coast were the principal targets.

Most of the day's drama on the Isle of Wight did not come until the early evening. The main preceding event had been the successful morning interception by Spitfires from 213 Squadron of a Dornier Do 17 as it neared the Island on a reconnaissance flight from 3./(F)31 at Nantes. It crashed into the sea south of Ventnor. Late in the afternoon, a force of Ju 88s crossed the

Channel with a Bf 110 escort, heading for the Hampshire airfield at Middle Wallop. Spitfires from 609 and 234 Squadrons were scrambled to meet the threat.

Shortly before 6.30pm, as the raiding force was returning to France, the ARPO at Ryde reported that an enemy plane had been brought down south-west of the town, at West Ashey Farm. Incorrectly described in succeeding reports as a Junkers Ju 87, this was actually a Messerschmitt Bf 110, from 2/ZG76 at Rennes. It had crashed in a ploughed field north, and just below, the road from Ryde as it turns sharply right near the sea mark on the top of Ashey Down. Within minutes – for the first and only recorded time in the war – a German serviceman had been shot dead on Isle of Wight soil.

He was the Messerschmitt's gunner, Feldwebel Bindorfer. The manner of his death was contained in a single sentence from the ARP authorities in Ryde. Having had time to assess the situation at Ashey, they reported that the military had the matter in hand, adding: "One of (the) crew shot by military as he was interfering with controls and would not desist."

Piloting the plane was Uffz Max Guscheweski. In a letter written by him in the late 1970s – now in the archives of Tangmere's Military Aviation Museum – he described how an attack from two Spitfires had left the 110 with a burning right motor. "Then our left one was hit and the propeller stopped." Guscheweski tried to bale out but then lost consciousness after being hit by a machine gun bullet. He came to as the plane landed in the field at West Ashey:

I could not move. Soldiers of a Scottish infantry regiment arrived. Two soldiers lifted me from the cockpit. I still had my parachute on; they could not release it – the device, of a British design, was jammed. I tried to stand but could not; my left side was paralysed. An officer of the Scottish infantry gave me cigarettes as I lay on the grass. The officer – I do not know his name – and his soldiers were most kind to me. They stayed with me, but I could not understand much English. They brought some bottles of beer and more cigarettes. Later, I was taken in a motor and put in a police prison cell for the night.

Guscheweski, who spent the majority of the war's remaining years in Canadian prisoner-of-war camps, did not refer in his letter to Fw Bindorfer's death; it is fair to speculate that the pilot was unconscious at the time and did not witness the incident. Few other official details of the shooting have come to light. The "Scottish infantry regiment" to which Guscheweski referred was almost certainly the 6th Black Watch, who had men stationed – as part of the Island garrison force – at nearby Havenstreet during this period.

Vernon Scambell, who has made extensive notes on wartime incidents in the Island, claims the Bf 110 – by implication, Bindorfer – fired on the soldiers as they approached the plane, which was then riddled "from end to end" by bullets from a Vickers machine gun deployed on the road above. What is certain is that the Messerschmitt, and two planes which came down in the sea off the Island's coastline, contributed to the Luftwaffe's overall tally that day – including its losses in a disastrous raid on the north east – of some 90 aircraft lost or damaged. It was *Black Thursday* for the German airforce. The RAF had lost 41 planes in combat and another 16 in attacks on 11-Group airfields.

Attack on the Pylons – 2

Friday 16 August saw renewed attempts by the Luftwaffe to knock out the southern airfields – and a great many bombs littered the fields of the Isle of Wight. In the early hours came reports of explosions in the West Wight, and livestock was lost as the result of a bomb which fell at Vittlefields Farm, on the Yarmouth road west of Newport. Then, shortly after 1pm, came news of a second raid on the radar station above Ventnor.

There had not been time since the raid of 12 August to put the Island's vital link in the home radar chain back on the air before the raiders struck again. Somewhat ironically, ample warning of the Luftwaffe's approach on the 16th had been given by other coastal radar stations, but, east of the Island, the German formation split up, and the RAF's defensive force found itself deployed on several fronts. A substantial number of Ju 87s turned eastwards to wreak havoc – though not without heavy cost – on the sector airfield at Tangmere. Others dived on the Royal Naval Air Station at Lee-on-Solent, west of Gosport, and the remainder veered off to the left to begin their dive on the St Boniface Down pylons.

The Air Ministry's official historians record that seven high-explosive bombs were accurately dropped on the site by five Ju 87s. Following the attack, all but two of the buildings above ground, and every one of those below ground, were unusable. The pylons themselves were seriously damaged. It was not until 23 August that the gap in the radar chain was replaced with the opening of a reserve facility at Bembridge. Meanwhile, unexploded bombs near the St Boniface site again hampered repair work — and the railway station below was again temporarily closed.

Much else was taking place in the sky above the Island. Just the other side of the Solent, Gosport's Naval Air station was attacked by a force of Ju 88s, with a Bf 110 escort, and Islanders did not have to strain their eyes to see the results of this raid, and that inflicted on neighbouring Lee by the Ju 87s; fires burned furiously at both airfields. As the German planes turned for home, many crossed the Island at a terrifyingly low altitude.

As the afternoon progressed, bombs were dropped harmlessly near Newport, and, later, a low-flying German plane skimmed the rooftops in the town's Barton district, machine-gunning houses in Barton Road and Robin Hood Street. A shell splinter ripped through the roof of a house in Castle Street, Ryde, smashing windows in the process; machine gun bullets tore a hole in the roof of the ARP post in the town's Union Street, and a frantic search began for an unexploded shell which fell between Mitchells Road and Lower Bettesworth Road. In Osborne Bay, East Cowes, a minesweeper was sunk in the crossfire and its casualties were landed on the Island. Later, in the West Wight, eight bomb craters were found in open country north of the Newport-Freshwater railway line near Lower Watchingwell Farm; a further two high-explosive bombs had dropped in a field 200 yards south of the searchlight site at Calbourne.

Every so often on this drama-packed day came news of a plane crash on the Island. There were three, two involving RAF aircraft and one German casualty; the Luftwaffe also lost aircraft in the sea off the Island's coast. First to crash on the Island was 43 Squadron's Hurricane N3521, which was reported down — in flames on Horsebridge Hill, Newport — at 1.40pm. The pilot, Flying Officer C.A. Woods-Scawen, es-

caped with only slight injuries. Some four hours later a successful sea search off Bonchurch was mounted for Flying Officer H.P. Connor, who had baled out before his Spitfire (266 Squadron's X4016) had crash-landed in flames 250 yards north of The Heights, on the Whitwell road, near Ventnor.

The Celebrity Messerschmitt

It was a report from the RAF at Ventnor that alerted the ARP authorities to the unplanned arrival on Island soil of the day's German casualty. Somewhat surprisingly, perhaps, they identified the stricken plane incorrectly as a Dornier when it was actually a Messerschmitt Bf 109e of 2./JG53 at Rennes. Employed on fighter escort duties, it had fallen victim to a 234 Squadron Spitfire and crashed at Bathingbourne Farm, south-west of the main Newport-Sandown road between Apse Heath and the Fighting Cocks Inn.

Suffering from shock, but with no serious injury, the pilot, Feldwebel Christian Hansen, was soon in police custody, but was allowed to recover his composure over a drink in the Fighting Cocks Inn before being driven to Newport.

His plane, in relatively undamaged condition, was destined for celebrity status on the Island. Removed from Bathingbourne by the fire service, it was put on public display at fire brigade headquarters in Newport. Many young (and some not so young!) Islanders paid 6d to sit in the cockpit and thereby raise cash for the local Spitfire Fund before the 110 eventually left the Island for the RAF's No 6 Maintenance Unit at Sealand. An enterprising Island printer boosted the fund further by producing, and then selling for 3d each, mock *In Memorium* cards, which bore the legend: "In joyful remembrance of the fate of the Messerschmitt 109, one of Hitler's Nazi Circus, which finished its aerial career at Bathingbourne Farm on Friday, August 16th, 1940. May its end be followed by many others."

Sunday 18 August saw a renewal of the aerial bombardment on the airfields of Southern England. The Isle of Wight was caught up in the action in mid-afternoon when Ju 87s and 88s, escorted by Bf 109s, carried out raids at Thorney Island, Lee-on-Solent and Gosport. On the

Island, Newport, and particularly Hearn Street, was machine-gunned by a solitary low-flying Bf 110, which inflicted a glancing head wound on a local man, and the first accounts of the many enemy planes to crash either on the Island or in the sea surrounding it that day came shortly after 2.30pm, when one was reported in the sea about a mile off Dunnose Head, on the Island's south-eastern corner. A Ju 87 from 2./StG77 at Caen, it had unloaded its bombs before striking the sea and made an unsuccessful bid to rise clear of the water before disappearing beneath it with the loss of its two-man crew.

Some 30 minutes later a dramatic message was on its way to County Control from the ARP wardens in the West Wight, who reported a crashed German aircraft on fire at Tapnell Farm, east of Freshwater. It was a Bf 109 from Beaumont-le-Roger's 6./JG27, whose pilot, Oberleutnant R. Mullerfriedrich, had baled out to a safe landing on Brook Down — and a military reception committee. Also taken prisoner-of-war was another Bf 109 pilot from 6./JG27, Leutnant Julius Newmann, whose plane came down on St Martin's Down, east of Wroxall village (he surrendered to a couple of Home Guardsmen), and Leutnant Gerhard Mittsdorfer, rescued by a local boat after his Bf 109, from 1./JG27, plummeted into the sea at Monks Bay, south of Dunnose.

The Luftwaffe lost a Ju 88 in the Solent, off Puckpool, on 19 August, when Southampton Docks was the enemy target. In mid-afternoon, four bombs were dropped on Ventnor by a Junkers with fighter escort. A bungalow was wrecked in Zig Zag Road, Belgrave Road was blocked by a crater, a gas main was severed, telephone links with the nearby villages of Niton and Wroxall were cut, and an unexploded bomb lay dangerously close to the front of Ventnor's Royal Marine Hotel. This attack had caught the town unprepared — there was no air raid warning and no anti-aircraft fire — but the only casualties were said to be suffering from nothing more serious than shock. The *Isle of Wight Mercury*, Ventnor's own newspaper, was soon calling for the provision of more air raid shelters in the town — a "vitally urgent necessity," it said.

Killed — By Enemy Action

Further minor casualties, and more damage to property, were reported at Ventnor the following day when a delayed action bomb exploded in Alpine Road. Unexploded bombs were discovered at Ryde and at several West Wight locations. Meanwhile, the Luftwaffe lost more Ju 88s as their return journeys from mainland bombing raids ended in the sea off the Island's coast. On an otherwise quiet 21 August, with the weather unfavourable for aerial assault, the only real incident of any note on the Island was the explosion of a delayed action bomb at Carisbrooke; the following day, another went off above the railway tunnel on St Boniface Down. Then, on Friday 23 August, the Island was recording its first two civilian deaths of the war.

Portsmouth, Thorney Island and RAF Tangmere, all in the proximity of the Isle of Wight, were among the Luftwaffe targets that day. A 609 Squadron Spitfire from Tangmere came down in the West Wight, at Broad Lane, Tapnell, the pilot baling out safely, and, shortly before 7pm, several high-explosive bombs desce· led on the north-east of the Island. A German raider, desperate to escape the attentions of two Spitfires in hot pursuit, dumped five on the corner of Priory Drive at Nettlestone. Another eleven bombs finished on or near West Green at St Helens, and five more were soon reported to have exploded further south, at Sandham Grounds on Sandown seafront.

The Nettlestone bombs killed one man who was taking cover in a wooden shed at the back of his home at West Priory Cottages. The other fatal casualty was 55-year-old Edith Clarke, a widow who, with sad irony, had left her North London house for her sister's Sandown home to escape the anticipated air raids on the capital. She had been taking tea in a beach hut facing the seafront, close to Sandham Grounds, when the bombs were dropped. About a dozen huts were wrecked in the raid, which also damaged a breakwater, smashed countless windows and brought down several ceilings. Among injury victims at Sandown were a local girl and a gunner from the nearby Culver Battery, who were walking along the seafront at just the wrong moment.

The Plane in the Well

Recent poor weather cleared on 24 August, paving the way for the Germans to renew their offensive. Despite the intervention of Fighter Command and the AA barrage, Portsmouth was devastatingly bombed. Some 70 high-explosive bombs fell in the space of five minutes; 125 people were killed.

The day was destined to produce one of the most amazing acts of the Isle of Wight's eventful aerial war — one that has become part of local folklore. It involved the Bf 109e of 6./JG2's Feldwebel Gerhardt Ebus, based at Beaumont-le-Roger, which had been badly damaged by a 238 Squadron Hurricane in a dogfight above the Island. The start of the Messerschmitt's descent to the unlikeliest of crash-landings at Great-woods Copse, south of Shanklin, was seen by Hedley Vinall, who worked then in the Surveyor's department at Sandown-Shanklin Urban District Council:

My uncle was a farmer at Cliff Farm, Shanklin, and he had a spare piece of land right at the top of Victoria Avenue, about half-a-mile north of Greatwoods, which was one of the council's water-gathering areas. I was on my uncle's land this Saturday afternoon with a friend; we were watching the air raids going into Portsmouth and saw numerous enemy aircraft attacked. This particular plane was obviously in trouble. It was getting lower and lower. We watched the pilot coming down on his parachute, drifting towards Shanklin. The plane levelled out near us, then passed over the top of us and disappeared. We knew it must have come down nearby, so we got on our bikes and shot down Victoria Avenue, Westhill Road and Cowlease, which runs alongside Greatwoods.

On the way they met a council colleague who told them he had been at the Greatwood reservoirs when the Bf 109 had careered through the trees of the copse and, amazingly, plunged into the top of an old well, bored during tests for water some 45 years earlier; its exact position had been in doubt for some time! While their colleague set off to notify the police, Hedley and his friend made for the crash scene. He adds:

The plane had made a fair-sized hole in the tree cover and, sure enough, had gone right into this well, which was about 2½ metres across and had been covered with sleepers and the like. It had gone in at an angle; pieces of the wings and the tail fin were sticking out of the well, and there were other bits of debris lying all around it. I remember seeing cannon shells pitted in the trees nearby, which had presumably been thrown out by force when the plane hit the well. A military unit arrived and put a guard on it; those cannon shells were dropping everywhere!

Much of the doomed Messerschmitt's fuselage and its engine, which had completely disappeared into the well, were eventually removed, although some parts — including a cannon — were to remain there for over 40 years before air enthusiasts finally launched a successful bid to retrieve them. Fw Ebus, despite his frantic attempts to avoid it, came down in the sea half-a-mile south of Dunnose. A motor boat from nearby Bonchurch set off, with a soldier in attendance, in pursuit of the fast-drifting parachute, but nearly an hour had elapsed before the unfortunate airman could be hauled aboard. He was at first thought to be British, but a short message from Ventnor's ARP wardens soon corrected this assumption: "Military reports the pilot is a Bosche — and alive." Sadly, the young German, severely wounded, died shortly after his rescue.

Another Island aircraft casualty that day was 234 Squadron's Spitfire N3239, from Middle Wallop, which came down in a field between

Shot down in the sea off Hanover Point, near Brook, during a mainland raid on 26 August 1940, the five-man crew of Heinkel He 111 G1+GN from 5./KG55 at Chartres were saved by a patrolling German air-sea rescue launch. Two of the airmen, Leutnant Von der Hagen (seated, left) and the pilot, Leutnant Karl Brütnning (standing, right) are pictured with members of the launch's crew. (Andy Saunders)

Merstone Junction and Little Budbridge Farm, north of Godshill. Its Polish pilot, P/O J. Zurakowski, suffered only slight injuries after successfully baling out.

The 24th saw a new development in the battle. For the first time the Germans sent a massed force of planes against London, although they appeared to have no specific targets in mind, causing widespread damage and casualties. Churchill retaliated the following night by ordering the start of a series of raids in the heart of Nazi Germany, and Hitler raged: "Since the British attack our cities, we shall wipe out theirs."

There was no shortage of aerial activity over the Island during the remainder of August and early September, and bombs − mainly incendiaries − continued to fall indiscriminately on the Isle of Wight from enemy planes prevented from attacking their mainland targets by the British defences. Searchlight sites at Ashey, Godshill and Calbourne were among the many locations bombed, as was Ningwood Station, on the Newport-Freshwater line, and the old life-boat house at Brighstone.

A Significant Saturday

The whole course of the Battle of Britain was to change dramatically on Saturday 7 September. The Luftwaffe assembled the largest force of aircraft ever seen in the history of aerial warfare − an incredible 965 planes, some 20 miles wide in formation − and set off in the afternoon across the Channel. Despite the huge increase in British fighter production, this was more than the battle-weary RAF could muster in its entirety. Fighter Command put up every available Spitfire and Hurricane − more than 400 from 21 squadrons − to meet the monstrous challenge. And then it happened. To the surprise of the awe-struck people on the ground below, the Luftwaffe flew over the southern airfields and headed straight for the nation's capital. The Blitz had begun.

On that same Saturday night, it seemed to the people of the Isle of Wight − and on the South Coast in general − that the unthinkable had occured. A misunderstanding led to the issue in the South of the codeword *Cromwell*, the signal that a German invasion force had landed in England. Local defence forces were immediately mobilised, and it looked like the big test had arrived for Churchill's Home Guard. Hedley Vinall, who had joined the East Wight Home Guard Battalion's 'C' Company as a young recruit at Shanklin, recalls being led onto the seafront by the Regular Army. "We were taken along the Esplanade, which was closed to the public, to man a pill box on Chine Hill, below the Chine Inn. Well, we manned it all the rest of that weekend, until we were ordered to 'stand down' at the end of Sunday afternoon. There hadn't been an invasion after all."

Invasion Postponed

By Sunday 15 September, the Germans had assembled more than 1,500 barges across the Channel for the planned invasion of England, already postponed several times. On that day Fighter Command "cut to rags and tatters," as Churchill put it, "separate waves of murderous assault upon the civil population" to gain a great and hugely significant victory. Two days later Hitler again postponed Operation *Sea Lion* and the Luftwaffe knew it had finally lost the battle for the air supremecy demanded by the invasion planners.

On the Isle of Wight a welcome lull continued, broken on the 17th by a report from an indignant ARP warden in Brighstone, who described being fired upon by a soldier on sentry duty while cycling round the village and blowing his whistle to alert residents to an air raid warning. The sentry missed him! On the following day the Admiralty warned the Island's ARP authorities that the enemy was dropping magnetic mines by parachute. "No metal − not even tin hats − or tools should be brought near, and all vibration (must be) avoided," read the warning.

Late on 23 September a combination of high-explosive, oil and incendiary bombs descended on Shalfleet Quay, in the West Wight; a cow's hind-quarters needed the attention of a vet as a result. The 24th saw renewed action through the decision of the Luftwaffe to mount a raid with some 100 aircraft against the Vickers-Supermarine factory at Woolston, Southampton. Damage and casualties were both substantial, and a number of enemy aircraft ended up in the sea off the Island's coast.

Woolston was again the target on 26 September for a large force of He 111s, from KG55, with nearly 100 Bf 110s providing their fighter escort. Several aircraft, from both sides, were to end up on the Island. Reported down in flames at Tapnell Farm, near Freshwater – setting a field alight in the process – was a Bf 110 from 7./ZG26; its two-man crew (Lt Konopka and Uffz Eiberg) were both killed. A sister plane, this one attached to 1./ZG26, crashed in a field half-a-mile from the Chequers Inn, south of Rookley, in the centre of the Island. Soldiers took the crew (Fw Rohde and Fw Both) prisoners-of-war and attended to the time fuse they had set in motion before leaving the plane.

A third Bf 110, from 4./(F)14, crashed in the sea just off Thorness Bay, on the north-west coast, and sank without trace; only a patch of oil was visible on the surface of the water when a rescue boat arrived on the scene. Although one of the two airmen (Lt Pank and Uffz Schmidt) baled out of the stricken Messerschmitt, his parachute failed to open. Both were killed.

The British crash victims were luckier. Pilot Officer R.A. Kings baled out of 238 Squadron's Middle Wallop-based Hurricane P3830 before it crashed at Colemans Farm, just south of Porchfield, and was unhurt; his plane was a total wreck. To the south-west, Flight Lieutenant C.E. Bowden safely left Hurricane P5208, from Tangmere's 607 Squadron, before it plummeted onto the main road 100 yards east of the Sun Inn at Calbourne, opposite the village's searchlight post. 'Jock' Leal has also recorded the ditching of two Spitfires and another Hurricane off the local coastline that day, when the only bomb damage on the Island was broken greenhouse glass at Freshwater Fruit Farm in Wilmingham Road.

Late on the evening of the 27th, what was regarded as yet another attempt by the Luftwaffe to put Ventnor's radar pylons out of action left many houses in Wroxall, north of the town, with smashed doors, windows, slates and out-buildings. The six high-explosive bombs which fell in the village also damaged the local electricity supply and led to some temporary evacuations.

The 28th was notable for the loss of three Hurricane fighters in a dogfight which culminated near the Island's east coast. Two crashed

into the sea off Bembridge – one of the pilots was rescued – while a third came down in flames on Culver Down, having been initially hit above Fareham, in Hampshire. Sgt S. Eric Bann, aged 26 and a veteran of the RAF's earlier fighting in France, managed to bale out from 238 Squadron's V6776 over the Island, but died in the marshes at Brading after his parachute failed to open. He had been married just five months.

The Final Phase

By now the Battle of Britain had entered its final phase. The Isle of Wight had been spared the awful devastation and dreadful casualties endured by cities on the mainland, but it was still a hazardous place to be in during October. There were reports on the 8th of two German planes flying very low up Wootton Creek from Fishbourne, machine-gunning all the way. Then, on 12 October, there was drama three miles off the Island's southern coast when a trawler, heavily shelled by enemy destroyers, began to sink. ARP Warden Fred Gould, of Bonchurch, set out in a motor boat and returned to land safely 25 members of the crew. On the other side of the Channel Adolf Hitler had ordered the postponement of Operation *Sea Lion* until the spring of 1941.

The last fortnight of the Battle of Britain – officially deemed to have ended on 31 October – saw still more plane crashes on the Isle of Wight. Returning from a mainland raid on 15 October, Feldwebel Horst Hellriegel, from 3./JG2, crash-landed in a Bf 109 on Bowcombe Down, west of Newport, having been successfully intercepted by a 145 Squadron Hurricane. 'Jock' Leal tells how the Luftwaffe pilot surrendered to the driver of an empty coal lorry on Bowcombe Road and was driven by him to the Waverley pub at Carisbrooke. There, Hellriegel was given a glass of beer by the landlord while the police were summoned to take the German away as a prisoner-of-war. Hellriegel was not flying his regular aircraft that day. It was unserviceable and he had, instead, borrowed the Bf 109e of Fw Franz Jaenisch, who was spending 15 October celebrating the completion of his 100th mission of the war. The plane (Yellow 8+), endearingly customised by Jaenisch with a picture of Mickey Mouse in

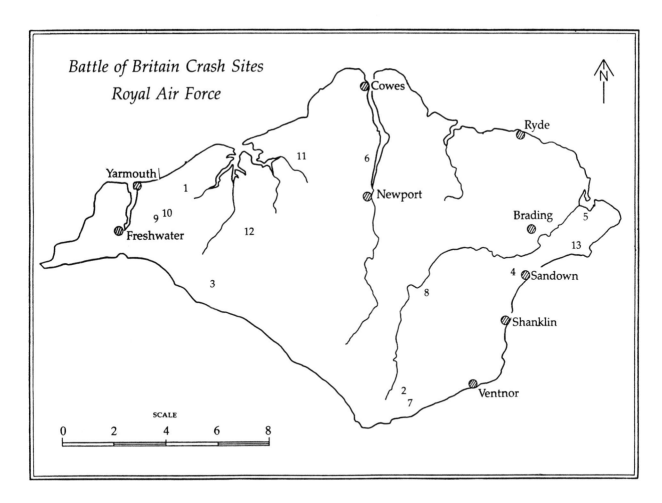

Battle of Britain Crash Sites
Royal Air Force

boxing gloves beneath the cockpit canopy, had incurred little damage on landing − but suffered substantially from local souvenir hunters before it could be protected by the military!

Some 40 buildings at Ventnor, including the Globe Hotel, suffered minor damage when high-explosive bombs were dropped on the town during the evening of the 26th. One day later the Luftwaffe again attacked Portsmouth − and another crop of planes were to end their battle involvement on or near the Island.

The crash of principal interest was that of Flight Sergeant D.K. Haire, flying Hurricane V6888 from Tangmere's 145 Squadron. The plane came down in the sea less than 100 yards from the cliffs at Foreland, the Island's eastern tip, and was quickly submerged, although its radio equipment was salvaged by locally-based soldiers. F/S Haire waded ashore, unhurt. Two other Hurricanes from 145 Squadron were also lost off the Island's north-east coast, but further out to sea. The pilots had contrasting fortunes.

Map showing distribution of RAF crash sites on the Island during the Battle of Britain: 1 Hurricane P3681 − Cranmore; 11 July. 2 Hurricane P3267 − Ford Farm, Whitwell; 8 August. 3 Hurricane P3164 − Mottistone; 11 August. 4 Hurricane P3172 − Fairway, Lake; 11 August. 5 Spitfire N3175 − Bembridge Aerodrome; 12 August. 6 Hurricane N3521 − Horsebridge Hill, Newport; 16 August. 7 Spitfire X4016 − The Heights, Whitwell; 16 August. 8 Spitfire N3239 − Little Budbridge, Godshill; 24 August. 9 Spitfire L1082 − Near Tapnell Farm; 24 August. 10 Spitfire (u/i) − Broad Lane, Thorley; 24 August. 11 Hurricane P3830 − Colemans Farm, Porchfield; 26 September. 12 Hurricane P5208 − Calbourne; 26 September. 13 Hurricane V6776 − Culver Down; 28 September.

Note: u/i denotes unidentified aircraft

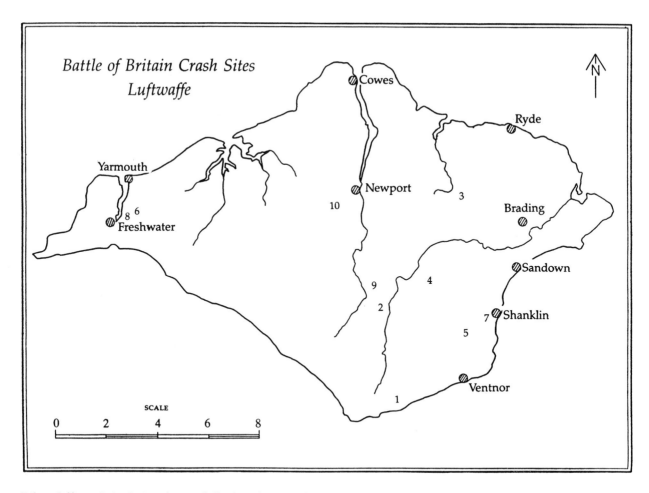

Battle of Britain Crash Sites
Luftwaffe

Cowes

Ryde

Yarmouth

Newport

3

10

Brading

8 6

Freshwater

9

4

Sandown

2

7   Shanklin

5

Ventnor

1

SCALE

0   2   4   6   8

Pilot Officer J.A. Jottard was killed in his crash near the Nab Tower, but P/O F. Weber, whose Hurricane came down off Seaview, baled out in time and was rescued by a launch. The Bf 109e piloted by Oberleutnant Wolf, of 3./JG2, claimed the unfortunate distinction of being the last Luftwaffe aircraft to crash in the immediate vicinity of the Island during the Battle of Britain when it was shot down in the sea that day by anti-aircraft fire. The pilot was killed.

Overnight, high-explosive bombs fell both sides of the railway line between Newchurch and Alverstone, and a suspected delayed action bomb lay just 15 yards from the track. Rails were fractured, debris littered the permanent way and the train service between Merstone Junction and Sandown was temporarily replaced with a bus. It proved to be the last incident of note on the Island during the Battle of Britain (although

Map showing Luftwaffe crash sites on the Island during the Battle of Britain: 1 Ju 87 S2+LM − The Shute, St Lawrence; 8 August. 2. Ju 88 9K+AA − Bridgecourt Farm, Godshill; 12 August. 3 Bf 110 MB+BP − Ashey Down; 15 August. 4 Bf 109 Grey 2+ − Bathingbourne Farm; 16 August. 5 Bf 109 Yellow 6+ − St Martin's Down; 18 August. 6 Bf 109 (u/i) − Tapnell Farm; 18 August. 7 Bf 109 (u/i) − Greatwoods Copse, Shanklin; 24 August. 8 Bf 110 3U+AR − Tapnell Farm; 26 September. 9 Bf 110 U8+HH − Near Chequers Inn, Rookley; 26 September. 10 Bf 109 Yellow 8+ − Bowcombe Down; 15 October.

Note: u/i denotes unidentified aircraft

the Luftwaffe did take another swipe at nearby Portsmouth on 29 October). For the moment, the invasion scare was over, but the Isle of Wight was still in the front line − and the months which followed would see a ferocious underlining of the fact.

FOUR

1940: The Sting in the Tail

The beginning of November 1940 saw the Luftwaffe intensify its night raids on London and the nation's major industrial centres. *En route*, the raiders passed repeatedly over the Isle of Wight, where the continuing vulnerability to indiscriminate bombing was graphically illustrated on the first night of the month, when London and Birmingham were the principal targets.

Shortly after 8pm high-explosive bombs were reported to have fallen at Shanklin. Water pipes had been fractured, telephone wires had been brought down and, with damage also inflicted on some buildings in the town − and delayed action bombs suspected − temporary evacuations to the Town Hall were organised. St Saviour's Church had escaped serious damage from a bomb which had fallen in its grounds, while another HE bomb had come down at the rear of the Napier House Hotel on the Esplanade.

The unoccupied building appeared to have survived intact. Then, apparently mistaking it for another hotel, a soldier called there after the raid. He rang the door bell, the building began to vibrate . . . and then collapsed altogether! All that was left of the hotel after its collapse − initially reported as a probable cliff fall − was the porch, which probably saved the life of one badly-shaken soldier.

There was high drama, quite literally, on the afternoon of Wednesday 6 November when a large Messerschmitt force crossed the Island on its way to attack Southampton. Soon afterwards, Arreton's ARP post was reporting a plane down in flames near Perreton Farm. Within minutes, a message to County Control from the wardens at Ventnor outlined the crash of an enemy aircraft in the sea at Monks Bay, Bonchurch; simultaneously, the Havenstreet post was logging details of a plane crash on the north side of the downs above Duxmore.

The crash at Perreton, not far from Haseley Manor, claimed the life of 145 Squadron's Flight Sergeant Haire, from Tangmere, the Hurricane pilot who, just ten days earlier, had safely waded ashore from his submerged plane off Foreland. 'Jock' Leal records:

His aircraft, attacked by a Bf 109, was seen to be on fire as it flew over the centre of the Island. He could see that the plane, which was now ablaze, was going to crash among the houses in the village of Arreton. Instead of baling out he stayed in the cockpit and steered the aircraft away from the village into open fields. Only then did he bale out. However, he had left it too late for his parachute to open fully and he fell to the ground, only yards away from the blazing Hurricane. He died before help could get to him.

It seems that the Messerschmitt responsible for the attack was itself shot down by another Hurricane immediately afterwards, and was almost certainly the aircraft reported in the sea off Monks Bay − a Bf 109e from 5./JG2. The pilot, Feldwebel H. Klopp, was killed. More fortunate was F/S J. Weber, at the controls of the Hurricane (145 Squadron's R4177) that crashed at Duxmore. He escaped unhurt.

The Messerschmitt double act, a large force of Bf 110 fighter-bombers escorted by 109s, crossed the Island again the following afternoon, heading this time for nearby Southampton. Again, the Hurricanes of Tangmere's 145 Squadron were scrambled to make the interception. At Ventnor, Mary Watson had been recording 'dog fights every day . . . right over our houses' in her diary. 'It was a thrilling sight, with several fights going on at the same time . . . the trails of smoke in the blue sky look lovely.'

Such were the images of aerial warfare in November 1940. Behind them, the harsh reality was the loss of more young lives. Just west of Ventnor, at Woody Bay, Pilot Officer A.N.C. Weir died when Hurricane P2720 crashed into the sea. Nearby, at Old Park, St Lawrence,

41

The removal of a large delayed-action bomb from its crater at Whippingham. A number of bombs were jettisoned in the area by a disabled Messerschmitt as it sought sufficient height for a getaway on the night of 17/18 November 1940. (CCM)

Flying Officer D.B. Sykes was more fortunate when making a crash-landing in sister plane P2924; he escaped with relatively minor injuries. To the north, in a disused chalk pit on Ashey Down, Pilot Officer J. Ashton survived, unhurt, a crash in a third Hurricane, P2683. Another came down off Littlestairs Beach at Shanklin, injuring its pilot, and the Luftwaffe lost a Bf 109, together with the pilot, further out to sea, south-east of St Catherine's.

Another British fighter plane was seen to ditch in the sea off Foreland on 8 November, but that was to prove the Isle of Wight's last aircraft casualty until the end of the month. The Island, however, continued to serve as a dumping ground for frustrated Luftwaffe bombers as the big raids on mainland England carried on unabated.

At Ryde on the 15th, Fred Kerridge's private log filled up with details of another four raid warnings — taking the total past 275 — between early afternoon and late evening, when a further attack on London kept the Isle of Wight in a state of alert throughout the night. By the time he had logged warning 300 on the evening of 23 November, many more high-explosive and incendiary bombs had fallen on the Island. But that raid on the 23rd was the first significant one to involve Ryde.

The warning sirens were heard in the town at 6.15pm. Fred Kerridge recorded "heavy AA gunfire soon after start, and continuous till 9.20," and went on to list a catalogue of both high-explosive and incendiary bombing incidents. It was 11.25 before Ryde was given the 'All Clear.'

Seven fires were reported in the town that night as a direct result of falling incendiaries.

The most serious was at St John's Lodge, Appley, where evacuation was deemed necessary; it was from here that the night's only casualty — a man with leg burns — was taken to hospital. In the same area, six houses in Arundel Road suffered bomb damage, largely confined to windows and doors, and a family was evacuated from Gordon Villa in Marlborough Road owing to the presence of a suspected UXB at Farrington House in nearby High Park Road.

High-explosive bombs were reported in the Marlborough Road-Arundel Road-High Park Road area, and near Ashey Waterworks, causing damage to two houses and the waterworks itself. Incendiaries had fallen at Westhill Road, St John's Wood Road and Gatehouse Farm, Upton. Not far from Ryde, a high-explosive bomb had exploded at the rear of Station House, St Helens, causing slight structural damage. An incendiary bomb which pierced the roof of Westfield, in Wootton High Street, and entered a bedroom, was safely disposed of by the occupant. Bombs had also fallen elsewhere in Wootton, and in the Cowes and Newport areas.

Throughout the next day a crop of UXBs were reported. A day later, there were still 28 on the Island, the vast majority near the railway at Whippingham, awaiting the attention of the bomb disposal squads. But it was quieter overhead, and would continue to be so until Thursday 28 November.

The Death of a Legend

On the afternoon of the 28th a force of Bf 109s was plotted south-west of the Island. They were from Stab/JG2, the headquarters flight of probably the most famous of all Luftwaffe fighter units. At their head was JG2's Kommodore, Helmut Wick. Aged 22, he had been promoted to the rank of Major the previous month and was the youngest German serviceman to have attained the status. As he approached the Island in his personalised 109e, Wick could claim 56 earlier victims among the ranks of the Allied air forces. But Thursday 28 November was to see his undoing.

Tangmere's 145 Squadron sent their Hurricanes to intercept the freelancing Messerschmitt force off St Catherine's Point. Fierce fighting followed, but Wick broke off the battle by

The famous Luftwaffe fighter ace Major Helmut Wick claimed several victories while in combat over the Island in 1940 before he was killed off the Needles in a dogfight on 28 November. The picture shows his Messrschmitt Bf 109 in northern France — with its tally of 'kills' on the rudder. (Andy Saunders)

ordering the 109s back to their Normandy base for fresh supplies of both fuel and arms. Returning to the same area, he then led his force in a diving attack on some of 609 Squadron's Warmwell-based Spitfires below them. What happened next has been a source of earnest debate ever since by historians in both Britain and Germany, leading always to the big question: who shot down Helmut Wick?.

Most sources credit the elimination of one of the finest fighter pilots of the war to Flight Lieutenant J. Dundas, of 609 Squadron, the man who led the Spitfire force that day. Wick had just dispatched Pilot Officer Baillon's Spitfire into the sea off the Island's south-western coast when Dundas attacked him. The German ace was soon plummeting into the sea himself — but was his resultant death caused by Dundas or, as was later claimed, by a colleague, Pilot Officer Marrs, in another Spitfire? Any clarification Dundas himself might have been able to provide was denied through the shooting down of his own plane by Oberleutnant Rudi Pilanz — an incident the Flight Lieutenant was not to survive; his Spitfire also ditched in the sea.

There was one crash-landing that day on the Island itself, Pilot Officer A.M. Lyall's 609 Squadron Spitfire hitting the ground at Rill Farm, just north of Whiteley Bank. An ambulance and first aid party were immediately sent from Shanklin, but their help was sadly limited to removal of the pilot's body to the Town Hall mortuary. In fact, none of the pilots shot down in the fierce aerial battle that day lived to tell the tale. It is, however, well told in the Battle of Britain Hall at Tangmere's museum, where the display includes a fine portrait of Helmut Wick, who became a legend at 22.

Drama to the End

The catalogue of bombs, exploded or otherwise, littering the Island continued as November drew to a close and the Luftwaffe's major mainland targets again included a battered Southampton. The prolonged, and devastating, overnight blitz of the city on 30 November/1 December produced a knock-on effect for the Island. The Southern Railway's Portsmouth-Ryde boat service was disrupted following the emergency commandeering during the night of one of the route's paddle-steamers, which was used to carry fire-fighting apparatus to the beleagured city.

Ryde came in for something of a battering itself on the wet evening of Thursday 5 December. The siren wailed out its warning at 6.15pm; before long bombs were dropping right in the heart of the residential area — miraculously without causing loss of life. The official ARP log book for this period of the war is missing, but Fred Kerridge's private log gives a summarised account of the major incidents. He recorded that twelve bombs fell in Bennett Street and another three in Riboleau Street, where a house was practically demolished and others damaged. Bombs also fell between Warwick Street and High Street, and in the Newport Street-Five Ways-Queen's Road area. The 'All Clear' was sounded at 9.15.

Again, the Luftwaffe had succeeded in disrupting the Island's train service. At 6.45pm a bomb had fallen on the double track just north of Ryde St John's Road Station, causing damage just in time to derail the locomotive at the head of the 6.35pm Ryde Pier Head-Ventnor passenger train; fortunately, there were no casualties.

The engine was successfully returned to the rails the following afternoon, when repair and clearance work was completed on the track.

Night raiders continued to cross the Channel as Christmas approached, heading for a variety of mainland target cities. The air raid alerts continued to mount up on the Island, and the bombs continued to fall. There was a two-night break on the 17/18 and 18/19 December, then more raids and more indiscriminate bombing of the Island before aerial hostilities temporarily ceased — over both Britain and Germany — for three nights at Christmas.

The only recorded plane crash in December had come shortly before midnight on 22 December, when a patrolling Bristol Blenheim 1F night-fighter, from 23 Squadron at Ford, Sussex, developed problems south of the Island. Although the three-man crew baled out, only the pilot, Flight Sergeant Loveridge, landed safely — near Ventnor. Flight Sergeants Newman and Southall drowned after coming down in the sea, and their stricken Blenheim finally crashed on Brading Down.

Dramatic to the last, 1940 finished with a massive fire bomb attack on London overnight on 29/30 December — and the Isle of Wight buzzed with the sensational news of the sentencing to death for treachery of a 42-year-old Sandown housewife.

Dorothy O'Grady, who lived at Osborne Villa in The Broadway, had been charged with nine offences, denying them all. Most were brought under the Treachery Act of 1940 and the guilty verdicts returned by the jury at Hampshire Assizes on 17 December left Mr Justice Macnaghten with no alternative but the passing of the death sentence. However, after a subsequent appeal early in 1941, Mrs O'Grady's life was spared. She was, instead, sent to prison for 14 years. An examination of this extraordinary and mysterious case appears in Part 4.

FIVE

The Night Raiders

The year may have changed, but it was 'business as usual' for the Luftwaffe at the beginning of 1941, with a continuation of the nightly attacks on the cities and industrial heart of Britain – and a constant interruption of sleep for Islanders below the raiders' flight path.

Thursday 9 January brought the first real drama of the new year. Wartime censorship restricted the *Isle of Wight County Press* to reporting the fall of several HE bombs and showers of incendiaries on the outskirts of "a town," but the Nazis had no such inhibitions. In their communique of 10 January a list of the towns raided the previous night accurately included "Newport, Isle of Wight." Eight houses were damaged on the main road to Ryde.

When Portsmouth Burned

On the night of Friday 10 January, Portsmouth was singled out for savage attention by the Luftwaffe. Some 300 enemy bombers made up the attacking force, pounding the city with an estimated 450 HE bombs – plus incendiaries – over a prolonged period. They killed 171 people, injured another 430 and left 3,000 homeless. Portsmouth's splendid Guildhall was gutted, and many other historic buildings were left as smoking ruins.

People on the Isle of Wight's north coast watched the unfolding tragedy on the other side of the Solent with a feeling of utter helplessness. Grocer Ernie Jolliffe, who was Ryde's Deputy ARPO at the time, recalls: "We watched Portsmouth burn. The sky turned completely red. We wanted to do something, to go over there and help, but we were told it would do no good because we didn't know the lie of the land and

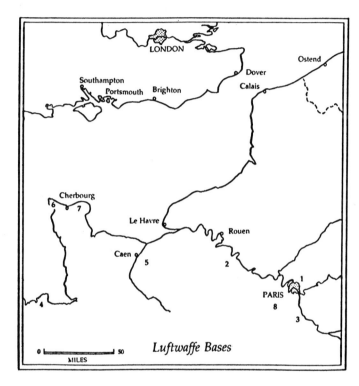

Map showing Luftwaffe headquarter airfields within Luftflotte 3's sphere of operations in northern France, as at August 1940. It was from these bases, and the many smaller satellite airfields attached to them, that most of the raids against the Island were launched. Headquarters shown are: 1 (Paris) Orly – KG51. 2 Evreux – KG54. 3 Villacoublay – KG55. 4 St Malo – StG 2. 5 Caen – StG77. 6 Cherbourg West – JG27. 7 Cherbourg – JG53. 8 Toussee-le-Noble – ZG2.

would only get in the way of the rescue operation."

Fred Kerridge, who made up his notes that night with shells falling all around him, recorded "almost continuous AA fire from 5.30pm until 1.40am . . . the noisiest raids to date."

Portsmouth was again singled out for heavy bombing raids on the evenings of 9 and 10

March – and that meant problems for Ryde. The county ARP record for this period of the war is missing, but Fred Kerridge's private log reveals the location of a number of bombs which fell at the heart of the Island town's shopping centre on the 9th. They were recorded in Spencer Road, near St Thomas's Church, in Union Lane and in the main shopping thoroughfare of Union Street – where a 500lb UXB was removed safely. Surprisingly little damage was caused.

One Man and a Bomb

On 11 March a suspected UXB was located on the double-track railway in Ryde, north of St John's Road Station. Traffic was immediately suspended between there and the Pier Head terminus while the Southern Railway called in the experts. Ernie Jolliffe recalls, however, that the incident was dealt with in rather less expert a fashion than the railwaymen had a right to expect:

I went into our report centre at Caversham House that evening and was told the railway company was requesting an expert in UXBs. However, as far as could be made out, the nearest bomb disposal people that evening were in Portsmouth, and they couldn't spare anyone. So I was told: 'You'll have to go instead.' Me? I had just come out of a grocer's shop. I didn't know anything about unexploded bombs! It was a wet, dark evening, I remember. I went down to St John's Road Station and was met by a group of very big men, including Bob Sweetman, who was foreman of the railway works. He knew I was his grocer, of course, but I had on my white helmet with the initials DARPO across it, and fortunately he didn't recognise me!

They gave me a hurricane lamp and suggested I walk down the railway line to where the bomb lay. So I set off along the track and walked towards the gas works. Behind me, following respectfully at a distance, came the railwaymen – some of the toughest-looking chaps I had ever seen, and all of them in awe of the 'expert' up front!. Eventually, we reached the site. There was a railway engine there, and steam all over the place. I was frightened to death, I can tell you! Anyway, I had a 'nose around' and told them I couldn't see anything that looked as if it was going to cause an immediate problem. I suggested it should be left until daylight – then I cleared off as quickly as I could!

Housewives were first urged to 'make-do and mend' on this wartime civilian economy poster. (IWM)

The Southern Railway's official record of the incident reveals that the offending object was an unexploded shell, about five feet deep. Emergency bus services operated between St John's Road and Esplanade stations, and passengers travelling on to the Pier Head terminus were conveyed the rest of the way by the pier tramway. A bomb disposal squad did finally arrive to deal with the shell, which was removed in time to permit a 10.30am re-opening of the line on 12 March.

Tragedy at Yafford – 1

Tuesday 11 March was punctuated by no less than nine air raid alerts on the Island – a record that would never be broken. The last of the day, just after 8pm, was the one that mattered.

It was virtually five hours before the 'All Clear' was sounded; by that time the tiny village of Yafford, in the Island's south-west, had suffered its first wartime tragedy. A lone raider, presumably aiming for a nearby searchlight post, dropped four bombs above the village. One thudded into the stone-built home of the Wadlow family, which was also used as a wartime billet for officers of the 19th Royal Fusiliers. Mrs Wadlow, her ten-year-old daughter and an Army officer were all killed, while a second officer and an officer's batman suffered injuries. Mr Wadlow had a miraculous escape, finding himself actually under the floorboards after the blast. Scrambling out from the ruins of his home, with nothing worse than a few scratches, he then assisted in the sad search for the bomb victims.

Two nights later, 13 high-explosive bombs thudded into the countryside just east of Billingham Manor, now military headquarters for the newly-arrived 214th Infantry Brigade. Another Island manor house was threatened on 14 March when 16 HE bombs, plus incendiaries, rained down at Arreton. The three which fell in fields near Arreton Manor caused little damage, but the incident did have a serious outcome. Two bombs exploded in the garden behind Box Tree Cottage, the home of 15-year-old Betty Howe and her family. Betty was treated for shock; the cottage required the services of the demolition party.

Islanders were learning the hard way that you didn't have to be particularly close to an exploding bomb to suffer the effects. Three HE bombs which came down in Whitefield Woods, south of Ryde, late on 14 March shattered the windows of houses at Haylands — two miles away.

Two Direct Hits

More lives were lost on the evening of 15 March when the Luftwaffe scored a direct hit on the searchlight post at Battery Road, Cowes, killing three of the soldiers manning it, and injuring two others. Twenty-eight houses were damaged in the attack. On the same night the searchlight battery on Ashey Down narrowly escaped when another HE bomb was dropped nearby. Then, on 17 March, the men manning the searchlights on Ryde Esplanade were evacuated from their post on the tennis courts following the discovery of an unexploded AA shell. By 6pm that day, the pock-marked Island soil was littered with 36 unexploded bombs or shells.

A Bristol Blenheim bomber (59 Squadron's V5396) from Thorney Island caused some excitement when it made a forced landing at Brook, south-east of Freshwater, on the morning of Saturday 22 March. The two-man crew escaped unhurt, and the plane, its undercarriage slightly damaged, was later dismantled and removed by an RAF maintenance team.

In the early evening of Sunday 23 March, 49-year-old Louisa Baker was serving tea at her home in Green Lane, Shanklin, to the elderly couple who lived next door. Shortly before 6pm a high-explosive bomb demolished the house — and killed all three people. Four others, two men and two women, were injured in the explosion, which also wrecked a neighbouring house and seriously damaged several nearby.

The 500th Isle of Wight air raid alert was heard during March. It was just one of the month's 109 warnings. The arrival of April did nothing to change the pattern. The relentless night offensive on mainland England showed no signs of abating.

Tragedy at Yafford — 2

An unidentified German aircraft released four bombs into the sea off Freshwater in the early hours of Saturday 5 April before plunging into the water itself, the victim of a British fighter plane. On the same night, the area between Whippingham Church and Kingston Farm escaped lightly from the descent of some 50 incendiary bombs — but Yafford was left to mourn its second tragedy within the space of a few weeks.

It was shortly before 2am when a combination of high-explosive and incendiary bombs fell on Yafford and neighbouring Brighstone. With cruel irony, John Ferrari, a 16-year-old evacuee from Portsmouth, died in his supposedly safe rural haven at Yafford of shrapnel wounds from an exploding HE bomb. A member of the local fire-fighting unit, he was endeavouring to put out a fire started by an incendiary bomb in an unoccupied cottage.

Less damage was caused by the eight bombs which fell at Brighstone, but a nearby house was quickly evacuated when a bomb in a field at Hunny Hill, west of the village, was found to be unexploded. Gunville, Carisbrooke, Parkhurst and East Cowes were also bombed that night, with little resultant damage, but the roofs of the farmhouse at Idlecombe, south-west of Newport, and an adjoining cottage, did need repairing after blast damage the following evening.

The isolated West Wight rail outpost at Ningwood − the scene of a disproportinate number of wartime bombing incidents − was again the centre of attention just before midnight on 9 April when a shed behind the semi-detached McCullagh and Draper cottages near the station was set on fire by incendiaries. The flames quickly spread to the thatched roofs, and the cottages were destroyed. Nobody was hurt, and the homeless couples were accommodated overnight by neighbours. The Women's Voluntary Service was on the spot to dispense tea and sympathy to both rescued and rescuers; its services would be much in demand over the succeeding months.

On 10 April, Maundy Thursday, the regional civil defence headquarters in Reading warned that there was "every reason to maintain civil defence and fire precautions over the Easter holiday . . . no relaxation can be permitted." It proved a masterpiece of understatement. The Luftwaffe had no intention of taking Easter off.

Good Friday 1941

Just after midnight, in the first few minutes of Good Friday, the blast from an HE bomb which crashed on the foreshore at Alum Bay, in the far west of the Island, smashed 60 windows at the Needles Hotel and its outbuildings. The hotel had been requisitioned by the Admiralty, but had been vacated only days earlier. At about the same time, reports were coming in of a plane "falling in flames" in the Ventnor area. The Island was about to claim its first night bomber victim − a Heinkel He 111 (6N+HL) from 3. KG100 at Vannes.

On its way back to the Brittany base after leading a raid in the Midlands, the Heinkel was shot down by Pilot Officer G.C. Budd in a 609 Squadron Bristol Beaufighter from Middle Wallop. It crashed at The Hermitage, near Whitwell, with the bodies of two of its five-man crew still

DURING BLACK-OUT HOURS

KEEP ALL BLINDS DRAWN.

KEEP ALL WINDOWS SHUT, except when it is necessary to lower them so that passengers may open doors to alight

MAKE CERTAIN the train is at the platform, and that you alight on the platform side

WHEN LEAVING THE CARRIAGE, close windows, lower blinds again, and close the door quickly. Doors leading to corridors should be closed at once after passengers have left the compartment and blinds readjusted, unless outside corridor windows are completely blacked out

DO NOT TOUCH ELECTRIC LIGHTS, except those under passengers' control. Please switch these off when not in use

ALL NECESSARY LIGHTS will be switched off in the event of an Air Raid warning

FOR YOUR OWN SAFETY

WARNING

•

Thousands of lives were lost in the last war, because valuable information was given away to the enemy through careless talk

•

BE ON YOUR GUARD

DURING AN AIR RAID

1. Close all windows and ventilators and pull down the blinds as a protection against flying glass.

2. If danger seems imminent, lie on the floor.

3. Never leave the train between stations unless so requested by a railway official.

4. Do not touch any outside part of a coach if a gas attack is suspected.

Three of the many notices put up in train compartments giving advice to Isle of Wight rail travellers − very timely in 1941 with the air raid siren an all too frequent feature of Island life. (Author / Ben Houfton)

inside. The others had all baled out, but only Feldwebel H. Hank succeeded in opening his parachute and, thus, became the solitary survivor of the crash. At 2.10am, County ARP Control was instructing district report centres to "notify all wardens' posts immediately that an enemy airman is at large on the Island. Every endeavour should be made to notify the public also — after daylight." Hank was at liberty on the Island until late the following afternoon, when he was captured at Ventnor.

Other dramas had been unfolding in the early hours of Good Friday, as more bombs fell in several areas of the Island. Then, at 3.45am, came the first news of serious bombing incidents at Ryde.

Nine HE bombs had been dropped in the lower part of the town, but details reaching County ARP Control from Ryde were initially sparse. There was a good reason for that — one of the bombs had fallen on the town's report centre at Caversham House, in Dover Street. Gradually, the news filtered through . . . "considerable damage to property in The Strand . . . evacuations from the Vectis Nursing Home . . . some trapped in Monkton Street . . . feared one or two casualties."

An update on the situation at Monkton Street, which links Ryde's seafront area with St John's Road Station, was not long in coming: "One man killed. Two women badly injured. All trapped." There had been a direct hit on the house at 99 Monkton Street, the home of 47-year-old town councillor 'Alfie' Williams. Further updates revised the casualty situation, confirming the death of Mr Williams — and also that of his 44-year-old wife. Her sister, who lived at the house, died later in hospital, although Mrs Williams's father miraculously escaped serious injury. A married couple were rescued, unhurt, from the ruins of their home next door. It was a sad loss for Ryde. Councillor Williams had been prominent in both the administrative and social life of the town.

Remarkably, casualties from the Ryde bombing were confined to the Monkton Street incident. Nobody was hurt in adjacent Wood Street, despite the fact that four of the bombs had actually landed there, and the evacuation of Vectis Nursing Home in The Strand — the rear of the building faced the seafront — was completed safely. An adjacent hotel, which bore the

By 1941 the Island's coastline was liberally punctuated with concrete gun emplacements like this 1989 survivor near Bembridge Point. (Ben Houfton)

brunt of the seafront blast, was badly damaged. Later in the day, one of three UXBs at another house on The Strand exploded, fortunately without casualties. Villages on the outskirts of Ryde had also suffered. Four HE bombs fell near Nettlestone and St Helens, causing blast damage, and another destroyed Seaview's fashionable Garland Club, eye-witnesses describing how pieces of the building were thrown "hundreds of feet into the air."

Altogether, 17 HE bombs and scores of incendiaries had been dropped on the Island in the early hours of Good Friday — but it wasn't over yet. Parachuted mines caused further problems as the morning progressed. Worst-hit in this phase of the attack was the Cowes area, where two mines extensively damaged property — including Gurnard Church — over a wide area. Another mine exploded near Nodes Point Battery at St Helens, also damaging property in the village. The 'All Clear' was finally sounded at 4.13am — after seven hours of Eastertide chaos.

Drama in Cambridge Road

At 9.50pm on Thursday 24 April, shortly after the day's third air raid alert had sounded, the rescue and first-aid parties were summoned to Cambridge Road, East Cowes, where the Oatley family's home lay partly in ruins following a direct hit from a high-explosive bomb. It quickly became clear that the four people inside were trapped.

Rescuers soon freed Mrs Oatley's 86-year-old mother, who was crouched beneath a table. After some difficulty they also managed to extricate Mrs Oatley herself from the debris. The women emerged with only slight injuries, thanks to the prompt and efficient response of their rescuers in a house liable to collapse at any moment. Its perilous condition had already claimed two further victims. The search for the Oatleys' two teenage sons was broadened when it became clear that Wardens Brinton and Cowburn, the first on the scene, had themselves disappeared.

Soon, reinforcements began arriving from other parts of the Island to help the rescue operation. The body of 18-year-old Everett Oatley was removed from the house after some three hours. Throughout the next day, and into the weekend, the rescuers toiled away in a hole excavated amid the debris. On the evening of Saturday 26 April the hole caved in and the desperate work had to be abandoned. Soon after the rescue operation resumed at lunchtime on the Sunday, the body of 19-year-old Edward Riddell, the Oatleys' adopted son, was recovered, but the two wardens were reported to have been "entombed by the subsidence." The excavation was now 20 feet deep. All realistic hope of finding the men alive had been abandoned.

Finally, at 4.30pm on Tuesday 29 April, the exhausted rescuers located the bodies of the wardens. By 9pm both had been removed from the wreckage. The 120-hour rescue operation was over.

It had been far from quiet elsewhere on the Island. In the West Wight, the fine Georgian fabric of Sir John Simeon's Swainston House had been gutted by incendiaries, while, at the other end of the Island, cottages at Nettlestone had been evacuated when a fire broke out in a bedroom. HE bombs east of Newport had smashed windows in houses at Buckbury Lane and caused blast damage at Little Pan Farmhouse – and at Ryde the dangers from straying anti-aircraft shells had been tragically demonstrated on the evening of the 27th.

A shell had exploded on the gateposts outside the north door of St John's Church, demolishing part of the church wall. A dislodged stone

fragment flew across High Park Road and killed War Reserve Policeman William Kelly, who was standing outside the telephone kiosk opposite the church. "It went right through the band of his trilby hat, and killed him outright, poor chap," remembers Ernie Jolliffe.

The Luftwaffe continued to threaten the Island's rich architectural heritage. On 4 May a quartet of bombs dropped uncomfortably near magnificent North Court at Shorwell, In the early hours of 8 May, Farringford, Alfred Lord Tennyson's former home in the West Wight, was even closer to disaster when a Heinkel He 111 from 2./KG27, on its way home after yet another night raid in the Midlands, crashed nearby. It was "completely smashed and burnt out," according to West Wight's ARPO, and, of the four-man crew, only Oberfeldwebel H. Laube survived to be taken prisoner-of-war by locally-based soldiers.

A Cowes Chronicle

Twelve days after the Luftwaffe lost a Junkers Ju 88 from 1./KG40, and its four-man crew, in a plunge into the Solent off Egypt Point, Cowes, a sister aircraft, taking advantage of low cloud cover, sneaked in from the east on the evening of Saturday 24 May and dive-bombed the riverside cement works between Newport and Cowes. Surprisingly little damage was caused by the nine bombs which were dropped, and the only casualty was a Home Guardsman who was struck on the head by flying debris. The raider evaded machine-gun fire and made its getaway. Not so fortunate was the 7.12pm Newport-Cowes passenger train on the adjacent railway. The locomotive and its two coaches were derailed, fortunately with no casualties, and the line was immediately closed until a successful re-railing operation the following day paved the way for a resumption of the rail service early on the 26th.

The next raid of significance, in the early hours of Tuesday 27 May, produced the most macabre incident of the Island's war. Four HE bombs thudded into the southern outskirts of Cowes, two of them exploding in the town's principal cemetery at Northwood. It suffered extensively, with headstones uprooted or smashed, many graves covered in clay, and both the chapel and mortuary damaged.

Vera Brown's father was a full-time ARP warden at Cowes, and she recalls him attending the cemetery on the night it was bombed:

This was a very nasty incident. The bombs had disturbed quite a number of the graves, and my father was considerably shaken by it. My uncle, who was also in the ARP, attended the cemetery at the same time. He contracted a very unusual disease and died within a few days. The doctors and pathologists said it had directly resulted from the cemetery incident, and his wife was awarded a war widow's pension as a result.

Another extraordinary incident at Cowes followed 24 hours later. As an outstanding story of escape from the clutches of death, it would appear to have few equals. This is how Minnie Spencer, a 33-year-old Cowes housewife at the time, remembers it:

My husband and I were asleep in bed at our Tennyson Road home, with our five-year-old son, Adrian, beside us. We used to turn the gas off before we went to bed and take a candle and a torch upstairs with us. We had done so on this particular night, and my husband had put them by his side of the bed. I don't remember any sirens that night – I think they thought it was just a reconnaissance plane going over. Anyway, at about twenty past one, I woke up and heard all this fizzing around my neck. I thought at first it was the candle, so I went to nudge my husband and ask him if he had forgotten to put it out.

But, as I sat up, something rolled down from my neck. It was an incendiary bomb! It had come straight through our roof and the ceiling of the bedroom. and had ended up on my neck. We hadn't heard a thing!

I then noticed that the bottom of the bed was on fire. My first thought was for my son, so I called out to my husband: 'Get Adrian!' It was then that I realised I had been injured. I said: 'I've lost my arm!' I couldn't feel my right arm at all, it just didn't seem to be there. I even looked under the bed for it! It *was* still there, of course, but it had a compound fracture, and all the feeling had gone from it.

We made for the stairs, but when I got to about the third step from the bottom, the Germans dropped a high-explosive bomb nearby, and it shook me hard against the wall. I eventually reached the bottom and sat on a chair with the child on my knee while my husband, having given me something to tie up my arm with, went back upstairs and tried to put out the fire. I went to the front door and called the wardens. They came in, coped with the fire and got in touch with the first-aid post at Northwood House.

Lead-up to a Major Incident

Sunshine on the first day of June was marred by a serious bombing incident at Cowes. The sirens wailed just before 2pm, coinciding with the dropping of the first of 16 HE bombs on the town. Two houses were demolished, another 20 suffered structural damage, and blast damage to buildings over a wide area was also reported. All of the nine casualties, however, suffered only minor injuries. Cowes was attacked again on 9 June, this time with a combination of high-explosive and incendiary devices. One of the former lay unexploded in Bernard Road, necessitating the evacuation of residents to the nearby Methodist Church. Altogether, some 100 houses suffered damage in this raid, although it was mostly of a minor nature – as were the injuries to the night's three human casualties.

In between those incidents, on 5 June, the spectacular descent of a fiercely burning German aircraft into the sea some six miles off Woody Point, near Ventnor, was reported by both the coastguards at Blackgang and the eagle-eyed plane spotters of the Royal Observer Corps.

Six nights later, it was Wootton's turn, with a combination of incendiary and HE bombs crashing to earth in an early hours raid. Soldiers at the searchlight post in Palmers Road narrowly escaped injury, but a civilian living at Little Canada Holiday Camp, off New Road, was not so fortunate; he was taken to hospital with "serious injuries." The evening of Friday the 13th was notable for a spectacular four-plane dogfight off Bembridge, and an apparent attempt to attack the Examination Vessel in St Helens Roads; two bombs just missed it. The next six nights, although all interrupted by the sirens, produced little in the way of drama, and, for a change, even the sirens were quiet throughout 20 and 21 June.

This unexpected lull proved horribly deceptive. Sunday 22 June was just 90 minutes old when the sirens wailed out their warning. The words 'Major Incident' were about to be used on the Isle of Wight for the first time in the war. For the town of Ryde, it was to be the worst incident of the entire conflict.

SIX

The Menace of the Mines

St Michael's Avenue, a pleasantly quiet residential street running between Upton Road and Bettesworth Road in the Swanmore district of Ryde, was known by another name in the 1939-45 war. A wall plaque erected there in April 1950 records that "the trees in this road have been provided, mainly through voluntary contributions made by residents of the district, as a living memorial to those who lost their lives by enemy action in the area on June 22nd 1941."

People who experienced the war years in Ryde always remember the incident that took place in the early hours of that fateful Sunday. It was the night Bettesworth Road School was totally destroyed . . . the night eleven people, including five children, lost their lives and 50 others were injured . . . the night the heart was ripped out of what used to be called Church Street.

The tragedy of Church Street was caused by a terrifyingly sinister weapon always referred to in wartime England as a land-mine. In fact, these were ordinary sea-mines, eight feet or more long and equipped with rows of horns at the top and bottom, which descended silently to earth by parachute. Many were dropped on the Island by the Luftwaffe, but none with such devastating results as the Church Street mines.

Ryde's 774th air raid alert disturbed its sleeping residents at 1.30am on a clear, but dark, summer night. Twenty minutes later a series of explosions rocked the town, and, at ten minutes past two, ARP headquarters in Newport received a short message from the Ryde report centre: "Land-mine exploded at top of Church Street, Swanmore." Twenty minutes later Ryde's police station was on the line with a dramatic follow-up: "Major incident . . . several houses demolished."

It was established that two parachuted mines had fallen in Church Street — although one

The wall plaque in St Michael's Avenue, Ryde . . . recording the loss of life in the 'land mine' attack of 22 June 1941, when the avenue was known as Church Street. (Ben Houfton)

failed to explode — and another in Bettesworth Road. Twenty houses had been either totally wrecked or severely damaged. The elementary school had been reduced to a pile of rubble on its corner site. As the early morning progressed, so the list of casualties grew. Many of the injured had escaped with wounds that could be adequately treated at the first aid post; others with more serious injuries were taken the short distance to the Royal IW County Hospital. But it had soon become apparent that several of the night's victims were beyond help.

Some of the dead were pitifully young. The first body to be positively identified was that of Michael Rhodes, of 22 Church Street. "Aged four years, male, single," read the text of the official ARP message. Two of the school's pupils were killed in their homes, and the injured included a 94-year-old woman. Yet, in spite of the awful unfolding tragedy, the wartime spirit of togetherness in adversity kept people going. "Civilian morale excellent throughout," reported the wardens at 9.30.

The rescue work continued throughout the day until everyone had been accounted for —

dead or alive. The final casualty figures were given shortly before 6pm: "Dead − five female, one male, five children. Injured − approximately 50." More than 130 people were suddenly homeless and many were given temporary shelter and refreshment at the town's Commodore Cinema. In addition to the appalling destruction in Church Street itself, damage to buildings throughout the town was reported.

Noreen Searle − formerly Miss Warne − lived at nearby Ashey Road at the time of the 'landmine' incident:

My mother, brother and myself were in bed when we heard all these terrible explosions. Then a blast blew me right out of my bed and I was knocked unconscious on the fireplace. Jack, my brother, carried me downstairs − or, at least. he tried to! It was very difficult because of the damage done to our house. The roof had gone, for one thing, and there was broken glass all over the place. Windows and doors had all been blown out. It was terrible. I eventually came round at my aunt's house further down the road, which hadn't been so badly affected. My brother lost all his clothes that night − we never found any of them. In the morning we just didn't know where to start clearing up; every room was the same, a terrible mess.

I had a dog, a little mongrel we called Rover. After some searching, we discovered him under the back door, which had been completely blown in. We had probably walked over the poor little thing several times. He looked a bit like a pancake, but all he had was bruising! After that, though, every time the air raid siren was sounded, he used to run down the middle of the road barking loudly − it was as good as a second siren!

There were other stories of miraculous escape. The elderly school caretaker, W.H. Fry, and his wife were trapped under the debris at their adjoining lodge, but their lives were saved by a dislodged heavy beam which prevented the rubble from burying them completely. ARP Warden Palmer was on patrol when the Church Street mine exploded just 20 feet from where he was standing − and flung him to safety in a passageway. It was the most hectic night of the war for the Ryde-based wardens, and for Ernie Jolliffe it provided the image that was to linger the longest: "I met this poor woman in Church Street, standing there and staring at where her home had been. She had nothing left but what she had on . . ."

The roof over the south aisle of St Michael's and All Angels Church, on the corner of Church Street and Wray Street, was ripped off in the raid, and many windows of the church were broken, but St Michael's was undoubtedly saved from total destruction through the protection afforded by the substantially-built school, just south of it, which bore the brunt of the blast. With so much debris inside the church, the vicarage lawn was used for the poignant church services held that Sunday.

Green Street and Trinity schools, elsewhere in Ryde, absorbed most of Bettesworth Road's pupils following the tragedy, but the Standard 1 and Infants classes were eventually re-located in the refurbished St Michael's Church Hall, where the only classes until then had been for the church's Sunday School. Incredibly, less than two years later, lightning − Luftwaffe-style − would strike for a second time at the self same spot.

A Quieter Interlude

A Hawker Hurricane (32 Squadron's Ibsley-based Z3396) crashed into a cliff at Freshwater Bay on a foggy 23 June, killing its pilot, Pilot Officer S. Szmejl. Three days later a combination of mines and high-explosive bombs were dropped on the Rookley area. Windows were blown out and slates dislodged in the village itself, while damage was reported to buildings at Sibden and Rookley Manor farms. The bomb disposal teams were busy again all over the Island − and were able to deal with the many reported UXBs during a period of relative calm on the Island. Indeed, when compared with the first six months of the year, the whole of the second half of 1941 was relatively − by wartime standards − incident-free.

While the night raids on mainland targets continued, and planes were seen to fall out to sea − three He 111s from KG100 ditched off the Needles on 7 July − about the only real occurrence of note during the next three months was the crash-landing of an off-course Junkers Ju 88 (4D+CH from 1./KG30) with an empty fuel tank on Bembridge Down. It had been returning from a raid on Birkenhead when the RAF successfully jammed the homing signals of the bomber force. 'Jock' Leal has unearthed an interesting sequel to the 24 July crash:

The P.S. Portsdown. *In September* 1940 *the* Portsdown *struck a mine off Southsea and sank with the loss of* 20 *lives.* (Author)

Second World War mines now serve as giant collecting 'boxes' on the Island for the Shipwrecked Mariners' Society. This one was pictured at Blackgang Chine. (Author)

Shortly after 0600 hours a youth out rabbiting on the down with a Sandown man stumbled on the aircraft. Carrying a double-barrel shotgun, they approached the plane. The crew were busy inside. Leutnant Diederich (the pilot) came towards them, telling them in perfect English to get clear as the aircraft was going to be blown up. With the three other crew members (Uffz Wiedermann, Gfr Riecke and Gfr Wildermann) they quickly got away from the area and the Ju 88 blew up. After this Diederich handed over his revolver and said he wished to be taken to the authorities as they were surrendering.

The Loss of the *Portsdown*

At 4am on 20 September the Southern Railway paddle-steamer *Portsdown* left Portsmouth Harbour for the mail run to Ryde Pier. She was destined never to complete the crossing. A book officially commissioned in 1946 to tell the story of the SR at war includes a graphic account of the *Portsdown* tragedy from the steamer's look-out man — his name was Jupe — that morning:

We left Portsmouth Harbour Pier at 4am. After we had cleared the harbour Channel buoys, the vessel was rounded up to go through the swashway to

continue our journey to Ryde. About a minute after this . . . I heard a sort of scraping noise alongside the port side of the ship, and then, after what must have been a few seconds, there was a terrific explosion. At this moment I was looking out across the port bow and I was thrown into the sea. When I came to the surface, I grasped a piece of floating wood and swam to the after port side sponson, where I climbed on board and assisted in getting out the lifeboats, both of which were lowered and loaded with passengers.

The *Portsdown* had struck a mine off Spit Bank Fort, Southsea. Although a Naval pinnace went out immediately after the explosion and saved 17 people, mostly servicemen, between 12 and 14 passengers and eight of the ship's crew of eleven were lost in the disaster. Built in 1928, the 342-ton paddler was so badly damaged in the explosion that she, finally, sank. Her remains were visible at low water for some years after the war.

Rescue at Steel Bay

A second potential disaster at sea led to the Island making the national news on the night of 10/11 November. The *Daily Express* had a man on the spot to provide a stirring tale of rescue and drama off the Island's south-eastern coast — just the stuff to boost morale on the Home Front. This is how he reported it:

Six British airmen, after battling with heavy seas for two days and nights in a rubber dinghy, drifted ashore at Steel Bay, near Ventnor, today. They were one of the 37 bomber crews reported missing after Friday night's heavy raid on Berlin and other parts of Germany . . . they had paddled and drifted between 150 and 200 miles in the two days. Their Wellington bomber, running short of petrol in the extremely bad weather conditions, crashed into the sea and broke in two, 30 miles from the Thames estuary. The pilot had been shot in the face and had injured his leg escaping from the bomber. But, as rescuers helped them out of the dinghy, he told them: 'Look after my mates. I'm okay. Give them my rum.' The airmen had been too weak to pull the stoppers out of the rum bottles.

Mr Lionel Martin, who lives in a cottage on the cliffs, had run down and jumped fully clothed into the breakers to carry a line to the dinghy. Helped by Fred Gould, of Bonchurch, and soldiers, he hauled it in. When the airmen asked him where they were, and he told them, one said: 'That's funny. I come from Ryde' . . . And a second, not to be outdone in cheerfulness, called out: 'I've always wanted to come

to the Isle of Wight!' . . . Soldiers carried the crew in their arms up the narrow path of a 200ft high cliff — a task involving considerable risk. At the top ambulances were waiting. In spite of their sufferings, the men kept cheerful all the time. The pilot was taken to hospital and the others were taken to a hotel and given dry clothing and hot drinks . . .

War and a little Peace

Early on the evening of 22 November two of 1 Squadron's Tangmere-based Hurricane fighters collided while patrolling over the east of the Island. One (Z3899) came down at Binstead Lodge Farm, west of Ryde. Flight Sergeant D.F. Perrin had successfully baled out and was only slightly injured. A search was then mounted for the second Hurricane (BD940), located soon afterwards at the rear of St Wilfred's in Ryde's Playstreet Lane. Its pilot, F/S L.J. Travis, was dead in the cockpit.

Sunday 7 December affected the whole course of the war, with the Japanese attack on the American fleet in Pearl Harbour extending hostilities into the Far East and bringing the mighty resources of the USA fully into the conflict. Britain and the USA formally declared war on Japan the following day, then Germany and Italy neatly rounded off the new battle line-up on 11 December with their joint declaration of hostilities against the Americans. Britain no longer stood alone.

Such momentous events had little obvious effect on the Isle of Wight, and, with the situation considerably less hectic than at the end of 1940, whole-time civil defence personnel on the Island were told that, all being well, they would be entitled to a special two-hour period of leave on Christmas Day. Nothing happened to spoil the seasonal gesture, and, apart from the discovery of two unexploded AA shells near Shorwell on the 28th, and the odd air raid alert, the year ended on a noticeably quiet note.

The first two months of 1942 followed a similar pattern. At Ryde, Fred Kerridge's log for January took up only five lines — one alert apiece on the 4th, 5th and 24th, and two on the 7th. It was a far cry from the 33 wails of the siren in January 1941. February was much the same, with seven alerts all followed within a matter of minutes by the 'All Clear.'

A New Aerial Threat

Islanders were not, of course, to know that the threat of invasion had finally been lifted, with the permanent cancellation of the German plans for Operation *Sea Lion*, and any lulled into a false sense of security by the reduced activity in the sky were in for a rude awakening when the arrival of March brought with it the first visit to the Isle of Wight of the Luftwaffe's 'tip and run' raiders.

These deadly radar-dodging low-level attacks by — initially, at least — the Bf 109s carried the combined threat of bomb, cannon and machine gun fire. It was mid-afternoon on a miserably wet Thursday 5 March when a brace of Messerschmitts from 10./JG2 tore up the *Back of the Wight* heading for Freshwater Bay. Two high-explosive bombs thudded down, killing three elderly people — two men and a woman — in a direct hit on The Porch, an old house formerly owned by Lady Ritchie, daughter of W.M. Thackeray. The house was totally destroyed and another adjoining it was badly damaged. The second bomb came down near the coastguard station, damaging many houses in the vicinity. but a fisherman on the beach was the only injury victim.

The West Wight was again in the firing line in the early hours of 17 April — this time with devastating results. A German bomber broke away from a mainland-bound raiding force,

Where to go for emergency rations at Gurnard in the event of a German invasion . . . a 1941-printed missive from the Ministry of Food. (Vera Brown)

dropped a flare above Brighstone's pre-war holiday camp, and followed it up with three HE bombs, demolishing with a direct hit Sea Breeze, a wood-built former hotel used by the military authorities for billeting soldiers. Twelve casualties resulted, ten of them fatal.

Later the same morning, another brace of HE bombs descended on one of the Island's oldest manor houses, at Great Budbridge, near Merstone. Fortunately, the damage caused was not severe. Nearby Newchurch reported several UXBs. On the 18th a bomb falling at Puck House Farm, near Fishbourne, shattered windows in neighbouring Wootton, and another, which came down in the sea off Sandown, damaged shop windows in eight High Street properties. An ack-ack shell plunged into a field just outside the walls of once-proud, but unoccupied, Appuldurcombe House, near Wroxall. The house survived that, but it was to prove only a stay of execution.

An enemy raider, whose arrival was not heralded by the siren, opened fire with his machine gun in the West Wight town of Yarmouth on 25 April, killing a Naval rating who had the misfortune to be on the pier at the time. Two other people were injured.

Then attention was focussed on Cowes, initially through a savage low-level attack on 28 April, which caused considerable damage and claimed several lives. Bad though this was, it was to prove merely the curtain-raiser for the awful Monday night of 4/5 May when the full horror and barbarism of modern warfare finally descended on the Isle of Wight.

MINISTRY OF FOOD
Southern Division
READING, Berks.

———— *Gurnard* ———— Parish.

TO HOUSEHOLDERS.
  Notice is hereby given that stocks of food have been stored for the above Parish as an Emergency reserve consisting of: biscuits, tinned meat, tinned soup or beans, tinned milk, sugar, margarine and tea. Authority has been delegated to local Voluntary Food Organisers to deal with such stocks; and, should it be necessary in the event of invasion to issue these, notice will be circulated locally by every means available. Should such notice be given, you should proceed to the address given below, taking with you:—
  (1) The ration books for yourself and other members of your household.
  (2) A sum of money representing 6/- for each ration book taken.
  (3) A basket or container in which to carry away the rations.

                                                        J. R. GALES,
Attend at { *Gurnard*
             Womens Institute } .   *Divisional Food Officer.*

•M4727 12/41 **702**

SEVEN

A Monday Night in May

"The public generally bore the ordeal with admirable fortitude and pluck, although the state of some of them next morning was pitiable . . ."
Isle of Wight County Press

The process of 'softening up' Cowes for its night of devastation one week later was achieved shortly before 7am on the morning of 28 April when seven Bf 109 fighter-bombers came in from the south, made for Newport and, flying just above the waters of the River Medina, roared on towards the Solent. Over the sea, the Messerschmitts made an abrupt turn and, in classic 'tip and run' fashion, attacked both Cowes and East Cowes with cannons, machine guns and, finally, their single high-explosive bombs. Returning the way they had come, the raiders added a post-script by machine-gunning Parkhurst, Newport, Carisbrooke and, as they departed the Island, a house at Atherfield Green. It was all over in a matter of minutes.

The Messerschmitts left in their wake a catalogue of serious damage and personal suffering. The prime industrial targets of J. Samuel White's shipyards and the seaplane production line at Saunders-Roe were both casualties. On the west bank, at Thetis Road, White's lost an entire boat-building shop in the raid, and the fire which broke out there quickly spread to houses in neighbouring Pelham Road, necessitating evacuations. It could, however, have been worse.

The Cowes-built Polish destroyer *Blyskawica*, which was lying alongside the works at the time, narrowly escaped serious damage when bombs dropped perilously close, wrecking the jetty which carried her gangway. (A week later the importance of the destroyer's escape from serious harm would be dramatically underlined.) White's East Cowes operations were also temporarily halted when an evacuation was ordered owing to the presence of an unexploded

bomb in a nearby street. Saunders-Roe, meanwhile, reported extensive, but mainly superficial, high-explosive bomb damage to its buildings. Two of the company's employees were killed.

Forty-two homes were declared uninhabitable after the raid, in addition to the four — all in Pelham Road — which the combined effects of fire, blast and bomb splinters totally demolished. It was in Pelham Road that six of the eight civilian deaths occurred, and two of those who lost their lives there were young children.

In one home four-year-old Dennis Bartlett was killed, together with both his parents. Two of the couple's other children escaped with minor injuries, and their one-month-old baby was recovered unharmed — shielded by the body of its mother, who died in her endeavour to save it. Five-year-old John Halliday was killed in the wreckage of his Pelham Road home, the bombs also taking the life of his father and seriously injuring his mother. Mrs Gladys Clark was the one other fatality in Pelham Road, but a nearby bomb which fell at the rear of a garage and motor works claimed the lives of another couple, whose children escaped with slight injuries.

The Interlude

While the twin towns at the mouth of the Medina licked their wounds, the Isle of Wight was able to enjoy some glorious spring sunshine on most of the succeeding six days. There was the odd raid alert, but nothing much resulted

57

during that deceptively peaceful period. A Bristol Beaufighter from Middle Wallop lost its propellor while patrolling off the south-west of the Island on 2 May and ditched in the sea near the Needles; the crew were saved. Then, on Monday 4 May, an unidentified British plane with fuel shortage made an unscheduled, and incident-free, landing south of Thorley School. It was still quiet.

The Blitz – Stage 1

Across the Channel that Monday, some 150 Dornier Do 217s were being prepared by the Luftwaffe bomber bases of KG66 and KG2 for an overnight raid on an important industrial target in the still sunny south of England. At 10.50 in the evening the first of them was approaching the Island, heading north through a clear and moonlit sky. The rising and falling note of the sirens wailed out its warning at 10.55. In Cowes, people thought Southampton was about to suffer yet another heavy onslaught from the air. Then, at exactly 11pm, the sky above the Island's most northerly towns, and out across the Solent, was spectacularly illuminated by chandeliers of parachuted flares. At that moment the awful realisation began to dawn on the residents of Cowes and East Cowes.

Blitz damage at Somerton Works and Aerodrome, Cowes. Hangars and planes were destroyed at the Island's only operational wartime airfield. (CCM)

In Beckford Road, Cowes, Vera Brown, then aged 16, heard the sound of planes. "Looking outside as the sirens sounded, we saw with horror and disbelief the huge flares hanging over the town and knew that this time it was us." Home Guardsman Raymond Tarrant remembers that "Cowes had had so much of it before, with the planes passing overhead, going up country somewhere. I suppose we didn't expect that this time it was actually ourselves who were going to get it." Inside with her young son at their Tennyson Road home, Minnie Spencer's realisation arrived with her husband. "He rushed into the house and called out: 'Get Adrian. It's our turn tonight' . . ."

Mr Spencer had hardly uttered the words when, at five minutes past eleven, the first wave of incendiaries rained down. Some fell on the aerodrome and works at Somerton, and were followed, almost immediately, by the first high-explosive bombs of the hour-long raid. The ARP report centre at Cowes (which also had responsibility for East Cowes) was given just enough time to pass this information to County Control before all telephone communication with the towns was lost. It was 12.25 before the next message arrived from Cowes – via a dispatch rider – urgently requesting rescue assistance, and adding: "All services out. All 'phones out of order. Electricity gone."

Incendiaries had started a series of large fires in waterside premises which, in turn, had provided the ideal illumination for the succes-

sive waves of high-explosive bombing attacks by the Dorniers. Rescue parties, first-aid teams and ambulances converged on Cowes and East Cowes from all other parts of the Island. Telephone engineers worked hard to re-establish limited communication with County Control from Cowes Post Office, while, with military help, a shuttle service of dispatch riders was put into operation. One of the riders arrived in Newport at 12.40 with the first official reference to casualties, although the message he carried from the Chief Warden at East Cowes contained no estimate of how many there were.

Slowly, as the rescue operation got into full swing, the confused picture began to emerge. The Luftwaffe had succeeded in inflicting damage on the shipyards and key industrial sites either side of the Medina. The Dorniers had also spread the destruction into many residential areas. Both in terms of damaged buildings and human casualties, it was clear in Cowes from an early stage that the Island had suffered by far its worst air raid of the war. The first attempt by the Cowes ARP Officer to summarise the situation reached Newport at 3.40am:

Extensive damage to works at Saunders-Roe, West Cowes. Direct hit on Saunders-Roe, Cornubia Yard, East Cowes. Gasworks and J.S. White's, East Cowes, still burning. Damage to GPO, Cowes High Street and Railway Station. Houses down in Baring Road, Arctic Road, Bernard Road, Mill Hill Road, Tennyson Road, Milton Road, Pallance Road and Gurnard. Unable to state number of casualties. Rescue parties still digging at three incidents. Assistance is being given by Cowes and Newport military, and Air Force units. Roads blocked at Cowes High Street, Medina Road, Pallance Lane, Broadfields Avenue, Three Gates Road; some by UXBs . . . Situation in general seems to be reasonably well in hand . . . Damage to water, gas and electricity service.

Vera Brown vividly recalls the raid:

The bombs were fitted with 'screamers' and were dropped in threes. A few mornings earlier we had had the reconnaissance raid, killing workers at East Cowes and dropping bombs on the local shipyard, J.S. White's, and this, of course, was the result. We had a chain of fire-fighters through our house in Beckford Road early on as the roof was alight, but Mother and I were firmly told to stay in our Morrison shelter, which Dad had erected in the kitchen. I cannot tell you of the screaming horror of that night – and we were among the lucky ones. Every road into both towns was bombed, making it difficult for the extra help to come in.

I remember that Dad, who was a full-time ARP warden, looked in after the raid, on his way to a nearby incident, where a shop and living accommodation had been demolished. The heavy rescue squad greeted him with 'Good old Ted – just the man we need!' It turned out that they were all on the hefty side and, although they had tunnelled so far into the wreckage, they could get no further. So Dad, being a little man, went through on his own and brought out the victims, whom he knew well. One of them, Mr

The results of a direct hit on a row of houses in East Cowes . . . a photograph taken at the rear of the properties on 5 May 1942. (CCM)

The wrecked Osborne Hall at East Cowes on the morning after the May 1942 raid. (CCM)

Fellows, was dead, but his wife lived for many years after that.

The Blitz – Stage 2

As news filtered through to County Control of serious bombing incidents in Newport itself, and with the catologue of UXBs at Cowes and elsewhere growing by the minute, the air raid sirens sounded again all over the Island. The notable exception was Cowes itself, still deprived of its electricity supply. From there, however, the new alert was clearly heard wailing on the mainland opposite. It was 3.45am.

Wardens at Cowes and East Cowes did their best to usher everyone – including the many people helping with the rescue operation – into the comparative safety of the shelters, but time was against them. The Dorniers reappeared overhead and, for the best part of the next hour, unleashed further bombs on the already beleaguered towns below. The 'All Clear' was finally sounded at 4.40, by which time the best part of 200 tons of high-explosive, and thousands of incendiary bombs, had been dropped in the two-stage assault.

The Morning After

It would be some time before the scale of the damage – to both people and property – could be properly assessed, but Cowes and East Cowes presented a profoundly pitiful sight as daylight arrived on Tuesday 5 May. Christine

Pitman, then aged 17, had just started work in the office at Groves and Guttridge's East Cowes shipyard, travelling daily from her Newport home:

Just before we reached Osborne on the morning of 5 May the bus was stopped by police and the Home Guard. We were told that both roads into East Cowes were closed, and that part of the town had been wiped out by incendiary and high-explosive bombs. A Polish battleship at J.S. White's shipyard had used its guns on the Germans very effectively, otherwise things would have been even worse, but there was still the hazard of unexploded bombs in the area. Just then a Fire Brigade officer arrived to say that the bus had driven through a nearby hamlet where two UXBs had just been located. Therefore, no-one could use the roads either way; passengers would have to make their way on foot through the grounds of Osborne House (then a convalescent home for officers), which were thought to be safe.

Later, as we approached the Saunders-Roe works slipway from the shore, we could see smoke and obvious destruction ahead. We had to wet handkerchiefs in the river to hold over our mouths and noses while we ran through the smoking remains of a factory to the main gate, then complete the last quarter-mile walk to our own shipyard. We passed more rubble, which had once been a cottage and small shop, then, when we hoped we were at journey's end, we were horrified to see that the shipyard, store and office block had been completely gutted. Charred timbers protruded from a cellar and the skeleton of a delivery van was visible under twisted metal. The launches and lifeboats under construction had disappeared.

Of the major overnight Luftwaffe targets, Saunders-Roe reported serious damage either side of the Medina. Its Cornubia Yard in East Cowes was said to be "burnt out" and the Solent Yard repair plant on the other bank of the river was described as "extensively damaged." Somerton works and aerodrome, the latter by then under the control of the Ministry of Aircraft Production, were badly affected, with three hangars and a number of aircraft destroyed. A request by Saunders-Roe for military transport assistance in the removal of bombed-out "workers' goods and chattels" to new homes immediately made available outside Cowes elicited the response that this was the duty of either the local authority, Saunders-Roe itself or the Ministry of Labour at Cowes. It was not a military responsibility.

The Polish destroyer Blyskawica, *the heroine of Cowes in May 1942, is pictured in her wartime camouflage paint.* (CCM)

More than 100,000 square feet of buildings were destroyed at J. Samuel White's premises. The damage at East Cowes, almost all of it caused by incendiaries, was substantial; the joiners shop, saw mills, mould loft and several other buildings were all lost. At the company's premises over the river, a high-explosive bomb which fell on the quayside considerably damaged buildings in the vicinity and superficially damaged the *Blyskawica*, still lying alongside.

The Polish Heroine

The name of the 2,144-ton Polish destroyer is still spoken with reverence in Cowes. People will tell you that, had it not been for the non-stop anti-aircraft barrage put up by her gunners that night, Cowes and East Cowes might well have been totally obliterated — although, for the sake of both completeness and fairness, it should also be recorded that the Royal Artillery's own ground-based AA gunners undoubtedly played their part. Often recounted is the story of how the *Blyskawica*, having left her moorings and dropped anchor outside the harbour, fired at the raiders with such fury that her guns, literally too hot to handle, had to be doused repeatedly with water. At one point her near exhausted ammunition stocks were replenished by boat from Portsmouth.

She was very much a Cowes ship. In 1935, against the keenest opposition from practically every other shipbuilding nation, White's had won the order for construction of the *Blyskawica* and her sister ship, the *Grom*. They were acknowledged at the time to be the finest super-destroyers in the world, and were the pride and backbone of the new Polish Navy. At the time of the May 1942 raid the *Blyskawica* was making one of her regular return visits to Cowes for re-fitting.

The people of Cowes have never forgotten the heroic deeds of her gunners and crew that night, and they were delighted when a number of the Polish seamen returned to the Island in 1982 to attend the 40th anniversary memorial service for those killed in the 1942 blitz. At least one member of the *Blyskawica's* crew has made a more permanent return to Cowes — by marrying a local girl. Raymond Tarrant's comments typify the feelings which have persisted in Cowes to the present day: "The only thing that really saved the town was that Polish destroyer in the harbour. Her people put up absolutely everything they had that night. I dread to think what might have happened had she not been there."

One result would certainly have been far greater industrial damage. While the destruction caused to the shipyards and works premises (one estimate claimed that 69 tons of bombs actually landed on the targeted industrial areas) was substantial, it could have been a whole lot worse. Touring the Cowes area soon after the raids, Sir William James, Commander-in-Chief at Portsmouth, regarded the comparartive lack of significant damage as "a minor miracle."

The bomb disposal squad pause for the photographer as they attempt to remove a UXB from outside the library in Beckford Road, Cowes, on 5 May. (Raymond Tarrant)

The Rescue Operation

The shipyards, and local war production. may have escaped relatively lightly, but the damage and devastation in general terms was far from insignificant. Following the second raid, the rescue operation in Cowes had, of course, to be re-launched; reinforcements and relief parties had to be organised. Not every town could spare its entire complement of first aid parties and ambulances – although they had been asked to do so two hours before the second attack. Newport, in particular, had problems on its own doorstep, with serious incidents at Shide, Parkhurst and on the main road to Ryde. Nevertheless, the Island's civil defence organisation, admirably aided by the Services and many others, rose magnificently to the nightmare challenge, both in the 'field' and back at administrative headquarters.

Reporting the raid the following Saturday – although wartime restrictions limited its description of the location to "a South Coast port" – the *County Press* commented:

It was by far the worst raid the district has experienced, and it is satisfying to be able to give whole-hearted praise to every branch of the civil defence service. They were faced with an exceedingly heavy task, necessitating a full concentration of all the personnel and equipment available, and untiring efforts amid great danger, but they never faltered, and those who suffered terribly as a result of the bombing were the first to pay tribute to their skill and bravery. The civil defence services were grateful for the prompt and effective assistance rendered by military medical units, which came to their aid immediately, without request.

As a "noble example" of this devotion to duty, the *County Press* related the story of Cowes ARP Warden Sydney Burchell: "The officer, who lost a limb in the last war, suffered a crushing blow early in the attack. His wife and her parents were killed, and his three-year-old son injured, when a bomb hit the private shelter in which they were taking cover; yet he refused to leave his post of duty, and carried on throughout the night and following day, giving an inspiring and heroic lead to his men."

Generally, the brick-built public shelters in the streets stood up well to the bombing, and there can be no doubt that they saved hundreds of lives. Some, however, were bodily moved by

62

blast, and there was one case of a shelter actually falling into a crater made by a bomb which exploded only a yard or so away. Although several people lost their lives in this incident, others escaped from it practically unharmed.

Rescue and first-aid parties, ambulance drivers and the National Fire Service − whose ranks were depleted by several casualties that night − worked ceaselessly with bombs falling all around them. In the thick of the action, the police − both regulars and specials − were later applauded for combining firmness with, as the *County Press* put it, "unfailing sympathy and helpfulness." The invaluable support from military units included some courageous work by members of the Home Guard, while both the British Red Cross and St John Ambulance organisations were there in force.

Co-ordination from County Control at Newport was hampered by the immense difficulties of communication with Cowes. Deputising for the wrecked telephone links, the dispatch riders faced lengthy detours round the bomb craters on all the main routes. While detailed information on the Newport area incidents was being regularly relayed, official updates on the situation four miles to the north were virtually non-existent.

In any disaster − and it was never so evident than during the 1939-45 war − the English turn to tea. It had not taken long for the issue of an urgent request for the Women's Voluntary Service to send all available mobile canteens (they were usually referred to as tea vans) to the stricken towns. The WVS was to play a vital role, later setting up emergency feeding stations in both Cowes (Trinity Hall) and East Cowes (Osborne Road Centre). Like everyone else, they toiled ceaselessly, regardless of the considerable risks. Tragically, one of the women was killed during the second raid while touring the stricken areas with a mobile canteen.

Another vital group of women were more fortunate, as Vera Brown recalls: "The volunteer ladies who ran the Forces Canteen in Cowes High Street dashed to a nearby street shelter when the second raid came over. They had a very narrow squeak − the canteen was completely demolished."

Fleeing to Safety

In the period immediately after the double-strike on Cowes, there was understandable concern on the Island that the Luftwaffe might attempt a follow-up raid. The attack had been sandwiched between those on the towns of Exeter and Norwich (two of the so-called *Baedeker Raids*) and, in both of those cases, the bombers had returned for a second night. Many people voluntarily left Cowes and East Cowes as a result − in addition to those who, having lost their homes, were officially evacuated to other parts of the Island. Special transport was arranged for the evacuees; those who had fled of their own volition to supposed safety had to make their own way. The *County Press* reported:

. . . they could be seen on foot, on bicycles, or in cars, making their way to safety with their portmanteaux and parcels of bare necessities. It was a pathetic spectacle, but everything possible was done to succour them, special billeting offices and feeding arrangements being put into operation in the places to which they trekked.

Throughout the daylight hours of 5 May urgent steps were taken to guard against the possibility of a second night of terror. This involved the re-location of some of the mobile ground defences, and Roy Brinton remembers a Bofors gun being brought into a field next to his house at Binfield. "We dreaded them having to fire it − all our windows would have gone, and probably a lot more besides! But no further enemy planes came over that night and, much to our relief, the Bofors gun was removed soon afterwards!"

With so many homes either destroyed or damaged, the offices for War Damage and Information were hard-pressed to keep pace with demand from anxious bombed-out residents, and a special Sunday opening was arranged for 9 May. The Cowes Blitz produced the only recorded incidents of looting during the war on the Island. Several complaints were made to the police some three weeks after the raid of people helping themselves to whatever took their fancy at damaged or demolished houses. Another distressing by-product was the large number of homeless, and in many cases owner-less, cats and dogs wandering the streets in search of food and comfort.

63

An enemy aerial photograph of the bomb damage either side of the River Medina . . . a picture published in both German and Italian newspapers soon after the raid. The Italian caption suggested Cowes was the "industrial centre of Britain"! (E.M. Weeks)

The Human Tragedy

But what of the human tragedy? It was nearly 9pm on the 5th before the first official hint, outside Cowes, of the scale of this was available. With considerable help from the Royal Army Medical Corps, which had made available all its Island-based ambulances, casualties had been dispersed to a number of hospitals, principally to Frank James and Osborne hospitals at East Cowes; the Royal IW County Hospital in Ryde; Parkhurst Military Hospital; and the Home of

Rest Hospital at Shanklin. At 8.55 the Parkhurst hospital authorities listed 15 civilian casualties, nine men and six women, in their care, aged between 19 and 76. Three of the men brought in had since been pronounced dead. It was the tip of the iceberg.

By Thursday 7 May the casualty picture was becoming clearer. In mid-afternoon, it was reported from Cowes that 63 deaths had been confirmed, while another 60 people had been seriously injured and 75 were slightly hurt. The post-script to this message added the two words: "Not final." Twenty-four hours later, the official death toll had risen to 64. Over the succeeding days, this figure was regularly revised upwards until, on Monday 18 May, two weeks after the attack, the combined total for the two towns had reached 70 deaths. In Cowes,

24 people had been killed outright and four had since died in hospital. At East Cowes the corresponding figures were higher in both cases – 36 and six, respectively.

With a further ten fatalities in the Newport area, the overall death toll from the night of 4/5 May was now exactly 80, and the total number of people reported as seriously injured in Cowes, East Cowes and Newport was 82.

With so many people killed in towns of relatively modest size, it was inevitable that the casualty list would include the names of some prominent local residents. Among those who fell into this category was George Cole, an Isle of Wight County Councillor, former Chairman of Cowes Urban District Council and one of the town's leading businessmen. His wife, Elizabeth, also died. The district council's Billeting Officer, E. A. Kersey, was killed, along with his wife and child, on what would have been his busiest night of the war. Among the casualties in the ranks of the fire-fighters was Colin

Weeks, the younger son of the Mayor of Ryde, who was one of two Ryde-based firemen – the other was Bert Dewey – to lose their lives.

Several people lost three, or even four, members of their family. The expanded columns of front page death notices in the *County Press* over the next fortnight were full of references to those killed "by enemy action." Did Gwennie Hughes, aged just four, even know who her enemy was?

Burying their Dead

Clearly, the sudden need to inter so many people at the same time in towns of this size had presented an unpleasantly awkward problem for the local authority. Cowes UDC proposed on 8 May that the air raid victims should be buried in communal graves, but added that relatives should be given the option of private burial if they so wished. This obviously practical solution met with general approval, and large graves were prepared at the cemeteries on either side of the river for the mass funerals which took place on 12/13 May.

A long procession made its way from Cowes on the wet afternoon of Tuesday 12 May to

Names of the victims of the May 1942 blitz (and other local raids) are inscribed on stones at the communal graves in both Cowes and East Cowes cemeteries. This one is at the Kingston Road cemetery in East Cowes. (Ben Houfton)

Northwood Cemetery. As it did so, the final indignity was inflicted on the mourning town. The air raid siren, which had heralded a night of so much suffering a week earlier, wailed out its chilling warning. Gunfire was heard in the distance. But Cowes was not prepared to be mocked in this way; the procession kept moving and the alert passed.

The coffins, draped in Union Jacks, were borne in motor wagons. At the cemetery, the procession, which included civic leaders and representatives of all the wartime services, had to by-pass several large bomb craters on the lengthy walk between the entrance gates and the communal grave. ARP wardens acted as bearers for all the coffins except one. The coffin of a cub scout, on which were placed his cap and neckerchief, was carried by senior members of the scout troop. The combined choirs of three churches sang at the graveside service, and the Island's Archedeacon gave the address.

On the Wednesday, a second graveside service was held in the much smaller cemetery directly across the river, at Kingston Road, East Cowes. The coffins for the raid victims of that town had been placed in the communal grave the previous day, and the grave itself draped by Union Jacks on either side. At both services the drab austerity of wartime was poignantly lifted at the gravesides by hundreds of floral tributes.

Large memorial stones were subsequently positioned by the communal graves at the two cemeteries. They list, with lettering now faded, the names of all victims of the 5 May 1942 blitz, together with those who died in the other air raids on the respective towns in the 1939-45 war. The stone at East Cowes commemorates not only the 43 people buried in the grave itself, but a further eight interred elsewhere in the cemetery and five more buried in other places. The corresponding stone in Cowes lists the names of 27 victims in the communal grave, one elsewhere in the cemetery and three in other places.

Silver Linings

But the blitz on Cowes was not exclusively a story of death and destruction. There were, for one thing, some remarkable escapes. One family whose house collapsed into a crater were extricated unscathed; a six-weeks-old baby was rescued alive from a wrecked house in which its mother and 14-year-old sister were killed; and members of the National Fire Service, working a pump during the second raid, and almost buried with mud thrown up when a bomb burst near them, walked away from the incident without injury.

There were also some remarkable demonstrations of the strange effects of bomb blast, as Minnie Spencer recalls:

After the blitz we had no roof on our Tennyson Road house at all; we just looked straight up into the sky. On our front room table we found a pepperpot, standing perfectly upright. The strange thing was, it didn't belong to us — it must have been carried from another house by the blast right through where our roof used to be and onto our table! Also, the clock on our mantlepiece was still going, although the mantlepiece itself was at the craziest angle. It was most peculiar the things that blast did.

The Other Tragedies

The sheer scale and widespread devastation of the attack on Cowes has, understandably, always tended to dominate recollections of the night of 4/5 May 1942 on the Isle of Wight. Yet, sadly, that same night was also notable for a series of tragedies elsewhere.

Soon after the first reports of raid damage in Cowes were logged at County Control late on 4 May, there were messages from both Ventnor and Newport report centres which suggested the activity that night was not going to be confined to the north of the Island. At Ventnor, incendiaries and high-explosives were dropped on the seafront area by a Dornier anxious to escape a British fighter plane in hot pursuit. Striking the face of a cliff between the disused gasworks and the pier, one HE bomb shattered glass over a wide area, blowing out completely the front windows of the *Isle of Wight Mercury* office in Pier Street and smashing the roofs of several seaside bathing huts.

The offending bomber later crashed in the sea, south of Dunnose — one of several brought down that night off the Island's coast. Back at Ventnor, the casualties were mainly confined to minor injuries from flying glass, but one woman, the wife of a postman and special constable, collapsed and died from shock. Ryde escaped that night with nothing more dramatic than shell damage to windows in Wood Street – but Newport had more serious problems.

The first were caused by the three high-explosive bombs jettisoned over the southern outskirts of the town just after 11.30pm. One fell behind the villa residences at the Shide end of Medina Avenue, demolishing three houses, seriously damaging half a dozen more and causing minor damage to many others. Somewhat miraculously, the only fatal casualty was music teacher George Kirkup, whose body was recovered from the ruins of his home at 123 Medina Avenue. Alone in the kitchen of the house when the bomb fell, he had been killed instantly when the building collapsed around him. Much luckier was Army Staff-Sergeant Chapman, rescued from his shattered home suffering from only bruising and shock. His wife and young son, and the sole occupant of the other house destroyed, had all made it to a shelter across the road minutes before the bomb exploded. One which didn't explode fell in Shide Station's goods yard – and halted the passenger train service until the end of the month.

It was the second visit of the Do 217s on 5 May which brought about the most tragic of the Newport area incidents. Two homes at Park-hurst were demolished, and, just after dawn, cottages at the Wootton end of The Racecourse, part of the main A3054 to Ryde, were reduced to rubble by a direct hit. The road was blocked – and ten people were said to be buried in the wreckage. In fact, 13 were eventually removed from the cottages, but only five of them were recovered alive. If ever a single incident brought home the horror of total war on the Island, this was surely it.

Living at Number 1 Point Cottage on The Racecourse were Wallace and Charlotte Chiverton and their eight children. Although injured, Mr and Mrs Chiverton survived the carnage, as did two of the children. The other six, Mary (7), Vera (4), John (3), the two-year-old twins Pat and Paul and baby Jean, born just five weeks

earlier, were all killed. At Number 2 Point Cottage, 65-year-old Frank Hendy and another child, five-year-old Joan Abrook, lost their lives. Her mother, Mrs Evelyn Abrook, was rescued after being buried amid the ruins of her home for six hours. but, tragically, she later died in hospital, bringing the total death toll for Point Cottages up to nine.

Military assistance with the rescue undoubtedly prevented this horrific incident from assuming even greater proportions. Soldiers were also used, at the request of Newport's Borough Surveyor, to clear the A3054, which had been blocked by the bombing. The Chiverton children were buried together on the Friday after the raid, the Mayor and Mayoress of Newport attending their funeral service. If such a harrowing story can be said to have a happy ending, it was provided some years later by Wallace and Charlotte Chiverton themselves. Living by then in another part of the Island, they had become the proud parents of a second large family.

Were They Warned?

There seems little doubt that the events of 5 May 1942 caught Islanders by surprise. However, it is worth noting that, shortly before the assault, in the dead of night, a Red Funnel vessel crossed from the mainland to Cowes with a cargo composed largely of fire-fighting equipment, to augment that already on the Island. There are some who believe this to be a firm indication of advance intelligence that a major raid was planned by the Germans.

Whatever the truth of that, the Luftwaffe permitted the Island a practically undisturbed three-week period in which to carry out its sad clearing-up operation after the blitz on Cowes. There would be no further raids on the Isle of Wight to match the savage intensity of the May 1942 attack, but the lives of many more Islanders would be lost as the Luftwaffe intensified its 'tip and run' bombing campaign throughout the remainder of 1942 and into the following year.

EIGHT

Tip and Run

A year-long period of 'tip and run' terror opened with a rare failure by the Luftwaffe. No enemy planes had been shot down on the Island during the attack on Cowes, but, by the end of the month, one had crashed near Sandown. Leutenant J. Fröschel, piloting a Bf 109f — the uprated version of the 109e — fell victim to a 41 Squadron Spitfire during an abortive afternoon raid with colleagues on the resort. The Messerschmitt, from 2./JG2, crashed in flames near Yaverland Manor, Fröschel had baled out over Culver, but too late for his parachute to open. His body was found near the sea wall at Yaverland.

Two 41 Squadron Spitfire pilots from RAF Merston crashed in the Island on the morning of 10 June. Flight Sergeant W.A. Wright came down at Rowborough Farm. Brading. and was removed, injured, from the aircraft (AR377) by soldiers. Shortly afterwards, Flight Lieutenant D.W. Wainwright's Spitfire (AD504) crashed at St Lawrence. He was taken to the nearby Royal National Hospital, but died there of his injuries. F/S D.C. Eva was more fortunate, escaping unharmed when his Spitfire (EN965), from 118 Squadron at Tangmere, crashed a week later in the south-west of the Island, at Atherfield. During this period there were several reports of aircraft — from both sides — ditching in the sea off the Island's south coast.

Ashore, stray shells continued to plague the Island. Thorne's Bakery in Wootton suffered when a cannon shell fell in its garage, striking a car and bursting the petrol tank — but it was 7 July before the next air raid of any note. It was an attack of particular significance.

Attack on the Troopships

At 6.15 in the morning, the Luftwaffe dropped four HE bombs in the western Solent off Yarmouth — five minutes in advance of the air raid alert on the land. The bombs fell near enough to cause casualties on board two assault ships lying at anchor with their troops. At first it was feared that the attack indicated German foreknowledge of the vessels' planned destination and purpose — a raid on the French port of Dieppe. This was later discounted, but the assault had, nevertheless, to be postponed for a month owing to unfavourable weather conditions.

The Island's 1,000th air raid warning of the war was heard at 5.30am on Tuesday 14 July, followed 12 minutes later by the 'All Clear.' The following Tuesday saw another apparent attempt by the Germans to knock-out the radar pylons at Ventnor. Two HE bombs missed the target, and caused only slight damage in the town below. Attention switched to the east of the Island a week later when two Gloster Gladiators (K7985 and L8030), from 2 Anti-Aircraft Co-operation Unit at Gosport, were involved in a tragic mid-morning collision while exercising off Culver. Both pilots, Flight Sergeant Chapman and Pilot Officer Flood, were killed.

Teatime Raid on Ventnor

At 4.15pm on 18 August, two Focke Wolfe Fw 190s swooped on Ventnor in typical low-level 'tip and run' fashion — so low that they almost

Severe bomb damage at an unidentified Island house. Note the air raid shelter in the foreground. (IWCC)

took the top off a telephone kiosk. There had been no warning of their approach. The 190s' single bombs thudded down on the town centre, scoring a direct hit on cottages in the High Street, and part of the police station next door. The latter was wrecked, along with seven other properties. Damage of only slightly less serious nature was caused to a number of buildings, including the labour exchange and Burt's Brewery, while shop fronts and windows were smashed over a wide area. Fishing boats in the bay were machine-gunned by the raiders as they left the shocked town.

Three people were killed in the attack, but good humour survived. The local press reported how an elderly woman, rescued from the wreckage of her home, emerged "cheerful, despite losing her false teeth . . ." They were later recovered!

The Disaster of Dieppe

As Ventnor came to terms that night with the savagery of the teatime attack, an Allied assault force of 6,000 men and almost 60 of the new Churchill tanks, massively supported from the air, was crossing the Channel. The Dieppe Raid, planned as the biggest test to date of the effectiveness of Combined Operations, was under way. It ended in disaster, with more than 3,500 men either killed, missing or taken prisoner by the far-from-surprised Germans. The tragedy of Dieppe was to have a profound effect on the people of the Isle of Wight.

Much of the final planning for the raid was overseen from Cowes, where HMS *Vectis* had recently been commissioned at the prestigious premises of the Royal Yacht Squadron as a headquarters for Lord Louis Mountbatten's Combined Operations Command (at the rent of one shilling a year). The Island also offered the ideal training ground for various components of the assault force.

It is widely-known, and commemorated by a plaque unveiled there in 1984, that the men of 'A' (Royal Marine) Commando – later re-designated 40 Commando – prepared for their part in the Dieppe Raid at Shanklin Chine. "We got to know them really well while they were here," remembers Teresa King (formerly Phillips), a wartime teenager in Shanklin. "What happened at Dieppe cast a terrible gloom over the town."

But it was not only the British commandos who prepared on the Isle of Wight for the ill-fated assault. Many of the Canadians, who made up the bulk of the raiding force, also came to the Island for their final training – providing many Islanders with their first sight of a tank.

Theo Pearson, a teacher at West Wight Central School during the war, remembers the Candians who were based at that end of the Island:

It became a familiar sight in Freshwater to see squads of Canadian soldiers creeping through gardens and along hedgerows. One morning, after a 'battle' in the Freshwater Bay area, they decided to call an armistice, and have their break outside Orchard's Bakery. They bought lots of doughnuts, and were about to enjoy them when a 'casualty' on a stretcher sat up to take his break, too. He was told: 'You caint do that, Sergeant, you're daid' – and pushed down again! Before finally leaving for the raid, they gave the children of the West Wight a wonderful party, collecting them in lorries and returning them afterwards, each wrapped in a blanket against the night air, and loaded with 'candy' and chocolate bars. The disaster of Dieppe followed.

Of the 4,961 Canadians at Dieppe, 3,363 (68 per cent) became casualties, as did 247 of the 1,057 British commandos – although 2,200 of the British and Candian 'missing' were taken prisoner. All 30 tanks which reached, or tried to reach, the shore were lost. Some of the men who escaped the carnage on the beaches themselves later fell victim to the Luftwaffe as the Germans chased the Allied force all the way home.

Dieppe Day brought little comfort to the Island, either, with the by now usual cocktail of machine gun fire and high-explosive bombs, but it did end the wartime flying career of Luftwaffe pilot Leutnant Erich Kegenbein, whose Junkers Ju 88 (M2+FH), from 3./KG106 at Chateaudun – already damaged in the attack on the retreating Allied force – ran into a hail of anti-aircraft fire over the fog-bound Island, and crashed in Wroxall Copse. Kegenbein and his crew, Uffz E. Ostereich, Uffz W. Arnold and Uffz W. Hase, all wounded in the crash, were taken to the Royal National Hospital at Ventnor, where Hase later died from his injuries. He was buried initially at Parkhurst, but his body was removed to the German Military Cemetery at Cannock Chase after the war. The others survived to sit out the remainder of the conflict as prisoners.

Ventnor Hit Again

The Ventnor area was again the focus of attention on 25 August – initially with the crash of another German aircraft at Wroxall. This one, a Junkers Ju 88d5 (4U+GH) from the 1.(F)/123 reconnaissance unit, came down on St Martin's Down, to the north-east of Wroxall village, shortly after 5.30am. Three of the crew (Lt Beeg, Uffz Schwarz and Gfr Scherler) were found dead in the burnt-out plane. The fourth, Uffz Mobias, was found by the wife of a local farmer, who tended the badly-injured airman until he was taken to the Royal National Hospital.

Mid-morning on 2 September, two Fw 190s flew in over the sea to carry out another lightning 'tip and run' raid on Ventnor. They announced their arrival by aiming machine-gun and cannon fire at the beach and town centre, then unleashed their solitary bombs. Sixteen people were injured – none of them seriously – but extensive structural damage was caused. Eight homes were flattened, including a row of houses in North Street, and several others were damaged. A number of shops in the High Street were demolished, and both the town's Liberal Club and Congregational Church suffered blast damage.

There were some miraculous escapes, perhaps the most remarkable being that of Percy Boxall, manager of a local building firm, who was buried up to his neck by a mass of bricks and debris in a passageway – but emerged with relatively minor wounds to his head and ankle.

Lofty's Last 'Op'

In the early hours of Wednesday 9 September a Heinkel He 111, probably from 15./KG6, was heading northwards across the Channel. As it got closer to the Isle of Wight, Warrant Officer Russell 'Lofty' Hamer took off from Ford, Sussex, in 141 Squadron's Bristol Beaufighter V8265. With him was his regular navigator/radar operator, Flight Sergeant Edmund 'Terry' Walsh. The two aircraft were destined for a dramatic confrontation.

A graphic account of subsequent events has been compiled by air historian Andy Saunders, Curator of the Military Aviation Museum at Tangmere, who describes how Hamer was ordered to patrol a line 25 miles south of St Catherine's Point at 8,000 feet. However, before he could get there, the approach of the Heinkel was plotted by radar and confirmed as hostile.The two planes were soon engaged, with 'Lofty' Hamer opening fire at about 300 feet and setting fire to the starboard engine and wing of the Heinkel. Part of the wing broke away, hitting the pursuing Beaufighter and making it swing to one side. The German gunner opened up, damaging the Beaufighter's cockpit area and starboard engine. Hamer renewed the attack. Finally, the bomber rolled over and, blazing fiercely, plunged into the sea some 25 miles south-west of the Needles.

'Lofty' Hamer had been badly injured in the fight. He could hardly use his left arm, and had no use in his right leg. He managed to feather the propellor of the damaged engine so that the fire died down, and headed for Beaulieu airfield in Hampshire, which had been specially-illuminated for him.

But the Beaufighter never made it. The dead starboard engine again erupted into flames, and, with the north coast of the Isle of Wight coming into view, Hamer ordered Walsh to bale out. He declined to leave the Beaufighter himself, even when the port engine cut out and the plane began to lose height rapidly. 'Lofty' managed to hold it at 1,000 feet long enough for Walsh to jump. Soon afterwards Hamer told ground control: "Afraid I'm finished − I'll have to go. Over." The aircraft then crashed and exploded at Boldre, near Lymington, killing its pilot instantly. Walsh, meanwhile, drifted down to land on the water's edge at Newtown (on the Island's north coast) − between two rolls of barbed wire entanglements.

Wet and bleeding, Walsh made it to a nearby farmhouse and, after managing, with some effort, to convince Farmer Pragnell that he was not a German airman, he was taken to the headquarters of the 345th AA Battery, his nightmare ordeal finally over. Walsh had undoubtedly been saved by the courage and self-sacrifice of his pilot and friend, 'Lofty' Hamer.

A Pause in the Action

The remainder of September was relatively quiet on the Isle of Wight, as was October − although Shanklin suffered a 'tip and run' raid on the 13th − but, on the foggy afternoon of 1 November, two 616 Squadron Spitfires from Westhampnett misjudged the height of Stenbury Down, west of Wroxall, as they flew in from the sea. They crashed within 50 yards of each other. Flight Sergeant S. Smith, flying BR186, was killed instantly. His colleague, F/S K. Rodger, piloting BR174, was taken to the Royal National Hospital with serious injuries.

Mid-November was a time for celebration. The defeat of Rommel's Afrika Korps at El Alamein had the church bells ringing out in the Island, as elsewhere in Britain, on Sunday the 15th. It was a welcome, if, for the moment, temporary, relaxation of the Control of Noise Defence Order, introduced at the height of the invasion scare in June 1940, which had reserved the use of church bells for local warning purposes only.

As Christmas 1942 approached, the main threat to the Island seemed, for a change, to be coming from the sea. with unexploded mines washing ashore at several points along the southern coastline. One went off on 16 December at Steephill Cove, Ventnor, smashing windows and bringing down ceilings at the nearby Royal National Hospital. The explosion which rocked the West Wight early on the morning of 20 December, however, was from something far bigger. A Halifax bomber had crashed at Eades Farm. south of Newbridge.

The Halifax (W7768), attached to 405 Squadron at Beaulieu, was beginning a regular morning patrol when the tragedy happened. Its six-man all-Canadian crew were all killed. Rescuers who rushed to the scene of the 7am crash retrieved only two of the bodies. They could do nothing to release the remaining airmen, whose outline could be clearly seen in the fiercely-burning plane by the distressed onlookers. The plane was piloted by Flight Sergeant L. Snarr, whose colleagues were Flying Officer F. Stollery and Flight Sgts H. Croft, N. Van Brunt, N. Fugere and G. Wagner. Bombs from the Halifax spilled out over the surrounding ground as the plane crash-landed. Their disposal was handled by experts from the RAF.

Islanders were able to enjoy the rare luxury of a siren-free week over the Christmas and New Year period. The final air raid alert of 1942 was sounded at 1.20pm on Christmas Eve, followed within a matter of minutes by the 'All Clear.' It was New Year's Day before the next warning was heard — and then, just two days later, the peace was well and truly shattered by easily the most serious 'tip and run' raid on the Island to date. The town selected for attack by the Luftwaffe was Shanklin.

Shanklin's Savage Sunday

Sunday 3 January 1943 was a pleasant day on the Isle of Wight, with plenty of sunshine. There were more people than usual to enjoy it, too, for a two-month relaxation of the ban on visitors to the Island had just started. At Shanklin the day had passed uneventfully, interrupted only by an air raid alert at 3pm which had come to nothing. When the sirens wailed out again shortly before 4.30, many people were attending the town's church services — brought forward during the war to beat the black-out. There was no time to take cover.

The attack was delivered by a quartet of Focke Wolfe Fw 190s based with SKG10 on the Cherbourg Peninsular. They flew in low from the sea and, in now familiar 'tip and run' fashion, strafed the town with machine-gun fire before unleashing their high-explosive bombs — with devastating effect. Direct hits destroyed both the Roman Catholic Church in Atherley Road and the town's Landguard Road Fire Station. When the casualty figures were finalised some days later, 23 people — 13 men, nine women and a young girl — were listed as dead.

A service was in progress when the bomb hit the church. Fortunately, the congregation was relatively small. Of the 26 people present, six — all adults — were killed. Many others, including children, were injured. The nearby Anglican church of St Paul's was damaged by the blast, just as a baptismal service was being conducted, but the damage wasn't serious. It was the bomb that fell on the National Fire Service headquarters (the former Gloucester Hotel and Garage) in Landguard Road which produced the raid's most tragic outcome. Nine firemen, two dispatch riders and one firewoman were killed. A further five firemen suffered injuries.

Elsewhere in the town, Grove Ground Cottages at Hyde were hit by another of the bombs, which completely demolished one home and

Bombs on the Wight

LOSS OF LIFE

Four enemy F.W. raiders flying in low from the direction of the sea on Sunday afternoon dropped bombs and machine-gunned a small south coast resort causing damage to residential and business property and loss of life.

A church received a direct hit and was practically demolished. At the time a service was being conducted by the minister, who was injured.

Fortunately the congregation was a small one, about 26 people being present. Five adults were killed and others, including children injured. Those fatally injured were Sister Claire, Mrs. Reddie Fraser, Miss E. West, Miss Eva Cheetham, Mr. Henry Rogers. The latter's wife was seriously injured, as was also Mr. W. Sheehan, Sister Veronica (who was at the organ) escaped with minor injuries, and Sister Alphonus suffered from shock.

Mrs. Rogers has since died.

Happily, the children's Sunday schoolroom, which was damaged and adjoins the church, was empty.

A terrace of workmen's houses were badly damaged, but the occupants escaped with their lives.

A former hotel and garage received a direct hit and it was here a number of

house. In the house on the other side a woman over 80 was badly cut with glass and she was among those taken to hospital.

Mrs. W. Brown said: "I was waiting for my husband to come home when I heard a tremendous bang which smashed the glass and threw me on the floor."

Richard Cronin, age about 13, an evacuee, who was in the bombed church when he heard machine-gunning. He pushed his little sister and another little girl underneath a seat and then himself took cover. They escaped with minor injuries.

Shelia Boyce was lucky not to have been at the church when it was hit. She intended going, but at the last moment decided to take some flowers to a grave at a nearby town instead.

The exterior of a hospital was damaged by cannon-shell.

TO THE RESCUE.

There were busy scenes following the raid. Rescue workers from adjacent places gave assistance. No time was lost in patching-up, at least temporarily, those houses in the vicinity which were not too badly damaged. Neighbours helped one

How Shanklin's local newspaper, the Isle of Wight Guardian, *reported the most damaging of the Island's 'tip and run' raids — the devastating attack of 3 January 1943 which killed 23 people. Technically, the paper was in breach of wartime censorship regulations by identifying the Isle of Wight in its headline — although the opening paragraph confines description of the location to "a small south coast resort."* (Eileen Foss)

seriously damaged two others. Of the seven casualties there, two — a mother and daughter — were killed. The injured were treated at Shanklin's Home of Rest Hospital, until the limited accommodation was exhausted, and transfers to other Island hospitals were required.

Ryde's Black Thursday

More 'tip and run' raids by the Fw 190s followed during the early part of 1943, with Ventnor (where seven people were killed in the town centre), Sandown and Shanklin bearing the brunt of the attacks. Then, on Thursday 4 February, it was the turn of Ryde. The siren wailed out its warning in mid-afternoon. For many it came too late.

Four bombs from a quartet of Fw 190s rained down on the residential area in the south of the town — and the nearby Royal IW County

Hospital prepared itself to receive the casualties. They came mainly from houses in West Street, Arthur Street, Queens Road and, most dramatically, Ashey Road — the setting for the final act in a remarkable bombing tragedy which brought more suffering to the Swanmore area devastated by the Church Street land mines of 1941.

St Michael's Church Hall had been utilised since the land mine tragedy — which destroyed the adjacent Bettesworth Road School — as a classroom for the school's displaced youngest pupils. By a cruel twist of fate this corner site in Swanmore was again in the firing line on 4 February 1943. Jack Harvey, who had celebrated his eighth birthday the previous day, was in the classroom that afternoon:

I recall that we were about to leave the school at the end of the day — we had just stood up in the aisles ready to file out of the classroom. Suddenly, the room was full of dust. I don't remember any noise. In fact, the next thing I recall is following the light of the door and making for Church Street outside. The roof of the classroom had fallen in.

Incredibly, a high-explosive bomb had passed right through the hall, above the heads of the children, without exploding. The damage it caused to the building injured about 20 of the youngsters. Most, like Jack Harvey — who had a small head wound — escaped with minor injuries. But seven-year-old Thomas Carswell was killed by the falling debris. He was to be the only Island child to die at school as a result of enemy action during the entire war.

The bomb which caused his death was soon to claim more lives as it continued on its eccentric course. Ernie Jolliffe, Ryde's Deputy ARPO at the time, describes what happened next:

After it left the school, the bomb hit the ground in the garden of St Michael's Vicarage , bounced in the air, passed through a house on the corner of Wray Street and Ashey Road — again, without exploding — and finally exploded the other side of Ashey Road, in front of Hazlewood. The second bomb which was dropped in that area passed between two houses in Ashey Road and exploded in a garden at the back of them.

Hazlewood, the town's former YMCA building, was used as a wartime billet for soldiers. Four of them died in the explosion which wrecked it. In all, eleven people were killed in the raid (the civilian casualties were three men,

Appuldurcombe House, near Wroxall, was reduced to a roofless ruin in February 1943 when a Dornier Do 217 on a coastal mine-laying mission inexplicably turned inland to drop a mine just west of the house before crashing on St Martin's Down. (English Heritage)

two women and two children), and another 62 were treated for injuries at the hospital. Several had suffered from the machine-gun and cannon fire which the Fw 190s, arriving from the south, had unleashed at the start of the attack. Literally hundreds of properties in Ryde were damaged — and five were totally wrecked.

Appuldurcombe's Ruin

On February 7 a mine-laying mission off the Island's southern tip ended in disaster for a Dornier Do 217 from G./KG2. The low-flying aircraft unaccountably turned inland, dropping its last mine just west of Appuldurcombe House at Wroxall before crashing on the nearby St Martin's Down. All four members of the crew (Fw Salx, Uffz Jendis, Gfr Gröschel and Gfr Teubner) were killed. Their final act had reduced once proud Appuldurcombe, already in a bad state of repair, to the roofless ruin it is today.

Apart from being officially banned, taking photographs on the Island was a virtual impossibility owing to the lack of materials. Shanklin chemist A.J.P. Pionchon had access to one of the few rolls of available film, and took several photographs of 'tip and run' bomb damage in the resort — although some time after the raids themselves. This one shows the wrecked Marine Villa on the Esplanade. (Hedley Vinall)

Damage from enemy action at the Royal Spa Hotel, Shanklin Esplanade. (Hedley Vinall)

Bomb devastation and general neglect at the south end of Shanklin Esplanade, looking up Chine Hill. (Hedley Vinall)

Shanklin's Vicar Killed

The eight Fw 190s responsible for the savage 'tip and run' raid on the morning of Wednesday 17 February evaded anti-aircraft fire when they swooped in from the south-west late in the morning — then strafed farm buildings at Wroxall with their own machine-gun fire as they

closed for the kill at Shanklin. One of the six bombs dropped in the heart of the town's residential area tore into St Paul's Church, high on its north side, passed clean through the building and exploded on the adjoining vicarage, which was practically demolished. Buried in the wreckage were the 64-year-old Vicar, the Rev Bob Irons, his wife and her 85-year-old mother. They were among the twelve people killed in the raid. Teresa King remembers:

The bomb had first of all bounced in Atherley Road, then passed through the gate and garden of a house and gone up over the top and into the church. When it exploded on the Vicarage, the rescuers weren't sure who was in there — they had to dig their way through all that rubble. In fact, they were still digging that night, having set up acetylene lamps. I was with a crowd of people there, standing on the vicarage lawn. Suddenly, we heard a plane overhead, and everybody stood absolutely still, all of us looking up in the sky. Nothing happened, but it was quite hairy for a few minutes.

It was not until the early hours of 19 February that the rescue operation at the Vicarage — sustained by hot soup, tea and sandwiches from the ladies of the WVS — was finally wound down with the discovery of Mrs Irons' body. Apart from the direct hit on the Vicarage, bombs had also fallen during the raid in Landguard Road, North Road, Queens Road, Crescent

Road, St George's Road (two) and Rylestone Gardens. Fourteen houses were demolished, and many others were badly damaged. In addition to the twelve deaths, another 19 people suffered serious injuries.

The Bishop of Portsmouth, the Rt Rev William Anderson, told the congregation at a funeral service for the victims, that the second attack on a Shanklin church within the space of a few weeks "must have been deliberate."

Raid on the Capital

March was noticably quieter — apart from the 8th, when a combination of high-explosive, incendiary and phosphorous bombs were dropped in the Nettlestone and Seaview area — but April was less than a day old when Ventnor was hammered once again by the 'tip and run' raiders.

Four Fw 190s attacked the Island's most southerly town at 4.45pm on All Fools Day. Their bombs badly damaged the Rex Cinema and several hotels, notably the Royal Marine and Trafalgar. Several houses were demolished. A lengthy rescue operation succeeded in extricating some people from the debris of wrecked buildings, but four people (two men and two women) lost their lives in the attack, and another ten were badly hurt.

And then it was Newport's turn.

The Isle of Wight's capital had hitherto escaped serious damage at the hands of the Luftwaffe, but on the morning of Wednesday 7 April a formation of eight Fw 190s from Jabo 10./SKG inflicted one of the the worst of the Island's 'tip and run' raids on the ancient market town.

Skimming the cliffs at Sandown just after 7.15am, the fighter-bombers roared on at a low altitude towards Newport, opening up with cannon and machine-gun fire as they approached the town. Swinging round in a half circle, each of them dropped a bomb and then made a fast getaway down the Bowcombe Valley, to the south-west of the town, and out over the coast at Chale. At least one was hit by the locally-stationed AA gunners, who produced a devastating burst of fire as the raiders arrived at Newport, and again as they departed little more than a minute later. Over the Channel the 190s were engaged by RAF fighters, and

Where they sheltered — Above: Several examples of this type of brick-built surface air raid shelter survive on the Island. This one — minus its blast wall — was photographed at New Street, Newport, in 1989. Below: Flat-roofed shelter pictured in a back garden at York Avenue, East Cowes, in May 1989. (Author)

one, maybe more, fell victim to a Hawker Typhoon. Behind them, back at Newport, a frenetic rescue operation was under way in the stunned town.

The bombs were well scattered, causing extensive damage, but it was worst in two rows of terraced homes — at Chapel Street and Clarence Road. Eight of the 16 people who were killed in the raid died as a result of these two direct hits.

Chapel Street lost five of its houses that morning. Six people were killed there — five women and one man — and children were

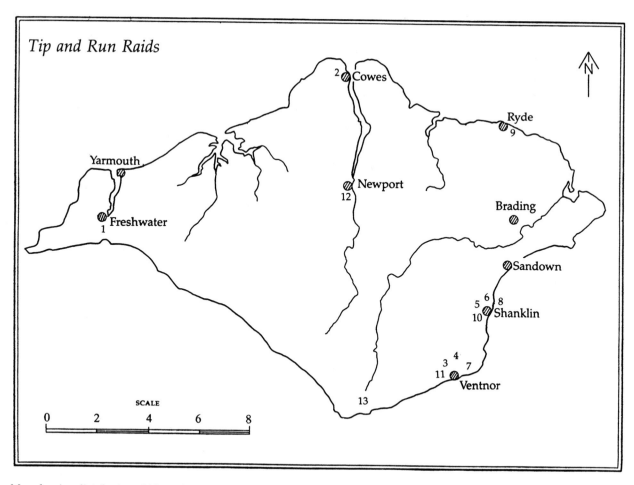

*Map showing distribution of 'tip and run' raids on the Island:
1) Freshwater Bay, 5 March 1942: 3 killed. 2) Cowes, 28 April
1942: 10 killed. 3) Ventnor, 18 August 1942: 3 killed. 4)
Ventnor, 2 September 1942: none killed. 5) Shanklin, 13
October 1942; none killed. 6) Shanklin, 3 January 1943; 23
killed. 7) Ventnor, 17 January 1943; 7 killed. 8) Shanklin, 20
January 1943: none killed. 9) Ryde, 4 February 1943; 11 killed.
10) Shanklin, 17 February, 1943; 12 killed. 11) Ventnor, 1
April 1943; 4 killed. 12) Newport, 7 April 1943; 16 killed. 13)
Niton, 1 June 1943; 6 killed.*

among the injury victims. Four homes were
wrecked in Clarence Road, where the five
fatalities included two children. Another three
men were killed in Morey's timber yard by a
bomb which bounced at least 200 yards after
first hitting the ground, passed through the roof
of a neighbouring house, struck the ground in
the garden of the Baptist minister's home next
door, ploughed up the soil for about three
yards, passed through a concrete wall and
richocheted over two roads and several houses
before finally exploding in the timber yard —
another dramatic example of the effects of low-
trajectory bombing.

The remaining two deaths were the result of a
direct hit on Bradley Lodge, the home of Dr
Arthur Straton in Medina Avenue. "Hardly one
brick of the large house remained on another,"
reported the *IW County Press* (without, of
course, identifying the location). The doctor and
a maid were killed, although Mrs Straton was
rescued from the debris, albeit with serious
injuries. In all, 17 people were listed as serious
injury victims, and another 200 were said to be
"slightly hurt."

In the High Street, a bomb passed through the
roof of the Medina Cinema, badly damaging it,
and then exploded next door, in Phillips' draper's shop, completely demolishing the building
and the adjacent electricity company's premises.
The Guildhall opposite and the nearby offices of
the *County Press* were also affected. Elsewhere,

Members of J1 Post, Royal Observer Corps, at Mount Joy, Newport, in April 1943. The men's C/Obs, W. Sibbick, is pictured with the salver. (CCM)

damage was caused to the requisitioned Southern Vectis bus garage in Pyle Street, the nearby Catholic Church, and Jordan & Stanley's grocery shop in St James's Street. Military help was sought to salvage the animal feed, tons of meat for human consumption and thousands of gallons of fresh milk stored at the roller mill in Petticoat Lane after a direct hit on the premises — but food was immediately available from the WVS, who set up two mobile kitchens in the town.

Planning the Offensive

After the misery caused by this serious attack on the Island capital, good news was needed to lift the gloom. It came on 15 April, when the Government announced that, "under present conditions," the ban on the ringing of church bells was to be suspended forthwith. The bells would cease to be the recognised form of local alarm signal "until further notice."

But, if the invasion of England by the Nazis was no longer considered a serious threat, the possibilities of invading occupied Europe in the opposite direction were increasingly taxing the minds of the Allied leaders.

The Last Raiders

As the tables gradually turned, so also did the 'tip and run' campaign draw to its close. The sting in the tail came late in the morning on Tuesday 1 June, when eight Fw 190s, taking advantage of low cloud cover, unleashed a vicious attack on the southern coastal village of Niton. They were no doubt attracted by the radar and wireless stations located there, but it was the large Undercliff Hotel, used as a wartime billet for the service personnel, which suffered the most. It was completely demolished by a direct hit, killing two soldiers. Rescuers toiled all afternoon extricating several people trapped in the wreckage.

Also hit was the emergency power house and boiler room at St Catherine's Lighthouse. All three keepers, by a cruel twist of fate, were together at the time, stacking bird perches they had just taken down from the tower. They all died, and were buried together in the local churchyard. A sixth fatality was a local man, whose home near the village school also took a direct hit. Another eleven people were injured, and several other buildings, damaged.

Remarkably, although a window in Niton Parish Church was smashed in the raid, it turned out to be the only one not made of stained glass! Maybe it was a sign from above — the 'tip and run' raiders were never to reappear over the Island

NINE

To D-Day . . . and Victory

As the Anglo-American team charged with planning the Allied invasion of Europe continued its deliberations, the Isle of Wight was already being invaded — with increasing regularity. During the latter half of 1943 all manner of weapons were fired across its once peaceful countryside, as a bewildering and ever-growing number of military units exercised and trained for the big offensive to come.

The rolling acres of much of Brighstone, Cheverton, Rowborough, Limerstone and Fore Downs, and ancient Gallibury Fields — all firing ranges in 1943 — shook to the harsh sounds of practice warfare. Mortars, rifles and machine-guns blasted out from the West Wight their promise of things to come on the continent of Europe. The gunners of Coast Artillery added to the cacophony with regular practice shoots at towed targets from the East Wight forts at Nodes, Culver and Yaverland; from the aged Spithead sea forts at Horse Sand and No Man's Land; and from Cliff End Fort, at the other end of the Island, and Hurst Castle, jutting out from the mainland opposite.

At HMS *Vectis* in Cowes, Combined Operations' Force J planned to avenge the disaster of Dieppe as its men practiced close support firing on the Tennyson Range at Freshwater, and staged mock landings amid the famous coloured sands of Alum Bay. Mine-laying techniques were perfected off the Island's coast, practice Very lights and flares frequently illuminated the night sky, and the Royal Navy also used Cowes Roads to rehearse fire-fighting operations, and much else besides.

The enemy, by comparison, was relatively quiet, and it was not until August that the Island was jolted rudely back into the war with, in the words of Fred Kerridge at Ryde, "the finest display of fireworks to date."

On the memorable Sunday night of 15 August, the air raid alert was heard on the Island at five minutes to midnight in response to a pathfinder force of Dornier Do 217s from 1./KG66 homing in on Portsmouth from the east. Fred Kerridge recorded practically continuous anti-aircraft gunfire, growing in intensity, throughout the hour-long bombing attack. Planes were caught in the criss-crossing searchlight beams, and the sky was further illuminated by the colourful marker flares which preceded the Dorniers' incendiary and high-explosive bombs — and successfully picked out the target area for a second wave of Do 217s. Watching the spectacular action at Ryde, a 36-year-old woman was killed when a rocket shell struck the town's parish church.

On the following evening the sirens wailed again to herald the arrival in the area of three Messerschmitt Bf 109s to photograph the extent of the previous night's raid on Portsmouth. Crossing the Isle of Wight on their return flight, the 109s ran into a heavy AA barrage, and one of the Messerschmitts was destined to be the victim of the Island's most spectacular ack-ack success of the war.

Thousands of Islanders watched as the planes were attacked by the 3.7 inch gun batteries at both Whippingham and Nettlestone (and probably by those at Binstead and Forelands, as well). Despite the fact that the Messerschmitts were flying at 36,000 feet (nearly seven miles up) the Island-based gunners scored an incredible direct hit, or at least one which was near enough to the leading aircraft to cause a spectacular explosion. The 109, piloted by Leutnant H. Jaschinski, broke up in the sky, spreading its wreckage over a wide area and giving the impression from elsewhere on the Island — one that persisted in some quarters for a long time — that all three planes had been shot down. The spectacle drew probably the largest cheer heard on the Island since before the war!

A couple of days later the national press was given the story. The location had, of course, to be non-specific ("over the South Coast") and the description of the gunsites limited to "mixed AA batteries," although some of the papers did devote considerable space to pictures of the six-strong gun crew credited with the feat. The question of whether they were from Whippingham or Nettlestone (the two principal contenders) has remained an arguable point on the Island, but the newspaper photographs did reveal that half of them were women — three ATS privates working alongside three Royal Artillery gunners.

The *Sunday Express* enthusiastically called the feat "a record kill" and added the following "official comment" from an unnamed Army source: "A remarkable achievement for an AA gunnery to score a direct hit at such a terrific height. It was the first time that a shell has met and blasted to pieces a raider at such extreme range for the type of heavy guns used."

The RAF crew of an Armstrong-Whitworth Albemarle medium-bomber (V1711) which crashed at St Catherine's Down on 13 March 1944. From left. F/S Knowles, F/S Muddeman, F/L Kingdon (the pilot), F/S Bishop and F/S Hulme. The photograph was sent with a letter of thanks to T.C. Hudson, who helped the men after F/L Kingdon called at his Chale cottage home on the night of the crash. "The pilot had misjudged the height of the land," recalls Mr Hudson. (T.C. Hudson)

Countdown to *Overlord*

With the Luftwaffe considerably weakened and demoralised by the Allied bombing offensive, the aerial dramas on the Island in the closing months of 1943 were mainly confined to a series of crash-landings by RAF or USAF planes.

By early 1944, the preparations for Operation *Overlord* were plainly evident all over the southern half of England, which seemed in real danger of being swamped by uniformed men and the complex panoply of 20th century warfare. The American forces — nearly a million men by now — were based mainly in the south-western counties. Their seemingly endless supply of everything the British people had been missing since the outbreak of war was thus largely denied to the Isle of Wight, which formed part of the area designated for the encamped British and Empire components of the invasion force. The only Americans to train in number on the Island were the 2nd and 5th US Rangers, who scaled the Island's cliffs during May in preparation for what turned out to be an heroic and bloody assault on the Point-du-Hoc gun batteries at *Omaha* beach.

Tented accommodation for the troops-in-waiting appeared all over the Island. At Thorness Bay, on the north-west coast, soldiers and Churchill tanks were put ashore in mock-Normandy landings. Meanwhile, mobile guns arrived to augment the existing ground defences.

Anybody on the Island still in doubt that the long-awaited Second Front was drawing near had only to cast an eye over the massive anchorage off the north coast. From Spithead, in the east, to the 'gate' beyond Hamstead, which controlled the western approach to the Solent, the sea was becoming ever more solid with the vessels of war. Soon somebody would first make the comment — one that is still often repeated today — that it was surely possible to walk across the Solent, hopping from deck to deck all the way to Portsmouth or Southampton! Nobody, of course, knew precisely where this huge mass of shipping was destined.

The guessing game on the Island was intensified by glimpses of the work involved in the construction of PLUTO (Pipeline under the Ocean), the brainchild of Lord Louis Mountbatten, when Head of Combined Operations. With

Four photographs showing men from the 1st Independent
Guards in a pre-invasion exercise at Thorness Bay. Above.
The first soldiers leave the landing craft. Below. Hauling the
guns, ammunition and Bren gun carriers ashore. Opposite
top. Churchill tanks are manoeuvred into position. Opposite
bottom. The men return to their troop carriers after the
exercise. (IWM)

some 14,000 vehicles earmarked for landing in Normandy on D-Day alone, it was obvious to the invasion planners that some means of transporting the millions of gallons of fuel required — other than in a vulnerable tanker fleet — would have to be found. PLUTO, an underwater 65-mile pipeline from the Isle of Wight to Cherbourg, was to be the answer.

Part of this ingenious scheme involved the transportation of oil to the Isle of Wight via a spur pipeline beneath the Solent (SOLO), which came ashore on the north-east coast at Thorness. The fuel was then pumped across the Island to a 620,000 gallon reservoir (TOTO) near Shanklin. It was from this town, and the neighbouring resort of Sandown, that the initial cross-Channel pipeline itself was built. (See Appendices).

On 1 April, at the insistence of General Eisenhower, the Supreme Allied Commander, one of the most irksome decisions of the Isle of Wight's war became effective. In a security-conscious move which met with an initially sceptical response from the British War Cabinet, the existing controls on movement within the south of England coastal belt were substantially tightened-up. Now the restricted area, ten to 20 miles deep, stretched from The Wash right round to Newquay in Cornwall, and the obstacles to movement inside it were suffocatingly-strict.

For example, Islanders found that even near relatives who lived on the mainland were prohibited from crossing the Solent to see them — and their own movement in the opposite direction was similarly impeded. Exceptions were made, but the required permit was hard to obtain. It was, commented the *County Press*, "a necessary but most inconvenient isolation."

The concentration of shipping off the Island was an obvious Luftwaffe target. It was finally attacked overnight on 25/26 April by a combination of Dornier Do 217s and the new Junkers Ju 188s. They mounted two raids and were met on both occasions, and particularly on the second, with a tremendous barrage of fire from the ground AA defences and the warships at anchor. The inevitable consequence was the jettisoning of bombs all over the Island. At Ventnor, Mary Watson wrote:

This was the worst air raid we have ever had. The

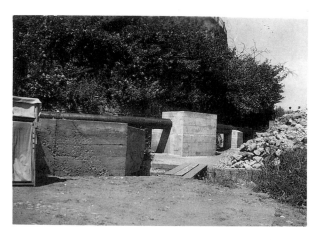

A section of the PLUTO pipeline — laid above ground at the bottom of Shanklin Chine. The photograph was taken in 1945. (Hedley Vinall)

noise was terrifying; the guns shattering. Naval vessels took part with their guns, and sometimes the rockets, flares and gun flashes made it seem like day . . . just as we got back to bed after the first raid, the other one started, and this was worse than the first. Altogether, 100 bombs were dropped on the Island; 29 in the Ventnor district alone. After it was all over, and we were back in bed, there seemed such a stillness, then a bird began to sing its spring song . . .

Another raid on the fleet followed on 14/15 May, when one of the many bombs dropped exploded on a row of town centre houses in East Cowes, demolishing six. Nine people were killed, eight of them — including three young children and their parents — in the same house. The Cooke family and the other victims were later buried together at East Cowes Cemetery, alongside the communal grave from the 1942 blitz. There were no casualties from the 2,000 lb HE bomb which dropped perilously close to Force J's Cowes HQ at the Royal Yacht Squadron, but considerable damage was caused inside the fine old building.

On the same night factory worker Arthur Moss, his wife and daughter were all killed by a bomb which fell in the road outside their Shanklin home. The raid also claimed the life of First World War veteran Albert Hyett, who died in hospital after a bomb exploded in a garden at the rear of a terrace of homes in Bembridge, leaving a dozen unfit for habitation. Many other buildings were blast-damaged in the attack,

The build up before D-Day. Naval transport and landing craft gathered in the Solent. (IWM)

notably Frank James Hospital and the Town Hall at East Cowes. Several bombing incidents disrupted the Island's railway network, the most serious tearing a hole in the roof of Newchurch Station.

The Bridgecourt Finale

The Isle of Wight sirens twice wailed their warning in the moonlit early hours of Tuesday 30 May — destined to be one of the more significant nights of the Island's war. The second alert heralded the arrival of a lone Focke Wolfe Fw 190. Over Godshill, it dropped its high-explosive bomb, which fell near disused Bridgecourt Mill, south of the village, seriously damaging the old buildings but causing no casualties. The plane disappeared over the sea. This bomb was to prove the last dropped on the Isle of Wight by a manned German aircraft. Indeed, the Luftwaffe would never again appear in the sky above the Island. It would not be

long, however, before the start of a terrifying last-ditch German aerial offensive which did not require the services of aircrew.

'OK, Let's Go'

As May drew to a close, the sealed military encampments across the south of England were at last opened and the troops released to begin their long-awaited journeys to the invasion ports. For those on the Isle of Wight, of course, the journey to their allotted troopships and landing craft was relatively short, and could be left almost until 5 June itself. Teresa King recalls that in those last few days before D-Day "the streets everywhere were full of the military. You couldn't walk on the pavements!"

Allied aircraft were seen day and night leaving on their bombing missions to France, while, on the water, the Solent and Spithead anchorages now contained more than 600 vessels, and smaller concentrations of shipping had sprouted at various points off the Island's coast, along its rivers and creeks, and within its harbours. A not

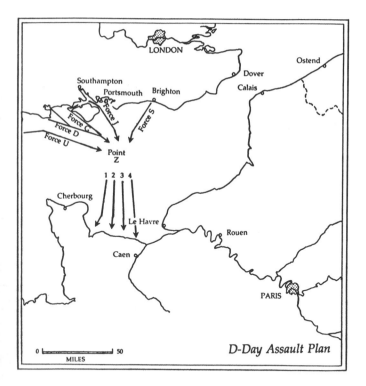

Map representing the initial D-Day assault — showing the routes to and from Point Z, the assembly area off the south coast of the Isle of Wight for the 6 June fleet. (1. US VII Corps; 2. US V Corps; 3. British XXX Corps; 4. British I Corps).

inconsiderable number of the craft had been built, or at least fitted-out, at Island yards.

Then the weather, the one thing the *Overlord* planners at their Hampshire base could do nothing to organise, played its card. Rough seas, poor visibility and low cloud were forecast for 5 June. General Eisenhower postponed the invasion for 24 hours until Tuesday the 6th, which promised better weather conditions. It was still raining heavily and blowing a gale when, at Southwick House in the early hours of Monday, the Supreme Commander confirmed the invasion was on for 6 June with the immortal words: "OK. Let's go."

In Groves and Guttridge's reconstructed ship-yard at East Cowes, there was something of a party atmosphere on 5 June. Christine Pitman, who had returned to the shipyard office after the 1942 blitz, recalls:

By late May 1944 several landing craft had come in for overhaul. These had been followed by stores and then the crews, in readiness for the anticipated landings, but the unfavourable weather meant that

no-one knew when the orders to join the fleet would arrive. The officers were very tense and, at lunchtime on 5 June, they set off for the local hostelry. Early in the afternoon they returned in a merry mood and, instead of walking straight through the office corridor and out into the courtyard, they opened office doors, grabbed the girls and started a conga dance all round the building and out into the nearest boatshop. The female staff were reprimanded by one of the directors, and the next day both craft and crews had gone. We will never know what happened to them.

The Isle of Wight, jammed full of soldiers up until the weekend, was now strangely quiet. A military exodus had taken place. However, by the evening of Monday 5 June, the Island found itself right at the centre of the world's stage. The crowded anchorages off the Island's north coast at last began to empty as the multitude of ships set off to join the greatest amphibian force in history, now converging from every conceivable direction on Point Z (or Piccadilly Circus, as it was soon tagged), the invasion assembly area some 20 miles south of St Catherine's Point. Tense soldiers took a last, lingering look at the Island's rolling countryside and wondered when, and perhaps if, they would see England again.

On the Island, 'Jock' Leal saw the move-off from the anchorages: "For the first time since the outbreak of war the lightship at Calshot Spit had its light flashing. There was a strange feeling that one was watching history in the making." Overhead, almost continuously throughout the night, could be heard the sound of wave after wave of aircraft — bombers, transports full of the paratroops who would lead the assault in the small hours, and the glider-towing C47 Dakotas. Each of the planes had its navigation lights on; a shining reminder of peacetime normality in the most abnormal of settings.

Then, just before 9am on 6 June, the unmistakable voice of the BBC's John Snagge confirmed on the wireless what Islanders had by now confidently assumed: "Under the command of General Eisenhower, Allied Naval Forces, supported by strong Air Forces, began landing Allied Armies this morning on the northern coast of France." The Germans had been taken by surprise.

6pm on D-Day plus 9 . . . Bernard Gribble's painting from an eye-witness account by Sir John Thornycroft, of Steyne, Bembridge, showing Normandy-bound vessels passing the eastern tip of the Island. Note the anti-invasion barrier running along the shore, the anti-aircraft gun in the left foreground, and the double-rainbow — exactly as Sir John described it to the artist. (T. Thornycroft / Ben Houfton)

The Island's Role

On the Isle of Wight the prevailing D-Day mood was something of a mixture. It swung from unbridled excitement at the great event unfolding so close to the Island's shores, coupled with wonderment at the plainly evident scale of it, to an unwelcome feeling of apprehension. Much of this was natural concern for the safety and success of the young men setting out to liberate Europe, but there was also the retaliation factor. The Germans would surely hit back. How, when and where? Again, Islanders keenly felt their proximity to the enemy.

They were, of course, unaware of just how significant a part the Island had played, and was continuing to play, in the drama. The role of the Force J specialists at Cowes (now led by Commodore G.N. Oliver) in planning, and training for, the landings (particularly for the Canadian-led assault on *Juno* beach) had been highly significant, while, at the opposite end of the Island, Niton's wireless station was the relay point for communications between Supreme Headquarters at Southwick House and the invasion beaches, It has been recorded how an anti-aircraft battery at Niton, in the process of fixing camouflage nets, managed to drive a stake into the telephone line from Southwick just before D-Day, temporarily severing all communications! Another gem among the many stories of this period was the loss overboard of a key to the safe — on a Normandy-bound transport off Yarmouth — which contained the secret landing instructions. It was eventually opened by an ex-burglar with a tin opener!

Sabotage by the enemy had certainly been expected — together with the possibility of a post-invasion counter-landing on the Isle of Wight. In the event, the fears proved unwarranted and the succeeding days saw back-up invasion equipment — including units for the artificial Mulberry harbours and the immense floating 'cotton reels' of yet-to-be-laid PLUTO pipeline — emerge unmolested from the Island's creeks and harbours. (The extraordinary response to the counter-invasion threat, a story inextricably linked with the history of the Island's resistance movement, is told in Chapter 13).

Dance of the *Doodle-Bugs*

As the largest concentration of aircraft ever seen above the Island, a bewildering variety bearing the black and white stripes of invasion, made for Normandy, Fred Kerridge recorded the momentous happenings in his log book with the supremely succinct one-line entry in capital letters: "INVASION JUNE 6." On the following Friday, in a simple, yet dramatic, personal expression of the mounting tension in the Isle of Wight, he again used capitals to write: "THE GREAT SILENCE."

Islanders expected the silence − only one air raid alert, lasting nine minutes, between 4 and 13 June − to end at any moment following the news that Hitler was preparing to launch his retaliatory strike against Britain in the frightening form of pilotless aircraft. It was on the evening of Tuesday 13 June that the V-weapon offensive began.

The V1 Flying Bomb, colloquially known as the *doodle-bug* or *buzz-bomb*, travelled at 400 mph, carried a 1,000lb warhead and could be expected to explode between five and 15 seconds after its jet engine cut out − although some could continue for a considerable distance in a shallow glide before finally dropping to earth. Of all the weapons flung at Islanders during the war, the *doodle-bug*, by common consent, was the most frightening. It was all right so long as you could hear it . . .

Map showing Island crash sites during the V1 offensive in 1944: 1) Duxmore, near Havenstreet; 25 June. 2) North Fairlee, Newport; 25 June. 3) Carisbrooke Road, Newport; 25 June. 4) Gurnard; 26 June. 5) Denness Road, Lake; 2 July. 6) Rew Down, Ventnor; 15 July.

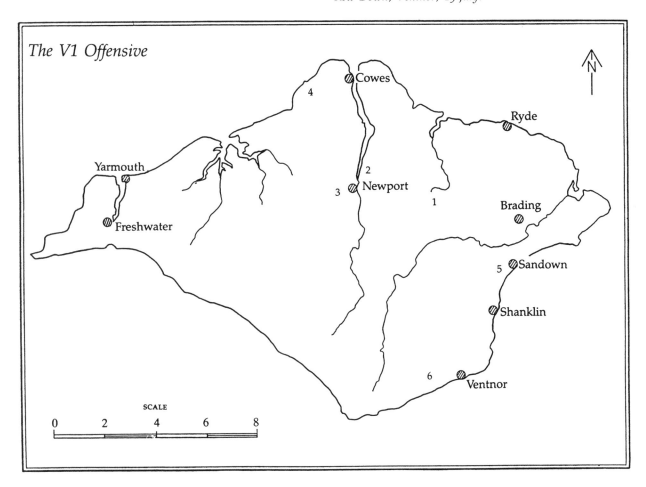

Before the advancing Allies overran the launching sites in France, the woeful inaccuracy of the V1 added to the Isle of Wight's war, as elsewhere in southern England, a short, vicious and damaging sting in the tail. Several landed on the Island between 25 June and 15 July, although the Government's policy of silence on the V1s — forbidding the release not only of details on the number landing or shot down, but also on casualty figures — meant the damage they caused on the Island was not publicly reported at the time. Information on the V1 attacks is also hampered by the absence of the county ARP log book for this period of the war, which would have recorded all relevant details. However, other records have survived and, from these, it is possible to piece together a fairly comprehensive account of the *doodle-bug* on the Isle of Wight.

It was on the miserably damp Sunday evening of 25 June that the Island became directly aquainted with Hitler's new terror weapon. The siren was sounded at 8.45 when a number of V1s were plotted crossing the Channel, approaching the Island from the south-east. A short burst of anti-aircraft fire was heard four minutes later, then nothing more until 9.10, when further intense gunfire preceded the arrival of a solitary V1 in the sky above Sandown Bay. Soon the flying bomb was crossing the Island, apparently heading for Southampton. It never made it.

The engine cut out at 9.25, and the V1 dived to the ground to explode at Duxmore, south of Havenstreet, shattering windows in the village, but causing no serious damage. It was not long before a second V1, following the same course, appeared above the Island. This one flew a little further than the first before its engine cut out at 9.50 above the eastern outskirts of Newport. The *doodle-bug* nose-dived to earth, exploding near the searchlight battery at Fairlee.

It was just the start. As the night progressed, the sirens repeatedly alerted Islanders to further threats from the flying bombs. Most flew over the Island without cutting out. Of those that did not make it to the mainland, three came down harmlessly on the Island's western coast and one sparked off the most serious of the night's incidents by plunging to earth near Carisbrooke Road at Newport, causing substantial blast damage in the area and killing a lone pedestrian.

The V1 alerts became less frequent after that initial burst of frenzied activity, but there were enough of them to keep Islanders on their toes. At Shanklin it was possible to follow the chilling progress of the flying bombs as they crossed the Channel. Teresa King did so from the Home of Rest Hospital, where her mother was Matron:

From the Home of Rest we could watch the *doodle-bugs* set out from the launching sites in Cherbourg, the speck of light from them getting bigger and bigger as they approached. We could usually work out where the target was by the direction they were flying, but, of course, they often didn't make it to Portsmouth or Southampton. I remember one dropped at Lake.

The Lake incident, in the early hours of Friday 7 July, was the worst of the Island's V1 onslaught. The flying bomb cut out soon after arriving above the Island and plummeted to the ground at Denness Road, which runs parallel with the main road between Sandown and Shanklin. A considerable amount of structural damage resulted, with four houses totally demolished and twelve casualties — one of them fatal. Those twelve people were to prove the final victims on the Isle of Wight of the enemy's wartime aerial offensive. Altogether, 214 people had been killed and another 274 seriously injured. Nearly 11,000 Island buildings, most of them people's homes, had been either destroyed or damaged.

The War Winds Down

Slowly — too slowly for many, who had believed, or at least managed to convince themselves, that it really would be "all over by the autumn" — the war was winding down in the Isle of Wight.

The sirens had sounded on only six occasion in August, without subsequent incident, and, on the 25th, the War Office had lifted the ban on entry to England's protected coastal belt, the Island included. It remained a regulated area, in which everyone over 16 had to carry their ID cards, no-one was permitted to use binoculars, telescopes or cameras without police permission, and certain beaches remained closed because of the still substantial presence of mines. But Islanders, as the *County Press* put it, "will breathe a sigh of relief" at the lifting of the visitors' ban, "a most encouraging sign of the good progress of the war."

There were no alerts at all in September, during which month Islanders went to church in substantial numbers to observe a national day of prayer on the fifth anniversary of the war's outbreak. Compulsory Home Guard parades ceased on the 11th; daytime fire-watching on the 12th. The first alert for nearly a month was sounded just after 1am on 24 October for no purpose apparent on the Island, and was insufficient reason to prevent the discontinuance from 31 October of night-time manning of the ARP warden posts and rescue depots by part-time personnel. The very last alert, the 1,603rd recorded by Fred Kerridge, followed on the evening of 5 November.

The winter and early spring of 1944-45 were bitterly cold, and, with a fuel crisis thrown in for good measure, Islanders, in common with the rest of the British people, approached the end of the war in anything but high spirits. The danger had passed, but so, too, had the excitement and much of that uplifting spirit of comradeship in adversity. The war had simply gone on too long. It was a dreary period.

One by one the wartime institutions came to an end. The Island's two Home Guard battalions had jointly held a stand-down parade in Newport on 3 December. By the spring of 1945, with victory in Europe imminent, the dismantling of civil defence was in motion. ARP's own stand-down took place on 2 May (although full-time staff would remain in employment until 30 June, and the top officials for a further month after that). The Royal Observer Corps throughout Britain, having contributed continuously towards the defence of the country since August 1939, was stood down on Tuesday 8 May — when Islanders joined the rest of the country and liberated Europe in the celebrations of VE Day.

By the time Winston Churchill formally announced Nazi Germany's defeat that after-

The war in Europe is over . . . and street parties like this one in Stephenson Road, Cowes, are held throughout the Island. (Raymond Tarrant)

VE-Day at Ryde . . . although there appears to be little sign of rejoicing on the faces of the civic dignataries assembled on the Town Hall balcony! Taking centre stage are the Mayor, Alderman Henry Weeks, and the Town Clerk, Mr Tommy Fawdry. Note the strings of coloured light bulbs. (Raymond Weeks)

noon, it was already like carnival time in Newport, with, in the words of the *County Press*, "a brave display of bunting everywhere." The Guildhall was "lavishly decorated by the Corporation employees and the NFS . . . the flags of the great Allies, Great Britain, the United States and Russia, were draped over the western balcony." Ryde Corporation's workmen "slung streamers of bunting across the High Street and Union Street in great profusion, until those two thoroughfares were a mass of flowing colours." Ryde went one better than Newport with its display of flags from the Town Hall staff — China's was there as well as the other three, a reminder of the unfinished business in the Far East. "Some of the licensed premises ran short of supplies," reported the *County Press*.

Celebrations in Sandown and Shanklin, by contrast, were "remarkably restrained," with people in the twin towns left largely to their own resources by the local authority. They "rose to the occasion with admirable zeal and ingenuity," said the *County Press*. In Ventnor there was "a spirit of quiet rejoicing," but Cowes was a picture of "gay scenes reminiscent of the great yachting festival of pre-war years." The palatial steam and motor yachts were replaced by large transports, tugs and small ships of war, but most of their crews had "dressed ship" for the occasion.

Out in the West Wight, Freshwater's Regent Cinema presented a free afternoon film show for the many troops stationed at the local forts (*Show Business*, with George Murphy, Eddie Cantor and Joan Davis). A bonfire was lit on the hill at Rancombe by the people of Limerstone hamlet — and an effigy of Hitler, made by the children, was placed on top. In the East Wight the Fuhrer was hanged "with some of his thugs" from the lamp standards at West Priory, Nettlestone. Nearby St Helens celebrated in gentler style with children's sports on the village green. On the Wednesday, a party of church bell-ringers toured the Island; the bells on this occasion signalled the friendliest of invasions.

Islanders who had been held prisoners-of-war by the Nazis began returning home in early May. Returning from the Island on 23 May as its re-elected Conservative MP was Captain Peter MacDonald, who had served during the war in the RAF Volunteer Reserve and, from 1942, as Secretary to the Parliamentary Air Committee.

The war's PS . . . like many other commodities, clothes remained on ration well after the fighting had ceased. (D. Corney)

The Island's vote did not affect the national political swing, for the British people as a whole had elected 393 Labour MPs to the House of Commons, thus removing Winston Churchill and his caretaker government — which had succeeded the dissolved wartime coalition — from office.

The Emergence of Peace

The distant war in the Far East, remote and now irritating to all who were not directly involved in its horrors, or knew people who were, held up the British people's quest for the 'new world' promised by the politicians until the atomic bombing of Hiroshima and Nagasaki brought it to a sudden and awesome end. The final Allied victory was announced by Clement Attlee, the new Prime Minister, at midnight on Tuesday 14

Arthur Street's VJ-Day party at Ryde in August 1945 was attended by the town's Mayor and Mayoress. (Raymond Weeks)

the rainy morning before becoming aware that the day was so historic, and then returned to drape their homes with bunting." At night on VJ-Day a flight of rockets was dispatched from the radar pylons on St Boniface Down at Ventnor. It was almost exactly five years since those same pylons, now brilliantly illuminated by searchlights, had been rendered inoperable by the two-stage German bombing strike at the height of the Battle of Britain.

The celebrations continued. some unashamedly wild, others quietly reflective, as the curtains came down on the Isle of Wight's eventful war. The events of 1939-45 will never, can never, be forgotten by those who lived through those incredible six years on the Island. They remember the deprivations and the fear, but they also recall the comradeship born of the common struggle, and — because those who look back on the war today were all young people then — they remember, too, the excitement and the laughter which carried them through.

August. Minutes later the bells of St Thomas's Parish Church rang out in Newport's town centre — the ending of war had shattered the peace in the Island's ancient capital!

Several more hours passed before the vast majority of Islanders woke up to the fact that the war was finally behind them. The truth dawned even later for some. At Ryde, reported the *County Press*, "many inhabitants stepped out in

PART TWO

The Garrison Isle

Soldiers from the Reconnaissance Corps training with a 3lb mortar near Shanklin in 1942. (Author)

TEN

The Military Presence

A sudden and dramatic increase in the military presence on the Isle of Wight came at the height of the invasion scare in June 1940 with the establishment of a garrison force by the men of 12th Infantry Brigade, part of the Army's 4th Division, under Brigadier D.M.W. Beak VC. Their principal brief was to equip the Island with full coastal defence protection against the soldiers and tanks of the Wehrmacht.

Initially, brigade headquarters was at Albany Barracks, north of Newport, but it was soon transferred to 18th Century Billingham Manor, in the south-west of the Island, owned by the novelist and dramatist J.B. Priestley. A little further to the west, one of 12th Brigade's

Evacuated from their own island in advance of the German occupation, men of the Jersey Militia were among the earliest troop arrivals on the Isle of Wight in 1940. A Lewis Gun team made up of Militiamen is pictured leaving an observation post in the West Wight to mount an attack during an exercise. (IWM)

constituent battalions, the 2nd Royal Fusiliers, set up its own headquarters in another of the Isle of Wight's historic houses – North Court, at Shorwell – and assumed responsibility for the western sector defences. With a similar role in the east of the Island, based initially in the Havenstreet and Wootton areas, were the men of the 6th Black Watch, while the southern sector was garrisoned by the 12th Battalion of The Royal West Kent Regiment,.

Of all the many infantry units stationed in the Isle of Wight during the war, it was the 6th Battalion of the famous Black Watch who made the most lasting impression. The men themselves look back on their six-month stay as certainly one of the better periods of their eventful war. It came, of course, almost immediately after the worst – the battalion's escape with 12th Infantry Brigade from the chaos of Dunkirk in May 1940. Frank Botham, ex-Black Watch, and now of Binstead, recalls:

Complete with their distinctive berets, 'D' Company of the 6th Black Watch assemble for this official photograph at their Fishbourne Lane encampment during the summer of 1940. (John Gibson)

'D' Company of the 6th Black Watch are photographed – this time unofficially – marching along Kite Hill at Wootton towards the camp on the corner of Fishbourne Lane. At the head of the men on the left is John Gibson, who now lives in Cowes. (John Gibson)

My company was stationed at Havenstreet, where we were encamped in a copse, Later on, during October, the whole battalion moved into winter billets at Ryde. During that summer, before we moved to Ryde, we had an infestation of lice; we all had to be disinfected, and they took everything from us. We were left standing there, alongside the road at Havenstreet Station, without any of our clothes, but with just our rifles and 50 rounds of ammunition! Of course, we were in full view of all the passing traffic, including the buses. There we were, 900 stark naked 'Scottish' soldiers defending the Isle of Wight!

Throughout their Island stay, the men were on ten minutes' standby, in case of enemy action, and had always to carry their rifles with them – even when off duty. Frank Botham remembers the problems these arrangements caused:

Because the 6th was so short of transport – it was abandoned in France at the time of Dunkirk – a bus, hired from Southern Vectis, had to follow us everywhere we went on the Island, in case of emergency. Later on, we were given these Hercules bicycles. Several photographs were taken at the time, and Raleigh, who made the bikes, used them for about ten years after the war as publicity and advertising pictures! As regards the rifles, the commissionaire at the Theatre Royal in Ryde always insisted on us opening the breaches to make sure there were no bullets in them before we went in the cinema!

Apart from the battalion's work on coast defences, the official war diaries reveal a number of special 'one-offs,' such as a demonstration of street fighting and house searching at Havenstreet, an exercise involving the 'recapture' of an aerodrome (the civil airfield at Ryde was used) from enemy parachute troops, and another in which the battalion had to hold an imaginary bridgehead at Wootton. A poignant red-letter day must have been 21 September, when the 6th Black Watch Pipe Band played the retreat at Havenstreet for the first time since the batta-

93

Men of the 6th Black Watch patrol the Island on their Raleigh bikes in August 1940 . . . one of a set of photographs later used extensively by the manufacturers to advertise their machines. (IWM)

The Defence of the Island

From January 1941 the Isle of Wight garrison force was provided by the newly-created 214th Independent Infantry Brigade, set up initially to provide a training centre for recruits, but, of necessity, later combining the role with that of a coastal defence force. On arrival in the Island, the 214th was commanded by Brigadier J.M. Grower DSC. By March, he had been succeeded by Brigadier J.O. Carpenter MC. Apart from the 6th Ox and Bucks, Brigadier Carpenter had three battalions of the Royal Fusiliers at his disposal — the 19th, 20th and 21st — together with the men of the 8th East Lancashire Regiment and the 156th Advanced Field Regiment RA. As senior officer commanding all troops in the Island, he also had overall responsibilty for a variety of support units.

At the end of April brigade headquarters was set up at Bellecroft, in Newport. Brigadier Carpenter's first missive from the new HQ was also one of the most important — the detailed plans for the defence of the Island in the event of a German invasion. Army policy on resisting enemy invasion was quite categoric — "to adopt the offensive, to inflict the maximum casualties, and to destroy the enemy ruthlessly and relentlessly . . . arrangements will be made for mobile divisions to destroy any airborne troops or parachutists who have landed . . . all troops, including Home Guard, allotted a defensive role will hold their positions to the last man and the last round . . . there will be no withdrawal."

Beach defences (already much in evidence thanks to the efforts of the men of 12th Brigade in 1940) included ditches, cement blocks or 'dragon's teeth' — some of which survive today — iron rails, cement walls, tubular steel scaffolding or anti-tank mines, "concealed wherever possible." Where practicable, all the beach obstacles were to be covered by gunfire — in the case of the tank obstacles, the cover would be by appropriate anti-tank weapons. "The endeavour must be to kill the enemy in his landing craft or on the beach," added Brigadier Carpenter. Wherever possible, the defences were to be concealed by either natural or artificial cover, and pill boxes provided for the use of light automatics and machine guns.

Detailed policy instructions set out the proce-

lion's return from Belgium. They left the Island in December 1940, eventually returning with distinction to the battlefields of Europe,

In addition to the three infantry batallions making up its main body, a large number of other military units were attached to 12th Brigade. Perhaps the most interesting was the Royal Jersey Militia. Removed from its own island following the British Government's decision to demilitarise the Channel Islands in June 1940 — a prelude to their, by then, inevitable occupation by the German forces — the Militia was later re-constituted as the 11th Batallion of The Hampshire Regiment.

Close-up of the Sandown Bay anti-invasion defences — a picture taken in 1940 on the foreshore near Sandown Canoe Lake. (CCM)

Surviving anti-tank 'dragon's teeth' on the beach at Bembridge in 1989. (Author)

dure for road blocks and the defence of aerodromes, and added: ''No bridge or railway will be demolished without an order from brigade headquarters. In most cases in the Isle of Wight, an efficient road block . . . will produce the same effect.''

More specific plans to defend the Island against attack from both air and sea were drawn up in August 1941. The coastline would, in the event of an invasion, be defended all along its vulnerable south-western and south-eastern stretches, from the Needles to St Catherine's Point, then round to Foreland (Bembridge) and Nodes Point. In addition, observation posts would be established on the high ground running across the centre of the Island from west to east. The town of Newport was earmarked for special attention. In the event of an invasion alert, it would be defended by ''manning certain road blocks, and the establishment of posts for observation, and from which patrols will operate.''

Plans were outlined in the August scheme for the construction of a defence line (the Yar Line) running from Freshwater Bay to Thorley village, in the West Wight. Most of the pill boxes which formed the line have survived to the present day, the best example of which stands alongside the Causeway, at the southern tip of the Western Yar.

A mass of detailed plans included a note that the piers at Ryde and Yarmouth, and the lifeboat pier at Bembridge, would be prepared for demolition, in the event of an imminent invasion threat. In conjunction with the Southern Railway, arrangements would also be made for rail blocks across the line at the two Ventnor tunnels; Shide Station; Gunville Siding; Cement Mills Viaduct; Sandown Station; Freshwater Causeway Crossing; and north of the tunnel at Newport. The Royal Engineers were detailed to build 72 'bent rail' road blocks, and a further eleven permanent blocks of reinforced concrete were planned for Newport (one), Sandown (five), Bonchurch (one), Ventnor (two) and Freshwater (two).

The Changing Units

The composition of 214th Brigade was constantly changing, as was the allocation of duties to the infantry units within the Island. In May 1941, the Royal Fusiliers held sway, with the locally-based battalions, the 19th, 20th and 21st, allocated to the three Island beach sectors, South, West and East, respectively. Making up the Island's Mobile Reserve at that time were the 156th Advance Field Regiment RA, the 8th East Lancs Regiment, the 6th Ox and Bucks (just

The Army's 'eyes' — the men of the Reconnaissance Corps — had a company stationed on the Isle of Wight in 1942. In this picture a line of Humberette scout cars is seen moving along a quiet Island country road, "with," to quote the official caption, "the gunners at the alert against possible air attack." (IWM)

transferred from South Sector duties) and an ITC detachment from the Hampshire Regiment.

Before long, the men of the 21st Royal Fusiliers had left the Island on their unit's re-constitution as a reconnaissance battalion. Taking their place were the soldiers of the 11th West Yorkshire Regiment. When the 8th East Lancs departed soon afterwards, the 10th Somerset Light Infantry moved in. By the end of the year, both of these replacement units had themselves returned to the mainland, as had the 6th Ox and Bucks. In came the 12th Hampshires and the 7th Wilts. Newcomers in 1942 included the men of the 2nd Essex Regiment, while both the 19th and 20th Royal Fusiliers moved out. This was to be the pattern for the remainder of the war — a complex cross-Solent shuffle of British infantry battalions.

In November 1942, with Brigadier H. Essame

MC now in command, the principal Isle of Wight-based battalions were the 7th Somerset Light Infantry, the 5th Duke of Cornwall's Light Infantry and the 12th Devonshire Regiment. Apart from their beach defence duties, the men had another purpose on the Island. That month, Brigadier Essame had been given six months to bring the whole brigade up to mobile operating efficiency. Every inch of spare ground was utilised for training purposes — including the cliffs at the Needles, which provided an excellent practice ground for climbing by rope. Among the several assault courses constructed was one at Parkhurst Prison!

Finally, in May 1943, the three battalions left the Island ready for action abroad. In the event, that was delayed until after D-Day in 1944, but then the Island-trained men distinguished themselves in bitterly-fought winter battles *en route* from the Normandy beaches to Northern Germany.

From June 1943, the Isle of Wight garrison. which had grown to more than 17,000 men, plus the two Home Guard battalions, was functioning as a sub-district under the aegis of 47th Infantry Division. Training needs — especially during the long build-up to D-Day — brought a bewildering variety of Allied military units to the Island. By then, properties everywhere, especially the seaside hotels and guest houses, had been requisitioned, either for military accommodation or servicing facilities.

One other building partly requisitioned for quite another reason was Parkhurst Prison. The military authorities had reserved short-term accommodation for up to 250 prisoners-of-war there. A strict procedure meant that a PoW was kept in the Parkhurst 'cage' for the minimum possible time, and would be transferred after initial interrogation to the mainland. The Army was strictly forbidden to interrogate senior Luftwaffe officers — that was the province of the RAF.

The Commandos

The specific role played by the Isle of Wight in the preparation of 'A' (RM) Commando for the ill-fated Dieppe Raid in 1942 is described in Chapter Eight — but the Island had an earlier association with the fledgling amphibian force, dating back to the days before the term 'commando' was first coined. Immediately after the evacuation from Dunkirk in 1940 Colonel Dudley Clarke formed the 11th Independent Company with the express intention of organising guerilla raiding parties to enemy territory. One of the first officers recruited by Clarke was Major Ronnie Tod — and it was Tod who settled the new Company on the Isle of Wight into the first *de facto* commandos.

Commandos were also much in evidence on the Island as the build-up to D-Day gained momentum. No 5 Commando was based at Shanklin towards the end of 1943, before leaving for service in India. In 1944, No 4 Commando was in the Island resort, pausing for breath in between its role — with 1 Special Service Brigade — in the Normandy invasion and the final Allied push into Germany.

Noting the use of the girls' school at Upper Chine as a headquarters for Shanklin-based commandos, the town's historian, Alan Parker remarks in *Shanklin Between the Wars* that "those who slept in the dormitories will doubtless recall the notice still pinned on the wall after the schoolgirls had been evacuated: 'If you want a mistress, ring the bell' . . .!"

Vulnerable Points

Special arrangements were needed to provide a 24-hour guard on the many military, and other, installations in the Island officially regarded as vulnerable. Much of this work was undertaken by the men of the Army's Vulnerable Points Section — the 'Blue Caps', as they were commonly known. Henry Williamson, of Binstead, was among them:

Each vulnerable point (VP) had seven men and one NCO assigned to it, the men working in shifts. We used to do eight hours on and 16 off. Since my home was on the Island, I would go home to the wife whenever I could, although there were always billets at the sites we were guarding. These included the PLUTO installations on Shanklin and Sandown seafronts, Seaview Esplanade, where we had to guard the telephone cables from the mainland, and Copse Lane at Freshwater, where guard duty at the ammunition dump involved us in walking up and down the lane all night.

At Niton, we had to guard the wireless station. I wasn't there the day it was attacked by the Germans. They machine-gunned it, but didn't really do any damage. There was another ammunition dump to guard at Brocks Copse, Whippingham, and I was also stationed for a while at the electricity sub-station at Brambles, between Newport and Cowes.

ELEVEN

The Forts and the Batteries

The countryside of the Isle of Wight, and especially its coastal region, was liberally dotted with the fortifications of earlier conflicts when the Second World War broke out in 1939. Many had been reactivated in the preceding months as war became increasingly likely, and to these were added the innumerable defences − the anti-aircraft guns and searchlights − commissioned to meet the new threat from the sky.

The Coastal Batteries

Forming part of the outer defences for Portsmouth and Southampton, the coastal gun batteries at either end of the Isle of Wight were ready for action when war was declared, having been continuously manned for the last ten days of peace.

The western batteries guarding the Needles Passage (the 'back door' to the Solent) were to form the sphere of wartime operation for the modern-day successor to the Island's own former infantry regiment, the Isle of Wight Rifles. Final conversion of the Rifles from Territorial infantry to artillery unit had taken place in 1937, when the Island men were first charged with the duty of manning the batteries of Needles Fire Command. An elongated title was adopted to reflect the new role while, at the same time, retaining the Rifles' historical associations. The men became known as 530 (Hampshire) Coast Regiment Royal Artillery − Princess Beatrice's Isle of Wight Rifles − and were allowed to retain their familiar green and black ceremonial dress.

Responsibility for manning the two six-inch guns at the new Bouldnor Battery, east of Yarmouth fell to the men of the Rifles' Newport detachment. The Cowes and Freshwater men were allocated to the reactivited batteries at Old and New Needles, while those from Ryde,

Sandown, Shanklin and Ventnor manned part of Warden Point Battery, Cliff End Battery and adjacent Fort Albert, and the reactivated battery at Hurst Castle, jutting out from the mainland on its narrow shingle bank.

Inevitably, the predominance of local men in 530 Coast Regiment was diluted by the posting of many of the former Island riflemen to other sections of the Army, and their replacement by gunners from the mainland. At times, owing to competing demands elsewhere, there was a severe shortage of manpower. A graphic illustration of this followed the drama of Dunkirk in May 1940, when only 15 men remained to man the 9.2 inch guns at the Needles, working 48 hours on, 24 off. It has been recorded that, in order to give the appearance of full manning at the depleted batteries − at Cliff End, as well as the Needles − scaffold pipe was rigged up to resemble anti-aircraft guns, and tailors' dummies 'stood in' for the gun crews!

Old Needles housed both the Needles Fire Command Post and the Port War Signal Station, the tower from which the Royal Navy policed the movement of all vessels entering the Passage. Protection from aerial attack at Old Needles was provided initially by a 3-inch anti-aircraft gun mounted on the magazines. A 40mm Bofors automatic AA gun replaced it in 1942, and a 20mm Oerlikon AA cannon on the edge of the cliffs protected the Needles lighthouse from low-level Luftwaffe attacks. The ubiquitous Bofors gun also appeared at New Needles midway through the war, replacing Lewis guns − and quickly notched up a notable success by winging a Focke Wolf Fw 190 at the height of the 'tip and run' offensive.

Today, it is possible to visit Old Needles Battery − now in the ownership of the National Trust − but New Needles, having served in post-war years as a testing site for Saunders-

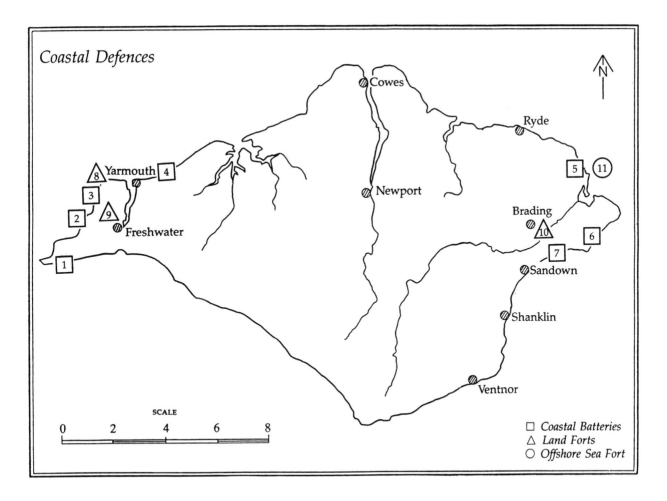

Coastal Defences

SCALE

0 2 4 6 8

☐ Coastal Batteries
△ Land Forts
○ Offshore Sea Fort

*Map showing the principal coastal defences of the Isle of Wight:
1 Old and New Needles Batteries. 2 Warden Point Battery. 3
Cliff End Battery and Fort Albert. 4 Bouldnor Battery. 5
Nodes Point Battery. 6 Culver Batteries. 7 Yaverland Battery.
8 Fort Victoria. 9 Golden Hill Fort. 10 Fort Bembridge. 11 St
Helens Fort.*

Roe's Black Knight space research rocket project, is deserted

North of the Needles, Warden Point Battery, built in 1862-63, was equipped with wartime searchlights, anti-aircraft guns (eventually a 40mm Bofors) and little else, its principal importance in 1939-45 being its role as headquarters for 530 Coast Regiment. It is now a holiday camp. Dating from the 1870s, Cliff End Battery, overlooking Fort Albert on Colwell Bay's northern headland, had been used by Territorials on summer camps in the period immediately preceding the outbreak of war. In September 1939 its fixed armament was reduced to a couple of 6-inch guns, following the removal of the last 4.7-inch weapons. A year or so later the gunners manning the battery had the enemy tantalisingly in the sights of those remaining guns, as Eddie Cooke recalls:

We were on the gun site one evening when a single German seaplane arrived in the area. The crew got out onto the wings and dropped mines in the water. We had the big guns and a Lewis gun trained on the plane, but we couldn't do anything about it. The order to fire was never given. It was very frustrating, but, had we fired, the Germans would have known of our positions − that's why the order didn't come. The mines were washed away on the tide. Unfortunately, a couple of days afterwards, a 10,000 ton ship hit one . . .

Cliff End acquired a Bofors gun in 1944 and was also equipped with searchlights − as was the brick-built Fort Albert in front of it. The fort had a pair of roof-mounted 6-pounders for its own fixed armament, later augmented by a Bofors gun on the adjacent hillside. Today, the

The men of 527(Hampshire) Coast Regiment's 'B' Battery formed their own wartime band, the highlight being a performance on the sea fort at Spit Bank for the BBC. They are pictured back in more familiar surroundings at Nodes Fort, St Helens. (Margaret Whitaker)

remains of Cliff End Battery have been largely swallowed-up by a housing development, but Fort Albert survives — as a block of luxury flats.

The batteries controlled by Culver Fire Command at the opposite end of the Island were manned from the start by mainland Territorials from Hampshire, who were eventually reconstituted in September 1940 as 527 (Hampshire) Coast Regiment RA.

Most northerly of the trio was Nodes Fort, built between 1900 and 1904 on Nodes Point, St Helens, and equipped when war broke out with both 9.2-inch and 6-inch guns. It was manned during the war by 'B' Battery, for whom additional accomodation was provided in 1940 — although further requisitioning of land was required at various stages. Early in 1940 Nodes was equipped for defence against a possible land attack. Today, the site of the fort is regularly invaded — by visitors to Nodes Point Holiday Centre, which took over the land following the demise of Coast Artillery in 1956.

Culver Fort, built in 1906 atop the Down of the same name, and protected to seaward by a virtually unclimbable cliff, was equipped with two 9.2-inch guns — with 6-inch guns positioned at the nearby Culver Down Battery. War diaries reveal a typical manning level of three officers and 116 other ranks, following the erection of new huts, and then permanent brick buildings, between the battery and the Port War Signal Station, covering the eastern approach to the port of Portsmouth. When the fort was vacated after the war by 118 Battery, it became the Royal Artillery (Coast) Practice Camp Cul-

ver. Its remains are clearly visible from the car park and turning area now used by motorists visiting the National Trust-tended Down.

Yaverland Fort, the last of the Sandown Bay defence works to be built, offered further 6-inch gun protection for the Eastern Passage. Commanded from Culver Fort, it was manned in the early part of the war by 28 gunners — and later by a battery from the East Wight Battalion of the Home Guard. Following the post-war dissolution of Coast Artillery, Yaverland remained in military use for many years, until its eventual sale to Sandown-Shanklin UDC. It is now the site of Sandown Bay Holiday Centre. The council also acquired the site of neighbouring Redcliff Battery, which had been used in the war to house an anti-aircraft gun emplacement

Fort Victoria

Fort Victoria. built on Sconce Point, west of Yarmouth, in the 1850s, had been inactive (in 'care and maintenance') for virtually the whole of the two decades preceding the Second World War, following the departure of the Royal Engineers who had manned its searchlights until 1920. However, the possession of its own pier led to the fort's reactivation in 1939, when it was used to land both stores and ammunition for the coastal batteries guarding the Needles

Passage. Between 1941 and 1943 Fort Victoria was the centre of activity for the Royal Artillery's 72 Coast Training Regiment, set up to prepare conscripted gunners for manning 6-inch gun batteries (and their searchlights) all around Britain's coasts.

As the tide of war turned, so the need for coast artillery training declined, and, as D-Day approached, Fort Victoria welcomed new tenants in the shape of the Royal Army Service Corps' recently-formed 42 Water Transport Un-

Coast Artillery gun crews are dramatically silhouetted as they rush to take up action stations at Culver's 9.2-inch guns during a practice shoot in August 1940. (IWM)

An end-of-war inspection at Yarmouth's Fort Victoria for the Royal Army Service Corps' 42 Water Transport Unit. The Quartermaster-General, General Sir Thomas Riddell-Webster, is seen with the men on Fort Victoria Pier in June 1945. (IWM)

it. It was, however, from Wootton Creek, on the other side of the Island, that men of the WTU's 626 Company sailed their harbour launches on 5 June 1944 to join the departing D-Day invasion fleet the next day; others followed within the week. The faster launches allotted to 624 Company crossed direct to Normandy from Fort Victoria on D-Day itself. Both companies – 626 in a ferrying capacity, and 624 in an escort role – performed with distinction off the invasion beaches.

Early in 1945, 42 Water Transport Unit expanded substantially at Yarmouth (to more than 1,500 officers and men) in preparation for the Allies' final push against Japan in the Far East – an exercise eventually rendered unnecessary by the atomic bombs in August on Hiroshima and Nagasaki. A year later, what remained of 42 WTU was disbanded at Fort Victoria, which was then – along with Golden Hill Fort at Freshwater – allocated to the RASC's Water Transport Training Company, its last military occupants, who remained at Yarmouth until 1962, leaving the Island without an Army garrison. Although minus its barrack blocks, Fort Victoria is now the centrepiece for a country park, from which runs the former military road (now a woodland footpath) to Cliff End Battery.

The Sea Forts

France, rather than Germany, was the feared aggressor when the prominent sea forts which still punctuate the waters of Spithead were built in the 19th century during the Premiership of Lord Palmerston. Collectively (along with the mainland fortifications on Portsdown) they became known as 'Palmerston's Follies' – oudated almost before they were completed and subsequently little used. Roles were, however, found for the quartet of forts (St Helens, No Man's Land, Horse Sand and Spit Bank) in the Second World War.

St Helens Fort, the nearest to the Island, was built on a spit of land jutting eastwards from The Bar, Bembridge Point's sandbank. It was the need to provide searchlight illumination for the shore batteries at Nodes Point and Culver which led to the fort's reactivation in the autumn of 1940. Its lights were operated by men of 527 Coast Regiment's 'B' Battery, which was

stationed at nearby Nodes. In 1943 the fort was equipped with a Bofors anti-aircraft gun. This was removed soon after the war, but the searchlights continued in periodic use to assist the training of Territorial Army gunners at Nodes Point until Coast Artillery was abolished in 1956.

Further north, the practically identical outlying sea forts on the shoals at No Man's Land and Horse Sand, largely redundant and neglected in the inter-war years, were equipped with searchlights during the Second World War, and linked by a submerged boom defence net, with fixed barriers from the Island and the mainland – Seaview and Southsea, respectively – on either side of them (See Chapter 16). An indicator loop was laid to detect the presence of enemy vessels attempting a 'break-in' to Spithead and the Solent.

Defence against air attack was limited to a token 3-inch anti-aircraft gun on Horse Sand. Even this was removed for a more pressing use – on a merchant vessel – in 1941, although Bofors guns were provided at both forts in 1943. The end of the war saw their immediate removal, and the 6-inch guns followed in 1951.

Spit Bank Fort, two-thirds the size of No Man's Land and Horse Sand, and the furthest of the sea forts from the Island, was already manned when war broke out in 1939 – by the Territorials of 154 Battery Hampshire Heavy Regiment RA, converted in 1940 to 123 Battery 529 (Hampshire) Coast Regiment. The fort, equipped with a 6-inch breach-loading gun at the outbreak, was later provided with a pair of Lewis anti-aircraft guns and, for the last two years of the war, with a Bofors gun. Spit Bank was given an important ship monitoring role during the war within Portsmouth's inner defence area, and also kept a look-out for mines parachuted into the sea by the enemy. All armament had gone by 1948, and the searchlight equipment was removed following Coast Artillery's demise in 1956. Spit Bank Fort has in recent years been opened to the public as a museum

The Land Forts

Bembridge Fort, dominating the local Down, was another of Lord Palmerston's expensive

A heavy anti-aircraft battery pictured under construction in 1940. This one was at Nettlestone, equipped initially with four 3.7-inch guns. (IWM)

19th century defences against the perceived threat of Napolean III. The fort was never re-armed following the early removal of its guns in the 1890s, although it was still in military ownership at the outbreak of war in 1939. Its principal use thereafter was as a Battery Observation Post (BOP) for the nearby batteries within Culver Fire Command. There was wartime accommodation at Fort Bembridge — as it was designated in the Second World War — for ten men at the BOP, plus another four to work in the various military storerooms which were also located at the fort. The soldiers were from 527 Coast Regiment's Culver-based 118 Battery. Bembridge Fort remains intact, and is now a base for light industry.

At the opposite end of the Island, on the high ground immediately north of Freshwater, the six-sided Golden Hill Fort owed its 19th century origins as a fortified barrack to a requirement for peacetime accommodation for soldiers manning the western coastal batteries — and the need to provide them with protection from the rear. Headquarters of the Needles Fire Command since 1932, and a training centre for Territorial gunners, Golden Hill provided accommodation for a number of military units during the Second World War. The Royal Jersey Militia (later the

11th Battalion of the Royal Hampshire Regiment) shared the fort with the Hampshires' 50th (Holding) Battalion during the invasion scare of 1940.

From 1941, the fort also served as one of the three Island supply depots for the Royal Army Service Corps (the others were at Ryde and Albany Barracks), and, in 1945, it was employed as overspill barrack accommodation for the men of 42 Water Transport Unit RASC at Fort Victoria. The Corps' Water Transport Training Company took over both forts in 1946, and Golden Hill was used by the WTTC until the fort was given up in 1962. It is now a major Island tourist attraction.

The AA Gun Sites

Purpose-built to meet the challenge of the Luftwaffe, most of the Royal Artillery's anti-aircraft gun sites on the Isle of Wight were constructed by the spring of 1940, although later additions were made. In August 1941, when a list of all defence forces on the Island was drawn up, the principal AA batteries at Nettlestone and Whippingham were shown in the care of the 57th Heavy AA Regiment's 213th Battery, the former manned by 185 men and the latter, by 120. Both sites were equipped with four 3.7-inch guns. Also listed in August 1941 was a troop of 66 men from the 137th Light AA

Much of the former anti-aircraft battery at Rew Street has survived on its isolated site south-west of Cowes. Pictured is a concrete magazine building. There were four 3.7-inch guns here. (William E.J. Parker)

Battery, who, equipped with Bofors guns, were located at Ventnor's radar station on St Boniface Down.

By June 1943, when the Island's heavy AA sites were under the command of the 35th Anti-Aircraft Brigade, ten sites were listed as operational. Apart from Nettlestone and Whippingham, they were at Rew Street (Gurnard), Dame Anthony's Common (Binstead), Lynn Farm (south-west of Havenstreet), Porchfield, Hamstead, Thorley Street, Cliff End Battery and Brighstone. All at that stage were equipped with 3.7-inch guns — four in most cases, although Rew Street had six — and a Bofors gun.

Other 3.7-inch sites are known to have existed at Forelands (Bembridge) and at St Catherine's Point, in the south of the Island. Later in 1943, Nettlestone's firepower was increased with the installation of four 5.25-inch guns, linked to radar control.

The Searchlights

Searchlight sites were strategically positioned during the war throughout the Isle of Wight. Their role was three-fold. The first, and primary, duty was to locate and illuminate hostile aircraft for the ack-ack gunners. Secondly, they were required, at the demand of the RAF, to provide 'orbit beacons' for night fighter operations; and, thirdly, they were expected to put up 'homing beacons' for Allied aircraft in distress.

The Island sites were manned at the start of the war (as they had been for several months beforehand) by the Territorials of the 48th (Hants) AA Battalion's 392nd Searchlight Company, attached to the Royal Engineers, formed entirely of local men and commanded by Major G.W. Garrett. By 1943 — by which time their unit had been redesignated 392nd Battery/48th Searchlight Regiment and assigned to the Royal Artillery, with headquarters at Northwood — the men's sphere of operation was wholly confined to the seven sites in the West Wight. The three East Wight sites — augmented by searchlights on the Spithead sea forts and others on the nearby mainland — were by then manned by two troops from Eastleigh-based 391st Battery.

A fascinating insight into wartime conditions on the Island searchlight sites was provided by D.R. 'Jack' Porter in the course of his entertaining autobiographical booklet, *I Remember . . . Looking Back 80 Years*. A First World War Royal Engineers veteran, 'Jack' joined 392 Company in January 1939, and was based at Shanklin, Arreton, Godshill, Thorness and St Catherine's Point during an eventful grand tour of the Island searchlight sites. It was at St Catherine's, he recalled, that, "one night, when I was walking about, smoking a pipe, and possibly flashing a torch for some reason or another round the Bell tent, I was told off by a Home Guard officer for showing a light — which I thought was rather futile since I was there for the express purpose of putting up a two-sized light with umpteen candle power!" (See Appendices).

TWELVE

Dad's Island Army

The Isle of Wight was more accustomed than most parts of England to the raising of local militia for the protection of its shores against a foreign invader. War Minister Anthony Eden's May 1940 broadcast invitation for men to enlist in a new Local Defence Volunteer Corps was the latest in a long line of appeals, stretching down the centuries, for the Island's civil population to take up arms. The big difference was that, on this occasion, invasion was feared from both the sea, its traditional route, and from the air. It was mainly to guard against landings by German parachutists that the LDV, destined to become the greatest of all the British wartime institutions, was brought into being.

More than 4,000 Islanders responded to Eden's call. Since just about the only qualifications for service were to be aged between 17 and 65, and to be blessed with "reasonable fitness," most of the applicants were accepted. Despite its numbers, many cynics doubted whether the LDV would be able to fulfil its primary function – namely "to hinder and harass the invaders as far as possible." The three initials, they confidently asserted, would soon stand for *look, duck and vanish!*

The five Island companies made up LDV sub-area number 4 within the five-area Hampshire and Isle of Wight structure. The Island companies and their commanders were as follows: 'A' Company (North-West Wight), Major-General W.R. Paul; 'B' Company (North-East Wight), Lieutenant-Colonel S. Davenport; 'C' Company (South-East Wight), Brigadier-General A.C. Aspinall-Oglander; 'D' Company (South-West Wight), Captain F. Neville-Jenkins; and, reflecting the wartime industrial importance of the twin towns at the mouth of the River Medina, 'X' Company (East and West Cowes), Major Musgrave. The Island's LDV headquarters were at Albany Barracks, Parkhurst.

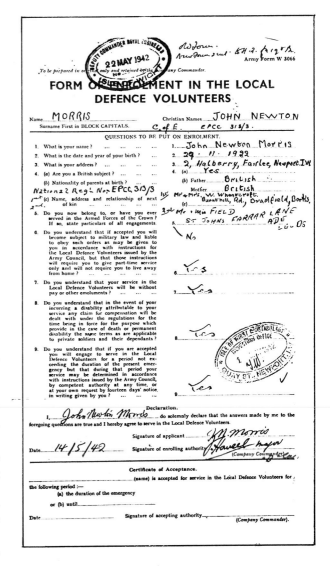

A 19-year-old Newport man joins the Home Guard's 19th (West Wight) Battalion. Although the enrolment form is dated May 1942, it is still headed by the organisation's short-lived former title – the Local Defence Volunteers. (IWCC)

As was the case with their mainland counterparts, this incongruous collection of local defenders, at both extremes of the adult age range, began with little more than armbands for uniforms and a motley collection of weapons. They shared in the June hand-out of half-a-million .30 calibre rifles from the USA, receiving 250 of the 1917-vintage weapons, together with 2,000 rounds of ammunition. The rifles had been in store for 20-odd years, and the grease used in the storage process had hardened in the barrels. In *The Isle of Wight — An Illustrated History,* Jack and Johanna Jones told how 'C' Company coped with this problem by sending the rifles to a Shanklin bakery and leaving them in the ovens on a high temperature setting to soften the grease and permit cleaning of the barrels!

Neither the initial organisational framework on the Island nor the original title of the organisation itself lasted very long. Winston Churchill declared on 14 July that the LDV "are much better called the Home Guard." By 28 July that had become their new official name. That same month, the Island acquired the status of an independent zone within the Hampshire Home Guard, and was allocated two battalions. With responsibility for the western half of the Island, the 19th (West Wight) Battalion set up headquarters at Fairlee House, Newport, under the command of Captain Neville-Jenkins, while the 20th (Nunwell) Battalion, covering the eastern half, was led by Brigadier-General Aspinall-Oglander from, as its name implies, Nunwell House, near Brading.

The battalions were divided into a number of companies, each covering a major centre of population. The companies were themselves divided into platoons, and the platoons broke down into sections, each with their own reporting post, and finally into squads. For example, Bryant's Hill served as the post for the village Home Guard squads in Sandford Section, which was part of Number 3 Platoon in 'C' (Shanklin) Company of the East Wight's 20th (Nunwell) Battalion.

Theo Pearson, a wartime teacher at West Wight Central School, has fond memories of the early days of the LDV / Home Guard in the far west of the Island. He recalls joining the rush to enlist following the War Secretary's broadcast appeal of 14 May 1940:

Teacher Theo Pearson, an early LDV recruit in Freshwater, contributed this amusing view of the Home Guard to a book of lino-cuts produced in 1940 by West Wight Central School pupils on the school's own printing press. (Theo Pearson)

The experienced ex-servicemen soon got things moving, and by the following night a 'guard' was on duty on a piece of rising ground inside a field on the far side of Norton village. Two of us, in our turn, reported for duty on the second night and found a tent, one rifle, five rounds of ammunition — and eleven pennies! Our instructions? In the event of a German invasion, one of us was to take the eleven pennies, run the half-mile or so down the road to the public call box in Norton village, and 'phone our CO, Charlie Merwood, in Totland, so that he could then 'phone the Army at Golden Hill Fort, Freshwater, to give them the news! I often wonder what happenned to those eleven pennies — and to the first rounds of ammunition!

Hedley Vinall was another teenage LDV rec-

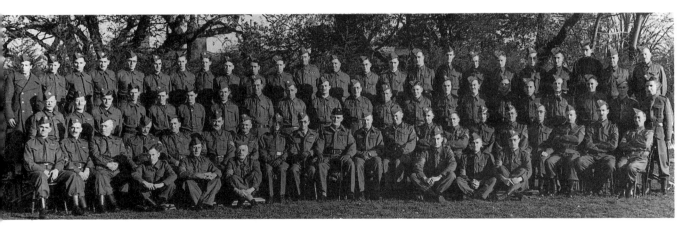

Home Guardsmen line up for the camera at Ryde. (R.F. Searle)

ruit, joining up at Shanklin and finding himself quickly allocated with some young colleagues to guard the telephone exchange in Collingwood Road:

We used to have a duty from 7pm until 7am. One or two of us would be on guard while the rest slept inside. The GPO men had been cutting the privet hedge by the exchange, and had left a lot of cuttings. A chap on duty had built it up to make a comfortable seat. At 2am there was an almighty explosion. I dashed outside, and there he was, just standing there, looking most perplexed. In the morning we noticed a great big smash in the garage roof of the nearby bus depot. My mate owned up. His seat had been so comfortable that he had nodded off — and off went his rifle, too!

The Home Guard take part in a Remembrance Sunday parade at Ryde. They are pictured approaching the Parish Church. (R.F. Searle)

To the Last Man

It was precisely this type of incident that television's *Dad's Army* so brilliantly re-created (with not as much exaggeration as some might imagine!), but, with more and better equipment becoming available to the Home Guard, there can be no doubt that it was soon regarded as a potentially serious — indeed, vital — component in the defence of the Island during the dark days when invasion was a constant threat.

Brigadier J.O. Carpenter MC, the senior Army officer on the Island while in command of the garrison force, underlined the local Home Guard battalions' "vital role in the defence of the Isle of Wight" when the overall local strategy against enemy invasion was confirmed in 1941. He defined that role as twofold. Firstly, a Home Guard platoon was responsible "for the defence of the village from which it had been raised." Secondly, it was expected to provide

"scouting and observation patrols . . . and . . . guides to assist field formations operating in the neighbourhood." Added the Brigadier in his 29 April briefing: "Every village of any size where Home Guards are available must be defended, and the enemy delayed in every possible way."

Home Guard Gunners

Some Island men, while remaining within the Home Guard structure, volunteered for operational Army duties outside the infantry sphere. Early in 1943, for example, the decision was taken to man the six-inch guns at Yaverland, overlooking Sandown Bay, with a Home Guard battery. Transfers to Yaverland were made from within the East Wight Battalion, 30 men from Ryde and 25 from both Sandown and Shanklin making up what was to be officially designated as 441 Coast Battery RA (HG). All were originally transferred with the rank of gunner, but were later able to earn stripes within the promotion structure of Coast Artillery.

Saro's 'G' Company

With the exception of the Auxiliary Unit specials (see Chapter 13). perhaps the most remarkable Home Guard contribution to the war effort on the Island came from the men of the East Wight Battalion's 'G' Company at Saro (Saunders-Roe), East Cowes. It began life as Saro VP (Vulnerable Points) Unit.

By the end of May 1940, it had enlisted 141 men, mostly from the company's own aircraft factory and shipyards. Their role, simply put, was to protect Saro's industrial sites from the enemy – a similar unit existed at J. Samuel White's. With considerable encouragement from the company, the Saro unit's strength grew rapidly, reaching 499 in July, by which time it was formally affiliated to the East Wight Home Guard Battalion. Saunders-Roe had purchased for the men an assortment of weapons – 12-bore shotguns, sporting rifles etc – from a variety of sources; others were loaned. A Bren-gun was somehow acquired, then the Ministry of Aircraft Production chipped in with four First World War Vickers machine-guns. Fifty Ross rifles and bayonets followed, and, in September, six Lewis automatics, with rough mountings for anti-aircraft defence, arrived – plus 3,600 rounds of ammunition.

By October, the unit's amazing arsenal even included two armoured cars, equipped with Browning automatic rifles – another gift from the MAP – and its men were setting-up their own network of posts, strong points and anti-aircraft defences. Many of the members of the volunteer force, which included a large number of First World War veterans, were manning these defences in addition to working a 70 or 80-hour week in the factories.

Inevitably, the German invaders' failure to put in an appearance either during 1940 or 1941 tended to have a cooling effect on the enthusiasm of the men. By June 1942 the unit's strength had dropped to 210. It picked up again following the introduction of conscription into the Home Guard. The first conscripted men arrived in August 1942; by January 1943, the unit had 347 members. In May 1944 it was officially re-designated 'G' (Saro) Company of the East Wight Home Guard, assuming responsibility for all Home Guard activity in East Cowes, and boosting its numbers still further by taking over a platoon which had formerly formed part of the Wootton Company.

What really set the men of the Saro unit apart was the involvement of some in bomb disposal duties. In September 1940, with the bomb disposal squads of the Royal Engineers hard-pressed to cope with the Island's demand for their services, a concerned Saunders-Roe management sought volunteers to dig trenches and erect walls etc in order to localise the danger from an unexploded bomb, pending the arrival of the Royal Engineers detachment who would actually deal with it. Some 30 men volunteered, courses were quickly arranged, and the Saro squad went into action.

The big test came in the spring of 1942. When the Luftwaffe 'softened-up' Cowes on 28 April in apparent preparation for the savage blitz one week later, there were no RE bomb disposal squads available, just a solitary corporal. Bombs had fallen either side of the River Medina, and a UXB lay dangerously close to a transformer station in an East Cowes street. All work was stopped at the nearby J. Samuel White's works, and the chain ferry across the river was halted. The factory bomb squad, hitherto confined to

Enterprising Home Guardsmen of the 20th (Nunwell) Battalion's 'C' Company at Shanklin produced their own magazine — Alert! Above: *the cover for the February 1941 issue.* (Hedley Vinall). Below: *An entertaining page from the magazine.* (Hedley Vinall).

HOMELY HINTS FOR HOME GUARDS

BROWNING AUTOMATIC RIFLE. Strictest economy must be used in the expenditure of ammunition. Remember, you can get rid of forty rounds in about a split second; therefore choose your target with circumspection. Don't fire a burst at one German—he's not worth it! Wait for a bunch of them!

DISTINCTION OF SOUNDS. It is important that sentries on night patrol should be able to clearly distinguish sounds. If you hear a creepy crawly sound it may well betoken the approach of an enemy, but if you only hear sundry grunts and groans with intermittent smacks—that may only mean the nearby presence of a courting couple.

RESPIRATORS. These should be worn when gas is present. Gas can be detected sometimes by faint smells like that of almonds, but don't confuse this with more obnoxious smells such as dead rats, old drains or Germans.

STREET FIGHTING. When the order "Fix Bayonets— Charge" is given keep your eye on the target, and let nothing divert your purpose. Don't stop for anything—even a passing "pub" must be ignored.

preparing the ground for the RE experts, went immediately into action. Under the lone corporal's supervision, they deputised magnificently for the Royal Engineers, and rendered the offending bomb harmless.

Then came the blitz of 4/5 May itself. On this occasion, the full-time bomb-disposal teams were much in evidence in the aftermath of the double-strike, but they were in danger of becoming overwhelmed by the sheer volume of work. Into the breach once more stepped the Saro squad. This time, without assistance of any kind, they dealt successfully with a 500 kilo bomb. In September of that year they were officially taken under the wing of the Saro VP Unit, the eventual 'G' Company.

Uffa's Private Army

Among the first Islanders to volunteer his services to the LDV at Cowes was the irrepressible Uffa Fox. It was entirely in character that he should, at the same time, also commit his entire workforce at the Medina boatbuilding yard, despite the fact that many of them were already working in their spare time with the civil defence services! Uffa had no time for anyone who didn't match his patriotic ideals. The Home Guard unit at Medina Yard was named by its leader the 'Uffashots.' Protecting the yard from the enemy was its brief, but Uffa also volunteered to protect the local grocer's shop, the police station — and (very much in character) the Duke of York pub!

The Flying Squad

When a new military communications link between the Island and the mainland was set up in March 1941, it was the men of the Home Guard who were entrusted with its smooth operation. There is little documented evidence to indicate its success or otherwise, but the service can certainly be said to have taken off — literally! There was, however, an obvious problem to overcome at the outset of the new carrier pigeon service. "All officers and other ranks who are accustomed to shoot pigeons must be warned accordingly," Island Home Guardsmen were told on 3 March.

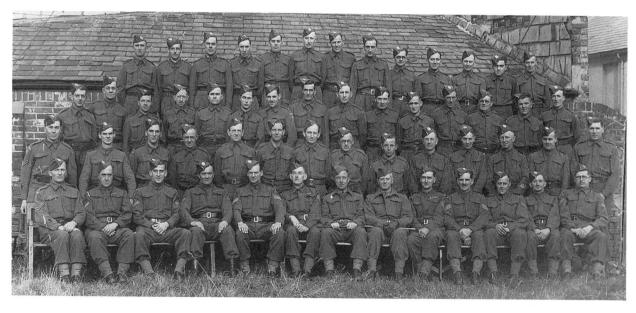

Number 4 Platoon of Newport's Home Guard was formed almost entirely of men from the Southern Vectis Bus Company. (Reg Davies)

It is a matter for conjecture as to whether the message penetrated sufficiently to prevent a considerable number of the birds ending up in the cooking pot! However, war records reveal that, in August 1941, there were some 80 birds available for front line service on the Island, 30 in the lofts of Home Guardsmen at both Newport and Brading, and the remaining 20 billeted at Ventnor.

Gone – but not Forgotten

The two Isle of Wight Home Guard battalions were 'stood down' on 1 November 1944,

although members were told the organisation had not yet been disbanded, "and, should the need arise, it is liable to recall." A joint stand-down parade was held at Newport's Victoria Recreation Ground on Sunday 3 December.

Today, some of the atmosphere of this amazing chapter in the military history of the Island survives in the cellars of Nunwell House, the former headquarters of the 20th (Nunwell) Battalion. With their blast wall and escape tunnel still intact, the cellars now serve as a Home Guard museum. Outside, in the grounds of Nunwell, stands one of the road blocks that might, had Hitler not changed his mind, have stood between the men of the Isle of Wight's Dad's Army and the German panzers.

For some Islanders who wore the Home Guard uniform, however, the arrival of a triumphant German invasion force on the Wight would not have signalled the end of their struggle – but the very beginning. The extraordinary story of the men of Home Guard 203 must now be told.

The remains of an underground hide-out built by an Auxiliary Unit in a copse on the southern outskirts of Ryde. This 1989 photograph, taken from what used to be the interior of the hide-out, shows one of the entrances, with the lintel above the doorway still intact. Part of the corrugated roof is still visible. (Ben Houfton)

THIRTEEN

The Island Resistance

"The possible advantages of limited operations before the general crossing (e.g. the capture of the Isle of Wight or of the County of Cornwall) are to be considered . . ." — Adolf Hitler

In remote areas of the countryside it is possible to find the relics of the most secret of all the military forces which operated in the Isle of Wight during the Second World War. Its operational bases were either built underground or utilised subterranean facilities (eg cellars and caves) which were already in existence. In all cases, these were cleverly concealed from friend and potential foe alike. Many remain so, the best part of 50 years later; others have succumbed to the ravages of time and given up their once closely-guarded secrets.

The men who made up the shadowy force who built and occupied the hideouts — men who had no claim to the protection afforded all other uniformed fighting forces by the Geneva Convention — were Islanders. They formed part of Europe's first and best-trained resistance movement. They were the men of Home Guard 203 — the battalion that never was.

Throughout the war, and for very many years afterwards, the British public had no knowledge of the resistance network which was organised in the aftermath of Dunkirk, when a German invasion of England appeared imminent — at a time when the country was totally ill-equipped to defend itself. The man entrusted with the task of setting it up in the second week of June 1940 was Major Colin McVean Gubbins, who had been working with the organisation known as MI (R) — Military Intelligence (Research) — and had already held classes for specially-selected British civilians in the art of 'irregular' (guerilla) warfare. The South Coast was his first priority.

Sector areas were drawn up, and officers were detailed by Gubbins to organise regional training centres in each of them. Only these officers would ever know the identity of all the men eventually enrolled in their region. They, in turn, appointed civilian subordinates, whose job it was to form local cells (patrols), usually consisting of a commander and five or six men. Security considerations demanded that each of the patrols should operate independently (although one patrol leader in every six was also given overall command of the whole group). They were to be known as Auxiliary Units, a deliberately vague title from which no indication of the true nature of their activities could be gleaned.

Nationally, the Auxiliary Units were grouped as three Home Guard battalions — 201 (Scotland), 202 (North of England) and 203 (South) — and the men were given Home Guard uniforms. This was solely to provide them with a convenient cover; the three battalions do not appear, and never have, on the official Home Guard lists. Although many presumed otherwise (and were given both Home Guard certificates, recording their service, and special lapel badges), the civilian members of the Auxiliary Units were never formally enrolled in anything. They, thus, stood a very real chance of being shot if caught on operational duty by the enemy.

Mr Watson's Secret Army

On the Isle of Wight the man selected to make the initial contacts was Sammy Watson, a well-known estate agent and valuer, who also had a useful — in this context — part-time role as Secretary to the local branch of the National Farmers' Union. With the help of her husband, Leslie, and Charles Holbrook — both members of the special wartime force — Mrs Eileen Foss (who lived during the war at the Godshill Park Farm home of her father-in-law, another Auxiliary Unit member) has compiled the following account of the subsequent progress of Mr Watson's secret army:

Those approached were mostly drawn from the farming community, and known by Sammy to be trustworthy and discreet men. They became the leaders of the patrols. The two men in overall command of the Island groups were Captain H.C.A. Blishen, of Arreton, and Lieutenant J.T.W. Fisk, of Brighstone, who was both a farmer and a member of the cattle-feed firm of Fisk and Fisher; he died only last year (1988).

An inaugural meeting was held at the White Lion, Arreton, in great secrecy. The topics discussed included guerilla tactics, and the making and laying of booby traps etc. The Island units spent many hours training under an Army 'top brass.' There were seven patrols in the East Wight and another seven in the West.

The hideouts were dug with much patience and determination − and also, discomfort! − using enamel wash basins to take out the earth after it had been dug with trowels etc. Hollow tree trunks, natural contours of the land etc were used to conceal entrances, and a system was set up to warn of approaching 'friends or foes.' One wonders now how these men could have spent so many hours training at night after working all day on the farms, producing much-needed food.

This clandestine night-time activity, particularly out in the countryside, was bound to arouse the suspicions of the forces of both the military and civil authorities − including the conventional Home Guard units. In addition to their identity cards, resistance leaders were required to carry special passes which made it clear that they would answer none of the questions put to them. The need for security was paramount if the Auxiliary Units, if called upon, were successfully to perform the tasks for which they were constantly being trained − to spy on, sabotage and, if necessary, kill the members of an invading enemy force.

Charles Holbrook has himself added further details to the story of the Auxiliary Units on the Island:

Inside the hideout, or observation base (OB), as it was known, we had four bunks and the means for cooking, with about 100lb of high-explosive, time delays, detonators, and both cortex and ordinary fuse − besides the Smith and Wesson revolvers and knives. We attended a meeting of all groups at the Drill Hall in Newport, when we were instructed in the art of assassination by Russian guerilla fighters, who had been through the thick of the German invasion in their own country. One of these stalwarts took the stage, waved a revolver in one hand and a knive in the other, and declared in good English: 'We call the revolver the wife, and the knife, mother.' When someone enquired why, his simple reply was: 'Mother is always faithful' − in other words, there was nothing in the knife to go wrong!

Other men known to have served as group leaders of Auxiliary Units on the Island include S.G. Taylor, of Arreton, and C.W. Burt, of Shalfleet, both of whom were told they held the rank of a second lieutenant in the Home Guard. However, since the Home Guard battalion to which they were assigned never formally existed, the ranks (and those supposedly held by Captain Blishen and Lieutenant Fisk) can be said to have existed on paper only.

The Men from the North

In May 1944, during the final build-up to D-Day, members of Auxiliary Unit patrols in Northumberland were issued with railway warrants and told to report, in Home Guard uniform, to a local station. Following secret movement orders, and travelling in reserved compartments, they began a long trek to the South Coast. Similarly-uniformed men joined the train at the many stops en route. Transferring at Portsmouth to a Southern Railway ferry, the resistance men crossed the crowded Solent to Ryde. It was only then they were told the reason for their journey.

A German counter-invasion of the Isle of Wight after D-Day was regarded as a very real possibility by the planners of Operation Overlord. If this transpired, the Auxiliary Units were under orders to destroy the invasion force from behind its own lines. In total secrecy, the men scoured the Island for possible landing sites, and for the best positioning of their own defences. That exercise completed, they dug in and waited. The D-Day invasion fleet sailed on 6 June, and the Germans' feared counter-strike failed to materialise. Two weeks later, as quietly as they had come, the men from the northern Auxiliary Units left the Island and headed for home.

PART THREE

In the Sky . . . On the Sea

*Newly-completed Sea Otter JM764 waits (in wartime
camouflage paint) on the slipway at Saunders-Roe's Columbine
Yard before the short testing flight to Somerton Aerodrome.*
(CCM)

FOURTEEN

Radar: The Vital Link

Inarguably the most significant contribution made by the Isle of Wight to the defence of Great Britain during the Second World War was its vital link in the nation's coastal radar chain. Inevitably, the Island's part in the pioneering wartime use of Radio Direction Finding – the name by which radar was first known – also served as a magnet for the enemy's aerial forces. A number of attacks were made on the principal installations throughout the war – but the Luftwaffe failed permanently to blind the Royal Air Force's Isle of Wight 'eyes.'

When the first coastal chain of 16 RDF stations was drawn up in the late 1930s, the approximate positions included the Island's St Catherine's Point as the most westerly location. Before long, the planned Isle of Wight link in the chain had moved slightly eastwards, to the summit of St Boniface Down, Ventnor, the highest point on the Island.

Radiolocation, the first abbreviated title for RDF, was highly secret. Thus, when tall pylons began appearing on the high downs above Ventnor and Bonchurch, local people were kept guessing as to their purpose. Rumours abounded throughout the last months of 1938 and early 1939 – some based on the few known facts and others founded on nothing but fantasy and wild imagination! Ventnor Chain Home (CH) Station had reached operational status, in an intermediate form, by the end of January 1939. Originally, there were eight pylons (later reduced to seven) – four 350ft steel masts for the transmitter aerials, and four 240ft wooden towers carrying the receivers. Equipment was initially housed in a cluster of wooden huts at the foot of the masts; later it would be accommodated in protected buildings.

The two attacks by the Luftwaffe on St Boniface Down in August 1940 – described in Part 1 – temporarily destroyed the Isle of

An early post-war view of Ventnor showing the prominent wartime radar installation on St Boniface Down, but with only six of the original eight pylons (350ft transmitting masts and 240ft receiving towers) remaining. (Roger Bunney).

Wight's vital link in the radar chain. While extensive repair work was being carried out at Ventnor, the gap was plugged on 23 August with the opening of a small reserve station in the east of the Island at Bembridge.

The WAAF at Ventnor

By 1940 all plotters at the RDF stations were members of the Women's Auxiliary Air Force, and from March 1941 senior posts were allocated to WAAF officers – one flight officer and three assistant section officers per station. These women had to be of "advanced scientific education" – up to graduate standard. At Ventnor, as the war progressed, and Air Ministry activity in the area increased, the local WAAF establishment grew substantially larger. Accommodation and facilities for the women were provided on a

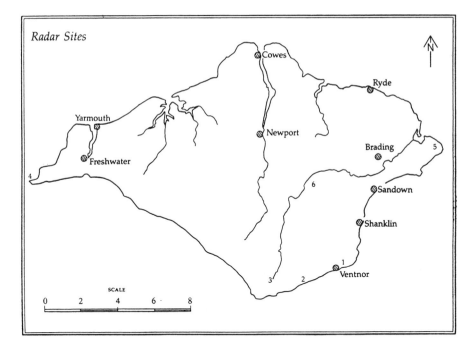

Radar Sites

Map showing location of wartime radar sites on the Island referred to in text: 1 St Boniface Down, Ventnor. 2 Woody Bay, St Lawrence. 3 Blackgang (Niton). 4 The Needles. 5 Bembridge. 6 Hale Common / Macketts Farm.

site at Down Lane, Upper Ventnor, a little to the west of the radar station. Later, properties on the northern side of St Boniface Road were requisitioned for WAAF quarters – no doubt somewhat more comfortable than the Nissen and timber huts on the Upper Ventnor site.

A far from confortable experience for the WAAF girls is recounted by A.T. Rodway, a wartime private with No 2 Special Services Battalion:

In the early 1940s Great Britain and Germany were trying to win the battle of radar. Many raids were made by the British Special Forces on various enemy installations to try and find out just how much progress had been made by the enemy. One such raid was on a radar installation at Bruneval in France, and, to make sure everything went to rights, an almost duplicate site was found here in England – St Boniface Down on the Isle of Wight. So a mock raid was successfully made on Ventnor's radiolocation station in the dead of night.

I was among the special forces who attacked it. Having successfully gone through the outer mine-field surrounding the station, we were then in control of the outer defences and, in turn, the inner defences. We then burst into the operations room, where amazed WAAFs and officers were still working at the operations table, plotting the flights of planes in the area. The boffins who had accompanied us proceeded to go around putting stickers on certain parts of the equipment they would, had the raid been for

real, have taken with them for future reference and comparison purposes.

That look of absolute amazement on the faces of the air force men and women was truly remarkable. I am sure their thoughts later were: 'Thank God it was only an exercise!' The mock raid was led by my superior, Colin Newman (who was later to win the VC in the raid on St Nazaire). As is well-known, the subsequent raid on Bruneval was to prove a very successful operation.

Triple Service Stations

The introduction of Triple Service Stations (designated CD/CHL) brought the Army and Navy into the wartime radar development programme. On the Isle of Wight the most obvious result was the setting-up, in July 1941, of a station at New Needles Battery, which greatly improved the Island's furthest west coastal battery's night-time operational capabilities, with regard to plotting both low-flying aircraft and ships at sea. Manned initially by the Army, the radar facility was eventually – in February 1942 – taken over by the RAF. The neighbouring Old Needles Fire Command Post was itself equipped with radar in January 1944, for the benefit of the gunners who protected the Needles Passage from either side of the Solent.

A rare photograph — on a commercial post card — of the wartime reserve radar mast at Woody Bay, St Lawrence. It is seen in the background on the left of this west-looking view from Ventnor. (Roger Bunney)

One local outcome of the Navy's involvement in radar was the February 1942 installation on St Boniface Down of the experimental Naval Type 271 ultra-high frequency RDF equipment, developed to improve further the detection of low-flying enemy raiders. Now, aircraft at a flying height of between 50 and 200 feet could be tracked up to 30 miles away, and occasionally, as far as 45 miles. On 23 May 1943 the equipment detected planes at a range of 34½ miles which were identified one minute later as hostile — 20 Fw 190s aircraft flying at 50 feet on their way to attack Bournemouth. Thus alerted, the anti-aircraft defences succeeded in destroying two of them. But the numerically small forces of planes used during this period on 'tip and run' raids against the Island continued to evade the radar plotters.

Blackgang's Role

Apart from the main installations on St Boniface Down, the reserve station at Bembridge and the Needles facility, radar masts also sprouted on the hills and cliffs overlooking the Channel near St Catherine's Point. The history of the sites at RAF Blackgang and RAF St Lawrence — the names by which the radar stations were known — is poorly documented in official records, although the Air Ministry's account of wartime

radar lists them both as eventually forming part of the extended Home Chain.

In fact, while St Lawrence was provided purely as a reserve facility for Ventnor, equipped with fixed aerials but, it seems, seldom used operationally, the role of RAF Blackgang was rather different. Situated on the Downs immediately north of Niton village — where its 100 or so personnel were billeted — it was equipped with a mobile rotating aerial, and cathode ray tubes, producing their luminous image on a fluorescent screen. Designated a Ground Control Interception (GCI) station, it reported direct to Fighter Command with up-to-the-minute information on the location of hostile aircraft in the area. The idea was to effect a closely-controlled interception, and was particularly useful at night.

The Germans were well aware of Blackgang's existence, and their 'tip and run' raid on Niton in 1943 was probably launched more with the destruction of the radar station in mind rather than with that of Niton's wireless signal station a little to the south. In fact, they missed both, but destroyed the Undercliff Hotel — where RAF and Army personnel were quartered — possibly under the impression that it housed the radar operations room. This was actually situated close to the aerial, and survives today as a shelter for cows.

The evidence of RAF St Lawrence, on the cliffs near Woody Point, is also plainly evident today, in the shape of the aerial stumps, bunk-

Built within a man-made mound, and all but hidden by trees, the largest of a series of surviving bunkers at the wartime St Lawrence radar station was pictured in 1989. Nissen huts also remain at the site. (Author)

The cast of Say Hullo, *RAF Blackgang's show in June 1943, are pictured on stage at Ventnor Winter Gardens.* (R.R. Trodd)

ers – again utilised by farmers for livestock – and surviving Nissen huts among the trees. More than 50 years after its own construction, the radar station on St Boniface Down remains operational. It is run today by National Air Traffic Services, a joint Ministry of Defence and Civil Aviation Authority venture. Many of the Second World War buildings survive, most of them in various states of disrepair.

The Army's Secret

Islanders may have puzzled over the specific function of Ventnor's radar station, but they could hardly have been unaware of its existence. 'The pylons' – as everybody called them – were conspicuous structures in a highly conspicuous setting. The RAF's smaller radar installations elsewhere on the Island were also at least partially visible to the inquisitive public eye. However, totally obscured from view at a secret East Wight location, was a radar site about which the public knew absolutely nothing.

So secret was the site that, even today, few Islanders are aware that it ever existed. Operated not by the RAF, but by the Army, it is virtually impossible to find references to it in any published material. No signs of it apparently remain. Fortunately, one of the men who worked there during the war was himself an Islander – the only one on the site – and he has vivid memories of its operation. Geoffery Searle, who now lives in Bembridge, served during the war in the Royal Electrical and Mechanical Engineers (REME) as a radar mechanic:

Crew 'A' at RAF Blackgang's radar station in 1943. (R.R. Trodd)

At the beginning of 1942 I was posted to the Isle of Wight. It was supposed to be for only three weeks, but I ended up staying for two years! Luckily, one of the mechanics there wanted to get off the Island, and, being an Islander myself, I wanted to stay. So we did a switch. The site at that time was at Hale Common, between Arreton and Apse Heath. It was a semi-static site, with the equipment actually housed in the back of lorries! There was a receiver in one lorry and a transmitter in the other, complete with aerials. At first, the artillery blokes guarding the site had to turn the aerials by hand; then we rigged up a small electric motor to do the job.

The idea of the radar was to provide an early warning to the Gun Operations Rooms at both Newport and Fareham. They would notify the various local gun sites, and the guns could then be trained on the target before it reached the area. We were plotting up to a 45-mile radius from the site. In the winter of 1942-43 we moved, in great secrecy, a little further south to a static site at Macketts Farm. Here, the equipment was properly housed in concrete buildings, with Nissen huts for accommodation about a quarter of a mile away. The aerial turning gear was in big underground compounds, with just the aerials themselves showing above the ground — there were 32 of them.

There were seven mechanics, under a single sergeant, 26 ATS women operators and the six-man artillery guard. We all had to sign the Official Secrets Act on taking up the post. Even my family knew nothing more than that I was working on a radar station 'somewhere,' although I was able to go home, to Ryde, every night. The public never came anywhere near us. We were issued with a machine gun for our direct defence only. On one occasion, when the low-level German force attacked Ryde in 1943, it passed immediately overhead, but we weren't allowed to fire — that would have given the game away.

We were at the Macketts Farm site the day the first *doodle-bug* flew over the Island in June 1944. We had been plotting it in, although we hadn't picked it up until it was very near the site because it was so low. Then, right above the site, the engine cut out. We dropped flat on the ground and held our breath. Fortunately for us, it was one of those that glided down, instead of plunging straight out of the sky. It passed over us and crashed near Havenstreet.

FIFTEEN

All Flights Suspended

The Isle of Wight boasted four active civil aerodromes prior to the outbreak of war in September 1939 – at Bembridge, Lea (Sandown), Ryde and Somerton (Cowes). Civil aviation was an early casualty of the conflict, and, of the quartet, only Somerton was deemed to have any wartime relevance. The remaining three were closed down for the duration, with their facilities rendered useless to a potential airborne invading force by the strategic positioning of obstacles on the landing strips.

Somerton, on the southern outskirts of Cowes, had been opened in 1915 as a works airfield by J. Samuel White's, who later sold the leasehold to Saunders-Roe. In the decade before the outbreak of war in 1939, it had been used to test their planes, and also those of Spartan Aircraft, following its own transfer to East Cowes. Scheduled passenger services had linked the aerodrome with London and other major centres.

With civil flying suspended, Somerton's principal importance in the Second World War was its role in the testing and dispatch of the many amphibious aircraft (Walrus and Sea Otter) constructed locally by Saunders-Roe. A newly-built plane would take off from the company's Columbine Yard slipway, near the mouth of the Medina, and fly the short distance to Somerton. From the aerodrome, once any problems had been ironed out, it would later leave for the mainland – flown by the pilots of the Air Transport Auxiliary – and eventual dispersal to its base. Some of the aircraft built by Saunders-Roe at its mainland factories in the South of England were also test-flown to Somerton.

The May 1942 blitz on the Cowes area caused serious damage at Somerton, both to hangars, three of which were totally destroyed, and aircraft. When the hangars were replaced later the same year, work also began on extending the airfield – which necessitated the closure of Three Gates Road (linking the A3020 and B3325 routes into Cowes) for the remainder of the war.

Somerton had been under consideration as an ALG (advanced landing ground) for the RAF, but a June 1942 report put it way down the priority list. While two landing strips were available, they were considered barely adequate, at 3,000 feet, for the role, and the Somerton area was obstructed by too many buildings. The other reason for its eventual rejection for ALG use was, of course, the seaplane production line – by then under the auspices of the Ministry of Aircraft Production – which was of vital importance. The aerodrome did, however, prove useful on several occasions during the war as an emergency landing ground for Allied aircraft.

It was closed at the end of the 1950s, and the site now forms part of the Plessey Radar complex. Two of the other Island airfields – at Sandown and Bembridge – have, however, survived. The former, known as the Isle of Wight Airport, is principally a base for pleasure flights, and the latter is the home of Pilatus Britten-Norman Ltd., manufacturers of the Islander aircraft and its derivatives.

The Decoy Airfield

The Isle of Wight also possessed a wartime airfield that never was! In a successful bid to fool the Luftwaffe, a decoy airfield was set up in the West Wight, in the vicinity of Newtown Bay. On at least one occasion, a number of bombs – probably intended for an operational mainland airfield – were dropped there during a night raid. Further details on this, one of the best-kept of the countless Island wartime secrets, have proved elusive.

SIXTEEN

Services at Sea

While the great naval battles of the war were fought many miles from its shoreline, the Isle of Wight's geographical position ensured it would have close associations with many aspects of the war on the sea – ranging from the building of warships for the Royal Navy to the planning of amphibious assaults on enemy territory. The Island also played an important role as a provider of vital sea rescue services.

The Admiralty

The Admiralty operated a number of Second World War shore establishments on the Island, the most prominent of which were the Cowes-based HMS *Vectis* – whose role in the interwoven stories of Combined Operations and D-Day is told in Part 1 – and HMS *Medina*, set up in the former Puckpool Battery, between Ryde and Seaview.

Another product of the 1860 Royal Commission into Britain's coast defences, the battery at Puckpool had been declared surplus to military requirements in the mid-1920s and sold in 1928 to St Helens Urban District Council, which opened it the following year as a public park. At the outbreak of war, Puckpool was again in demand by HM Forces. Together with the holiday camp behind, it became HMS *Medina* in 1939 and served for the next three years as a training establishment for the Fleet Air Arm. The Royal Observer Corps established a post at Puckpool, and Ryde's ARP Report Centre was there for the first year of the war, before its move into the town.

In her teens when the war broke out, Margaret Hicks (now Whitaker) found herself twice posted to Puckpool, a short distance from her Seaview home:

I was first there as a relief telephonist with the ARP, working shifts to give the permanent staff a break. We were in a sort of 'dungeon' right underneath the Observer Corps post. Then, in 1941, I joined the WRNS and went back to Puckpool. The Navy had gun emplacements all round the sea wall, and there was also a machine gun 'nest' on the Esplanade at Seaview.

The Fleet Air Arm was at Puckpool when I joined, but HMS *Medina* became a base for Combined Operations, under Lord Louis Mountbatten, in 1943. He used to come down to Puckpool, and I remember him telling naughty stories to the men. He used to say they weren't suitable for our ears, so, of course, we used to make a point of listening in the background – I can still remember some of them now!

Operating under the aegis of Combined Operations on the conversion of landing craft from barges were the men of 35 Maintenance Unit

The Women's Royal Naval Service . . . 1941 style. The photograph was taken at HMS Medina, *the wartime shore establishment in Puckpool Park, where the women worked in the Admiralty's base accountant's section. Note the hats – soon to be replaced with berets.* (Margaret Whitaker)

RN, who lived at Puckpool, but carried out their work at Wootton Creek. Margaret Hicks' own work in the Navy's base accountancy section was re-located from Puckpool to Ryde:

We took over the annexe of the Esplanade Hotel, which served as both the base accountant's office and a Naval supply office, and became known as HMS *Osborne* . . . We always paid a fortnight's pay on a Thursday. One day we had a message through telling us the men had to be paid three weeks' money. This was quite unheard of, but we weren't told the reason for it. It was June 1944 and, at the time, you could hardly see Portsmouth for the ships in Spithead; then, one day, they had all gone. D-Day, of course. That's why the men were paid the extra week's pay — they were off to France.

Air-Sea Rescue

The air-sea rescue service developed rapidly in the waters around the Isle of Wight — as elsewhere — during the Second World War. In 1940 it was being provided by a combination of local longshoremen, whose boats were often too slow and ill-equipped for the task, Naval launches based at Culver, near Sandown, and the amphibious aircraft just the other side of the Solent at RAF Calshot. In January 1941 a nationwide service was put into operation, utilising a dozen Lysanders from the Army, three Walrus flying-boats from RAF Coastal Command and 27 high-speed launches.

On the Island, a rescue unit (30 ASR) was set up with six launches at Marvins' yard in Cowes (also used in 1944 for traffic control duties when the invasion fleet was assembling in the Solent and Spithead for the D-Day landings). With outstations at Yarmouth and Bembridge, the local unit was responsible for rescue work in the Solent and in the coastal waters to the south of the Island.

Many of the Rescue Motor Launches (RMLs) were built in Island yards, among them Woodnutt's, at St Helens, and the Cowes yards of J. Samuel White's and Groves and Guttridge. The other local connections with air-sea rescue were the construction and repair by Saunders-Roe of the Walrus flying boats, and the development

A workshop barge belonging to the Navy's 35th Maintenance Unit is pictured at Fishbourne Creek in October 1944. (IWM)

and manufacture of the unique Uffa Fox-designed airborne lifeboats, which were built both at the yard of their creator and at those of other Island companies.

Uffa's Airborne Lifeboat

Uffa Fox (the surname was regarded as superfluous in Cowes — everyone always referred to him simply as Uffa) derived immense personal satisfaction in turning his concept of a parachuted airborne lifeboat into life-preserving reality. It was born of his deep-felt concern at the plight of so many British airmen, forced to ditch their planes, who were left drifting at the mercy of the sea — often to their death — in small inflatable rubber dinghies.

At first, Uffa conceived the idea of a folding boat which could be simply droped over the side of a low-flying aircraft to the men below. That was ruled out as impracticable, since the boat would break up on impact. His revised plan envisaged the use of parachutes. A self-opening, plywood-built motorised boat, reasoned Uffa, could be carried in the aircraft's bomb bay, then released automatically for the parachute descent to the sea. His biographer, June Dixon, tells how Uffa made his first test model out of "thick drawing paper and strawberry jam."! A more conventional model was later put to the test by the simple expedient of throwing it

Launch 198, one of the six allocated to the Island's wartime Air-Sea Rescue unit at Cowes. Note the deck-mounted armament. (Beken / CCM)

Uffa Fox . . . master yachtsman and designer. (Beken)

The gravestone of Uffa Fox in Whippingham Churchyard . . . depicting the airborne lifeboat he conceived, designed and built at Cowes during the war. (Ben Houfton)

out of the upstairs window at Uffa's Medina Yard at Cowes. It worked!

Uffa happened to be on friendly terms with Colonel (later Lord) Brabazon at the Minsitry of Aircraft Production. He wasted no time in outlining the scheme to him – and winning an immediate go-ahead to pursue it.

The 23ft unsinkable lifeboat was designed to withstand a gale, and to be easily manoeuvrable in the water. Uffa and his men worked round the clock to complete the first full-size prototype in three weeks. When the impracticality of carrying it in the bomb bay of a Lockheed Hudson became apparent, the plans were amended to permit transportation on the out-side of the plane. Flying tests were successfully carried out, and help from the Royal Aircraft Establishment at Farnborough was made available. Service chiefs descended on Medina Yard,

where the day and night working continued.

Finding an engine with which to power the boat through the sea was something of a problem. Specifications called for a unit capable of a loaded speed of six knots, and twelve hours' running from a maximum of twelve gallons of fuel. The Britannia Middy inboard motor met all the requirements and was regarded as ideal – but it was no longer in production. It was, however, to be found attached to a number of small pleasure boats, and several examples were accordingly obtained second-hand from inactive boating lakes. Finally, the Uffa Fox lifeboat was ready for its first major trial.

It took place in the Solent, off Cowes. on 12 September 1942. The lifeboat slipped smoothly away from the Hudson, while the aircraft was travelling at 110 mph, and dropped 600 feet on its three parachutes, at a 30 degree angle, to Uffa and his colleagues, anxiously observing its progress from a boat on the sea below. An explosion blew away the parachutes, and two rockets fired out the floating life-lines. It had all gone according to plan. A lifeboat production line was quickly set up, and the boats were later successfully fitted to a number of aircraft types – Avro Lancasters and Vickers Warwicks, as well as the Hudsons.

Later, Uffa developed a Mark II 30ft version of the lifeboat, increasing the capacity from 16 to 25 men. Fitted with the purpose-built Austin Airborne Lifeboat Engine, the new craft was eventually capable of covering up to 1,000 miles.

There is no doubt that many airmen in the latter part of the Second World War owed their lives to the imagination, brilliance and enthusiasm of Uffa Fox. He later wrote that developing the lifeboat was "possibly the greatest contribution I shall ever make to the happiness of others." Of all the symbols which might have been used to illustrate a life so rich in achievement, it seems particularly fitting that the gravestone erected in Whippingham Churchyard following his death in 1972 should depict the Uffa Fox airborne lifeboat on its life-saving descent.

The RNLI Lifeboats

Of the lifeboats based at either end of the Island during the war, it was the Bembridge boat which had the greater employment. The lifeboat station had taken delivery of the brand-new *Jesse Lumb* as late as July 1939. Over the next decade, she was to rescue 138 people from the sea – a large number of them during the war years.

The Bembridge crew were equipped with their own rifles for personal protection while on service, but, because of their sudden appearance at sea, they were probably in as much danger of being shot at by Culver Command's own coastal gunners as by a seaborne enemy. Eventually, the problem was solved by the lifeboat coming under Naval control – there was no way it could be launched without the permission of the Naval authorities, who would first alert the local gun batteries.

Among the more noteworthy wartime rescues performed by the *Jesse Lumb* was her call in January 1940 to the Naval minesweeper *Kingston*

Cairngorm, ashore on Chichester Bar. The Bembridge lifeboat took off the wrecked vessel's entire crew of 21 and landed them safely in Portsmouth, a feat which earned for Coxswain Gawn the RNLI's Bronze Medal. In June the *Jesse Lumb* rescued four airmen off Selsey; in August, she picked up another eight from an RAF launch disabled by enemy action. But it was the fixed boom defence barrier either side of the outer sea forts which caused some of the most spectacular problems for the lifeboat.

Captain R.C. Watson, former lifeboat secretary at Bembridge, later recalled its dangers:

The boom was constructed of old railway metals embedded vertically and diagonally in a concrete bed, so that the ends stuck upward like the spikes on the back of a hedgehog, and, as many of these spikes were submerged at high water, nothing could possibly escape destruction which had the misfortune to contact them. Some portions of this boom were further protected by spiked buoys of large dimensions, chained together so that neither submarine nor enemy E-boat could possibly raid the Spithead Anchorage.

. . . in December 1944 the Naval drifter *Minora*, in some unexplained manner, fouled the boom, and sank almost immediately, her crew of six scrambling for safety to the top of one of the large buoys . . . in which perilous position they remained for some six hours, for it was not until daylight that they were seen, and the lifeboat sent to their rescue. But the very purpose for which the boom had been constructed militated against the boat's approach to the fearsome spiked horror. The coxswain decided that the men had to be taken off, irrespective of any damage to the boat . . . to that end he drove the stern of the boat directly against the chain holding the buoys together, and . . . drew them in on either side of him.

But the lifeboat crew had considerable difficulties in getting the men from the buoy into the boat, as they had become exhausted by their night's exposure and could scarcely help themselves. The lifeboat returned to the station with her fore compartment flooded, as both bows had been pierced by the spikes on the buoy, but the coxswain and crew decided that the boat was still seaworthy, and she was reported ready for service . . .

On another occasion the barrier was responsible for the loss of a further two Naval vessels, and it was only the prompt action taken by the lifeboats of Bembridge and Selsey that prevented any loss of life. The sloop *Saltbury* was driven by the strong wind and tide right over the obstacle, and her bottom was badly torn apart by the spikes on the inner side. Then, when called to assist, the dockyard tug *Swarthy* also fouled the spikes and, as a result, foundered. The *Jesse Lumb* rescued the tug's crew of 14 before the two lifeboats, at great risk, took off the men of the, now, abandoned *Saltbury*.

Near the end of the war, a tragic incident occured which was to sour relationships between the Bembridge lifeboatmen and the Navy for some time. Two airmen were shot down in Spithead. While one made the shore safely, the other drifted with the tide towards Bembridge, passing within a few hundred yards of the lifeboat pier. His cries for help were plainly heard ashore. However, due to an apparent confusion in their minds between the man who had reached safety and his unfortunate companion, the Navy refused to sanction the launch of the lifeboat. The airman drowned, and the later acceptance of the entire blame for the tragedy by the Naval officer concerned only partially offset the ill feeling that resulted.

Yarmouth's lifeboat during the war was the *S.G.E. (II)*, built at Cowes in 1938. Her first wartime rescue was also the most dramatic. On the night of 14 November 1939 HM Trawler *British* went ashore in a gale on Ship Ledge, Brighstone. In a 13-hour rescue, the lives of 12 crew members were saved by the *S.G.E.* Coxswain Walter Cotton received the RNLI Bronze Award, and his mechanic, Albert Hayward, was commended for his role. Just over a year later, the lifeboat went to the assistance of the sinking SS *Kingsborough*, south-west of the Shingle Bank; 27 lives were saved.

Between May 1943 and May 1945, the S.E.G. was ordered elsewhere by the Admiralty. The reserve lifeboat, *Greater London*, had comparitively little to do, since most calls for assistance were dealt with by the Naval ships in the vicinity. However, in November 1944, with Stanley Smith now serving as coxswain, she took stores and equipment to the SS *Cantal*, when the stricken steamer put into Christchurch Bay.

French Footnote

The Free French Navy had a wartime base at Cowes — in Arctic Road — which added considerable colour to the town's social life! It also, of course, had its practical advantages. When the East Cowes-based Trinity House vessel was needed elsewhere, it was replaced locally by the French vessel *Andre Blondel*, British-manned and admirably suited for the role.

SEVENTEEN

Built at Cowes

Any account of the important wartime contribution made by the Isle of Wight's ship, boat and aircraft builders must start with J. Samuel White's, transferred to Cowes from the Thanet in 1802, but, sadly, now just a memory. White's was almost as synonymous with the name of Cowes as the town's famous yachting festival (the expression 'Cowes-built,' when applied to a ship or boat, invariably meant it had been constructed by White's). As a major employer, and flag-bearer, the company was of vital importance to the Island. As a highly-regarded builder of fine ships and boats, it was also of immense value to the country as a whole in wartime.

When war broke out in September 1939 the company was already working at full capacity on Naval construction, having endeavoured, in common with British shipyards everywhere, to keep pace with the accelerated expansion of the Fleet which had followed the Munich crisis. In *White's of Cowes*, the company's official historians have described how the change-over from peace to war had an important effect on production:

The chief difficulty which immediately arose was the provision of black-out throughout the works, involving the painting of acres of glass and the provision of innumerable shutters over windows and skylights. As shipbuilding is, to a great extent, an outdoor occupation, it was not permissible to provide sufficient lighting to carry on work at the berths after darkness, and this, therefore, imposed limitations on the hours that could be worked, a production-limiting factor which was never overcome throughout the war.

However, the provision of shelters, and the equipment and training of ARP personnel, was

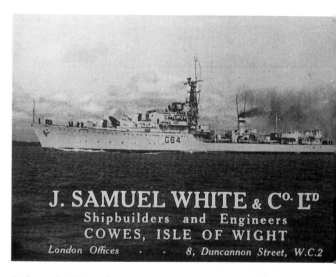

J. Samuel White's had a proud reputation for ship and boat building . . . one that was put to good use by the Admiralty during the war. (IWCC)

already at an advanced state when war broke out, so that the firm was prepared to meet any emergency. That September, its workforce was engaged on several important shipbuilding contracts. In addition to the destroyers *Kingston*, *Quorn* and *Southdown*, White's also had under construction the *Abdiel*, built to resemble a slow-moving County class destroyer, but designed as a fast minelayer, capable of laying her mines and making off at a high speed of around 40 knots. The 410 ft long *Abdiel* was the largest ship ever constructed at Cowes; with machinery boasting 72,000 shaft horse-power, she was also the most powerful.

The *Abdiel* was quickly to prove her worth. After completion, but before her running trials,

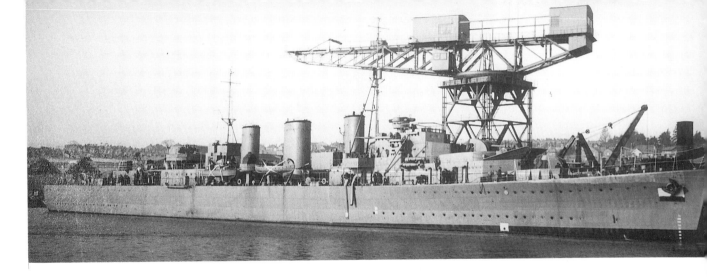

The fast minelayer HMS Abdiel, *completed in April 1941, was the largest ship ever constructed by J. Samuel White's yard at Cowes. She is pictured in the Medina, alongside the company's jetty.* (CCM)

she was urgently required to lay mines off the Port of Brest, in order to prevent the escape of the German warships *Scharnhorst* and *Gneisenau*. She left Cowes for the Clyde, collected a cargo of mines, and steamed direct to Brest at full power. Having successfully accomplished her mission, she returned to the Isle of Wight, but was soon sent to the Mediterranean, carrying out invaluable work in Crete and other parts of this theatre of war.

Under construction in another part of the yard were two destroyers for the Brazilian Navy. They were in an advanced state of construction, one having already been launched, when, within 24 hours of the war's outbreak, both were requisitioned by the Admirality. Completion was carried out to the requirements of the Royal Navy, although little modification was needed, and the two vessels were both at sea at the beginning of 1940 as HMS *Havant* and HMS *Havelock*. Subsequent wartime production at White's was almost entirely concentrated on the building of destroyers, principally of the Hunt escort class, but including three 'Q' class ships, the *Quentin*, *Quiberon* and *Quickmatch*.

Of the remaining vessels constructed by the company during the war, perhaps the most interesting was HMS *Grey Goose*, a very fast (35 knots) steam gun-boat with advanced machinery in a steel-built hull. She was captained by the naturalist Peter Scott (hence her name) and was originally designed to obtain much-needed supplies of ball bearings from Sweden. Small,

fast and silent, she proved well-suited to the task.

The Boatbuilders

As well as some 20 landing craft, the company's boatbuilding department also turned out 38 torpedo boats (MTBs) in the war period. These small and highly successful fighting ships were the subject of considerable intensive research and experiment, and the boats produced at Cowes to White's own design were widely regarded as the most successful of all the MTBs in Naval service.

Large numbers of smaller craft for Admiralty, RAF and War Office use were built, ranging in size from 6oft air-sea rescue launches to 16ft motor dinghies. Altogether, 317 boats were built and delivered by the company during wartime. Lined up, bow to stern, they would have stretched a little over two miles, and boasted a combined horsepower of 160,000!

In for Repair

In addition to the construction programme at J.S. White's yards, a great deal of repair work was carried out to ships − notably Tribal class destroyers − and machinery. With the approach of D-Day in 1944, it was realised that repair facilities at Cowes, with its obviously favourable geographical position, would be invaluable. Consequently, White's hauling-up slipway, which had been used as a building berth during the earlier war period, was again put into operation. From D-Day onwards, well over 100 ships were dealt with by the company (and several others by neighbouring Island yards), including tank landing craft (TLCs), tank landing ships (TLSs) and a number of the special vessels used during the invasion period.

White's engine works was heavily engaged throughout the war on the production of turbines and boilers for the vessels under construction in the Cowes shipyard, but the company managed to fit in a large amount of similar work for shipbuilders on the Clyde and North-East Coast. The fitting-out of vessels at these centres was undertaken by men sent from the Island.

The Bombers' Toll

The heavy air raids of April and May 1942 caused substantial damage at White's — as outlined in Part 1 — but repair and reconstruction work was put immediately in hand. In the meantime, in order to keep ship production going, buildings outside the works area were requisitioned for the use of the departments put out of action by the Luftwaffe bombs. As a result, there was no appreciable delay in the completion of partly-finished vessels. Work on the smaller craft in the boat shops, however, was severely dislocated, with a large number of boats either totally destroyed or damaged in the bombing.

Rebuilding the damaged sections of the works was complicated by the decision, taken not long after the raids, to build the world's first all-welded destroyer — HMS *Contest* — for the Admiralty, a task which required the provision of new cranes and the installation of a large amount of welding equipment and other necessary plant. The building and civil engineering work involved put a great strain on the supply of both labour and materials — already hardly sufficient to meet the demands of the builders who were reinstating the bomb-damaged buildings. The *Contest* was launched on 16 December 1944, but completed after the war had ended.

At the height of the war White's labour force was approximately 4,300. This included staff engaged at the company's Somerton Works on the production of airframes, rudder pedals, control columns and jettison fuel tanks for Spitfires; undercarriage parts and engine mountings for Mosquitos; elevators for the Lancaster bombers; towing arms and flare chutes for Wellingtons; and engine mountings for Oxford trainers. No company employees were killed on White's premises during the big raids, and, generally, the works' ARP organisation functioned well.

Before leaving the wartime story of J. Samuel White's an interesting Island sidelight on wartime history concerns the man who designed the Wellington bomber (and made possible the famous *Dambuster* raid). Dr Barnes Wallis began his long career in the drawing office of White's at Cowes. Sadly, the yard closed down in 1965, and Elliot Turbo-Machinery's takeover of the site failed to extend its life beyond 1981.

The products of Saunders-Roe — well illustrated on this poster — contributed significantly to the nation's war effort. (IWCC)

MEN O' WAR

Their medium — our heritage — the sea

Fighter Flying Boats—Flying Boats for all purposes

SAUNDERS ⟳ ROE LTD

WORKS AT :— EAST COWES, ISLE OF WIGHT • EASTLEIGH, SOUTHAMPTON • BEAUMARIS, ANGLESEY

Walrus amphibian 5658 awaiting repair at Saunders-Roe. The roundels beneath the cockpit denote the number of air-sea rescues made by the aircraft. (CCM)

The Saro Amphibians

Among the most tempting Isle of Wight targets for the Luftwaffe raiders were the various production and repair sites operated by the Saunders-Roe (Saro) company — now part of the giant Westland Aerospace organisation — and its subsidiaries. Principally known for its building of amphibious aircraft, the company was based at East Cowes. The majority of its wartime production was undertaken there (and at some 20 dispersal sites throughout the Island), but also on the mainland at Eastleigh and Weybridge.

Manufacturing work was concentrated initially on production of the Walrus single-engined amphibian, designed by Vickers Supermarine and used by the Fleet Air Arm for reconnaissance and air-sea rescue work. The 7,200 lb aircraft, its hull built of metal and ply, and its wings covered in fabric, was powered by a Bristol Pegasus VI engine, had a maximum speed of 135 mph and was equipped for catapulting. The company built 454 of these machines during the war, the peak coming in 1942

when 209 were completed — 25 being the maximum monthly output during that year.

Superseding the Walrus was the Sea Otter, another Vickers Supermarine design, but developed by Saunders-Roe. Powered by a Bristol Mercury 30 engine, it was substantially heavier and faster than its predecessor, weighing 9,600 lb and boasting a maximum speed of 150 mph. The hull of the Sea Otter was built entirely of metal, and the wings were, again, fabric-covered. Saunders-Roe completed 417 Sea Otters from 1943 onwards. Like the Walrus aircraft before them, all those produced on the Island were test-flown from Columbine Yard to Somerton Aerodrome. (See Chapter 15)

Some wartime work was also carried out at East Cowes on the S.RA1 jet-propelled single-seat fighter flying-boat, intended originally for the Pacific war zones. When eventually flown in 1947, it had an all-up weight of 15,500 lb, with a top speed of 512 mph, and proved to be the fastest flying-boat ever built.

About 6,000 people (4,000 in production and most of the remainder in the drawing office) were employed by Saunders-Roe on aircraft work in the war, 40 per cent of them women. A subsidiary company operated repair works at Solent Yard, West Cowes, and, after the yard was wrecked in May 1942, from a substitute site

The assembly line for the Walrus successor, the Sea Otter, is seen inside Saunders-Roe's Columbine Works at East Cowes. Otter construction began in 1944. (CCM)

at Forest Side, Parkhurst. Altogether, 435 seaplanes were repaired by the company during the war.

At Whippingham, another subsidiary, Saro Laminated Wood Products, produced no less than 40 per cent of the total wartime plywood requirements of the entire British aircraft industry, including components for gliders. The company also provided parts for motor launches, motor torpedo boats, air-sea rescue craft and folding boats. It supplied plywood for the pontoons used with the Army's Bailey bridges, produced two-man commando canoes and turned out large quantities of folding assault craft.

The principal effect of enemy action on Saunders-Roe in the Island, apart from several departmental transfers to the mainland, was the necessity to requisition some 20 establishments away from the main centre of operation to serve as the dispersal units. Churches, chapels and cinemas were among the buildings utilised. The savage bombing in 1942 took a heavy toll. By the end of that year, 200,000 sq ft of the total Cowes area establishment of 725,000 sq ft had been destroyed, necessitating the construction of machine shops and paint shops at Osborne, the erection of the repair works in Parkhurst Forest, and the establishment of the factory at Weybridge. Worst-hit of the subsidiaries was Saro Laminated Wood Products, which lost four million feet of veneer in the May 1942 blitz.

The Other Builders

While the activities of the two major industrial concerns, J. Samuel White's and Saunders-Roe, inevitably dominate the story of wartime production on the Isle of Wight, many smaller Island companies also contributed significantly to the war effort. In the Cowes/East Cowes area, the yards of Uffa Fox (nine vessels) — his first war contract had been for the supply of hundreds of pairs of oars — Clare Lallow (four), Simpson & Rooke (26) and Groves & Guttridge (nine) all built landing assault craft (LCAs); Woodnutt's yard at St Helens produced around 20 vessels of various types, including seven MTBs; and the Ranalagh Yacht Yard in Wootton Creek turned out a couple of motor launches. All these companies, and others, additionally built smaller craft and/or military structures — such as pontoons — and many were engaged in repair work.

EIGHTEEN

The Ferries go to War

"The little holiday steamers made an excursion to Hell and came back glorious." — J.B. Priestley

Virtually all the ships which formed the pre-war cross-Solent ferry fleets were on active service at some stage of the Second World War. Several of the well-known paddle-steamers were quickly requisitioned by the Admiralty, operating thereafter in minesweeping or anti-aircraft roles which took them far away from the Isle of Wight. Even those left in home waters to maintain the restricted wartime services were commandeered for the occasional, often humble, duty at the behest of HM Forces. But it was off the beaches at Dunkirk, in the desperate days of May 1940, that the Island paddlers, commissioned or otherwise, made their most gallant joint contribution to the war effort. Some of them died in the process.

The Isle of Wight fleets of both the Southern Railway and the Southampton, Isle of Wight and South of England Royal Mail Steam Packet Company — known to all as Red Funnel — were represented in strength at Dunkirk. Two of the requisitioned vessels, the SR paddler *Sandown*, built in 1934, and Red Funnel's much smaller *Gracie Fields*, just four-years-old in 1940, were among the first group of paddle-steamers to help lift men from the beaches. With them were two other commissioned paddlers, *Medway Queen* (which was later to find a home on the Island's River Medina) and the aged *Brighton Belle*.

For the *Gracie Fields* it was to be a tragically short operation. Having made a successful run back to Dover on 28 May, she was hit by a bomb in her engine room on her return to Dunkirk the following day. She was sighted soon afterwards by HMS *Pangbourne,* listing out of control, her rudder jammed. *Pangbourne* took off her troops, leaving only a skeleton crew on board, and

Red Funnel's 1891-built PS Lorna Doone *served in both minesweeping and anti-aircraft roles — heroically seeing off an attack by three Dornier Do 17 bombers in 1941 — before ending the war as an accomodation ship on the Clyde. She was returned to the company in a bad state, fit only for scrapping.* (Author)

began to take her in tow. But the jammed rudder kept *Gracie Fields* out on the starboard quarter, and she was steadily making water. It was obvious after an hour that there was no hope of saving her. *Pangbourne* took off the paddler's captain and the remainder of her crew, and *Gracie Fields* sank in the early hours of 30 May.

Sandown was more fortunate — the ship's immunity was ascribed by the crew to her mascot, the dachshund 'Bombproof Bella'! As well as rescuing 250 troops from HM Drifter *Golden Girt,* ashore on the Goodwin Sands, she survived incessant shelling off the beaches and returned safely to England for a second time with 910 soldiers.

The Gracie Fields, *with its namesake in the lifebelt. The paddle steamer sank off Dunkirk in 1940 after helping lift troops from the beaches.* (Author).

The railway paddle-steamer Whippingham *followed an outstanding contribution to the evacuation of Dunkirk in 1940 with Admiralty service in both minesweeping and anti-aircraft roles. She is pictured back in the Solent a few years after the war.* (Pamlin Prints)

Red Funnel's *Princess Elizabeth*, an early minesweeping requisition by the Admiralty in 1939, made a praiseworthy four trips from Dunkirk with troops; two DSCs and two DSMs were gained by members of the Naval crew. The Southern Railway's newly-built *Ryde*, another ferry-turned-minesweeper, also helped out.

Of the Isle of Wight ships called up specifically for Dunkirk, the Southern Railway paddle-steamer *Whippingham* was undoubtedly a star. Laid up at the outbreak of war as reserve ship in Portsmouth, she was hastily requisitioned, travelling at full speed across the Channel and arriving at Malo beach during a violent air raid. The flow of men to her via the small ferrying craft was painfully slow, so *Whippingham* attempted to put her stern on the beach. It proved impossible. Surviving repeated attacks from the air, she then moved into the harbour, making fast alongside the mole (pier) in heavy shell fire. Several members of her crew were wounded by shrapnel and pieces of flying concrete, but the ship herself miraculously escaped damage, and soon an estimated 2,700 soldiers were on board. The journey home was slow and, because of overloading, *Whippingham* listed violently every time she altered course.

Whisked away from the Solent for a rushed temporary commissioning at Sheerness into Naval service was the 1928-built PS *Portsdown*. Commanded by Sub-Lieutenant R.H. Church RNR, the paddler crossed to France totally without armament and still, of course, bearing the white paint of peacetime. Her Naval crew put the time on their hands during the crossing to good use, covering the paintwork wherever they could with brown and black canvas, draping the wheelhouse with kapok and cork life-jackets (to provide at least a minimal protection from flying shrapnel), and building a dummy anti-aircraft gun amidships!

Portsdown came under fire as soon as she arrived, but Sub-Lieutenant Church managed to put her nose on to the beach amd held her there, loading all the time until the tide began to ebb and nearly 500 troops were on board. Returning to England, she took off about 1,000 soldiers from a French vessel that had run aground near the Dunkirk breakwater, and finally limped safely into Ramsgate. Five of her crew were decorated for gallantry as a result of their actions. The paddle-steamer herself returned to normal service in the Solent — and an entirely undeserved fatal collision with a mine off Southsea in September 1941 (see Chapter 6).

The ill fortune of Red Funnel's evacuation fleet — with the honourable exception of *Princess Elizabeth*, company paddle-steamers made largely abortive runs to Dunkirk — extended to its last pre-war acquisition, the 1938-built motor screw vessel *Vecta*. She, too, travelled east to Dover, but, when crossing to Dunkirk, she broke down and was forced to limp back to port. The Southern Railway's little *Freshwater* made her only diversion of the war from the Yarmouth-Lymington service to help out — and the SR also sent two of its Fishbourne-Portsmouth car ferries.

The Little Ships

Down the scale — in size, but certainly not in endeavour — were the little ships used by the carriers Pickfords on their cross-Solent runs. There were five of them at Dunkirk — *Bee, Bat, Chamois, Hound* and *M.F.H.* Their crews varied from four to two, and, with just two exceptions, all Pickfords' men insisted on going with their vessels.

On 30 May, *Bat* picked up 15 of the crew from the French destroyer *Bourasque* and took them safely to Ramsgate. *Chamois* made two unsuccessful attempts to reach Dunkirk, beaten back by air attacks, before she succeeded in getting within two miles of the beaches. There, she encountered two transports in the midst of a heavy bombing attack by the Luftwaffe. *Chamois* went to the rescue of the survivors, mostly French and Belgian troops. The clothes of many were on fire, and ammunition in their pockets was exploding. The crew managed to rescue 170 men, transporting them to a French trawler for medical attention.

The following day, *Bat*, returning for the second time, put in close to shore on the west side, but found that all the remaining troops had been taken off in a destroyer. Proceeding to the east side, under continuous machine-gun and shell fire, she managed to take on board, from small boats, about 100 men, transporting them safely back to England. The crew had been without sleep for 92 hours, and the engine had been running continuously all that time!

Bee reached Dunkirk on the 31st, and, after lying three mies off the shore all one night, managed to take 360 British troops aboard, transferring them to a tug. Later, ten British and five French troops were taken from small boats and brought back to England. On her arrival, *Hound* sent the entire crew to the shore in a small boat to help the troops get away. It was dangerous owing to the number of men who tried to clamber into the boat, but, despite deaths caused by bombing, six were saved this way. For some time, *Hound* stayed alongside the remainder of one of the little piers, and took aboard about 100 French and Belgians.

When *M.F.H.* arrived at Dunkirk, there were about 80 German raiders overhead, dropping bombs on the beach 40 feet away. Troops were picked up and disembarked on to a larger vessel. *M.F.H.* then proceeded to the mole, took on board about 140 troops, and returned to England with them.

The Cowes Contingent

No record of the involvement of Isle of Wight ships at Dunkirk would be complete without reference to participating vessels actually constructed in Island yards. Many Cowes-built ships did valiant work throughout the evacuation, although the almost brand-new destroyer HMS *Havant* was lost off the Dunkirk beaches. Among the 'little ships' was the Thames firefloat *Massey Shaw*, constructed at White's some years before the war, which was instrumental in saving a large number of soldiers. The Cowes-built *Crested Eagle*, one of the famous Thames excursion steamers, also did magnificent work before her name was added to the list of shipping casualties.

Other War Work

At the time of the war's outbreak, the ferry links to and from the mainland were shared between the Southern Railway and Red Funnel. The SR ran the passenger service between Ryde and Portsmouth, the car ferry link to Portsmouth from Fishbourne, west of Ryde, and the western route between Yarmouth and Lymington. Red Funnel carried passengers and vehicles between Cowes and Southampton, as well as operating a cross-river service of launches between East and West Cowes, and an extensive summer excursion programme. Both companies had been required to relinquish vessels in the interests of the nation's war effort immediately hostilities were declared in September 1939. They were needed initially for conversion to minesweeping duties.

The shallow draught of the Southern Railway's 825-ton PS *Southsea*, introduced to the Ryde-Portsmouth passage in 1930, made her an ideal candidate for the task. She left in 1939 to earn herself a bit of glory — but never returned home to bask in it. The highlight of her war service came in November 1940, when, commanded by Lieutenant C.C.M. Pawley RNR. she was credited with shooting down an enemy aircraft which had attacked her. Just three months later, in February 1941, the *Southsea* struck a mine off the Tyne and was beached. An examination revealed her to be beyond repair, and she was declared a total loss.

Following her Dunkirk exploits, *Southsea's* sister ship, PS *Whippingham*, was again called up in 1941 for minesweeping service (pennant number J136), but was further converted in 1942 for new duties as an anti-aircraft vessel. She survived the remainder of the war in that role, and was returned to the SR in 1946. The *Whippingham* was eventually broken up in 1963.

The requisitioning of the 684-ton SR paddler *Sandown* for minesweeper conversion (pennant number J20) was immediate, although she, too, was later given an anti-aircraft role. Her visit to Dunkirk apart, the *Sandown* was mostly confined to the Firth of Forth. She was returned to the SR, following a refit, in 1945 for further service both on the Ryde-Portsmouth ferry passage and the railway's summer excursions. Breaking-up followed in 1965.

PS *Ryde*, the Southern's final pre-war acquisition for the Ryde passenger route — indeed, its last traditional Isle of Wight paddle-steamer — had been in service only since 1934 when the war whisked her away for minesweeping work alongside *Sandown* in the Firth of Forth (pennant number J132). By 1942 she had become another anti-aircraft conversion. The *Ryde* returned safely to her home waters, where, suitably refitted, she remained in service until her eventual withdrawal in 1969, and preservation as a floating bar and discotheque on the Medina.

Their wheelhouses protected with concrete, it was left to the oldest, and smallest, of the ships on the Ryde-Portsmouth route — the 1928-built, 342-ton sisters *Merstone* and *Portsdown*, and the 412-ton *Shanklin*, of 1924 vintage — to operate the restricted wartime passenger service.

The *Merstone* enjoyed an uneventful war, the only diversion from normal duties being her use in the period immediately before D-Day as a means of ferrying Normandy-bound troops to the transports anchored in Spithead. Laid up in 1948, she was scrapped four years later. In contrast, as related above, the *Portsdown's* Dunkirk adventure was, sadly, followed by her tragic sinking in 1941. She was replaced on the Portsmouth service by the diminutive 161-ton PS *Solent*, transferred from the Lymington passage (and, later, also used to ferry the D-Day troops). The *Shanklin* strayed off the route only long enough to help with the troop-ferrying in 1944. She was broken-up in 1961.

Called up in 1939 with *Gracie Fields* for mines-

The last paddle-steamer built for the Southern Railway's Ryde-Portsmouth passenger route, the PS Ryde, *was requisitioned by the Admiralty at the outbreak of war, firstly for minesweeping duties and then in an anti-aircraft role.* (Pamlin Prints)

weeping duties (pennant number J111), Red Funnel's slightly smaller 1927-built PS *Princess Elizabeth* survived the Dunkirk experience and was further converted for anti-aircraft duties in 1942, returning to the company at the end of the war, and eventual preservation on the Thames.

Requisitioned in December 1939 for minesweeper conversion was the company's venerable 1891-built excursion ship *Lorna Doone* (pennant number J135), a veteran of First World War Naval service, whose wartime exploits this time were to leave her fit only for the breakers' torch. Transferred to anti-aircraft duties (and renumbered 4.402), she provided an example of her suitability for the job when, in 1941, she engaged three Dornier Do 17 bombers off the Essex coast. Her gunners shot down one of the raiders, damaged a second and saw off the third. But *Lorna Doone* did not escape unscathed, and to the damage she sustained in this raid was added still more just four days later when the Luftwaffe mounted another attack while she was berthed at Harwich.

Red Funnel's speedy flagship, the 1900-built paddler *Balmoral*, was another First World War veteran, having served as a troop transport in that conflict. The 427-ton vessel, capable of 20 knots, did not get her Second World War call until April 1940, when the Admiralty signed her up for anti-aircraft duties (number 4.241). She,

too, was operating off Harwich when her gunners were credited with the shooting-down of a Heinkel He 111. Ending the war as an accomodation ship, she was finally scrapped in 1949. The *Bournemouth Queen* (anti-aircraft ship number 4.270) was another of the Southampton fleet to take part in both wars.

The PS *Duchess of Cornwall's* long career had included a spell of Admiralty ownership, but the Second World War service of the 302-ton 1896 veteran lasted a mere month before she was returned to Red Funnel as unsuitable. As if that wasn't enough, the unfortunate vessel was then sunk by the Luftwaffe at Southampton's Royal Pier during a raid later in 1940. However, she was raised, returned to service and given the honour in July 1945 of operating the company's first excursion to Ryde for more than five years. Scrapping followed in 1950.

Less fortunate was the venerable paddler *Her Majesty*. Built in 1885, used in the First World War as a minesweeper, and converted for car-carrying duties in the late 1920s, she, too, fell victim to the Luftwaffe bombers while moored at the company's Southampton repair jetty in December 1940. She was raised — but only for eventual scrapping.

Red Funnel retained the use of the aged paddle-steamers *Solent Queen* and *Princess Helena* (although both went to Dunkirk). Along with the motor vessels *Medina* and *Vecta*, the two paddlers, built in 1889 and 1883, respectively, maintained services between Cowes and Southampton, with the latter also loaned for a brief period to the Southern Railway for use as a relief vessel on the Ryde-Portsmouth route. They

One of the most famous Dunkirk paddle-steamer veterans, the PS Medway Queen, *found a retirement home on the Island's River Medina as a floating night spot. She later fell into disrepair and was photographed in a sorry state before the mounting of a successful salvage operation.* (Author)

both outlasted the war by a few years – the *Helena* surviving until 1952. The company's remaining paddle-steamer, the ancient (1876) *Lord Elgin*, a cargo-carrier since 1911, performed a vital wartime role in this capacity, and was still running up to ten years after the end of the conflict.

The company's war sacrifices extended to its smaller vessels. A little over a year before the war's outbreak, Red Funnel had modernised its cross-river service between East and West Cowes with the introduction of the smart motor launch *Norris Castle*, built of wood at the Cowes yard of Clare Lallows (she was framed throughout with Isle of Wight oak). The standby vessel was the veteran launch *Precursor*, built in 1898. Both were requisitioned by the Admiralty in 1939 and taken away for service in the Mediterranean. They failed to return, and the company never resumed its short Medina passage.

A former Medina ferry, the Cowes-built steam launch *Princess Louise*, used latterly by the company as a tug for towing coal barges, had her career terminated in a collision with a landing craft at Southampton during the build-up to D-Day.

PART FOUR

The People's War

Wardens outside their heavily-sandbagged ARP post in
Medina Avenue, Newport — converted from an annexe of the
Bethlehem Hall. (Shirley Pitman)

NINETEEN

The Civilian Forces

The civil defence of the Isle of Wight in the Second World War was organised by the county council, and run from heavily-sandbagged ground floor rooms at County Hall, Newport – headquarters and control centre of the Island-wide Air Raid Precautions (ARP) network. This formed part of an area group based in Portsmouth, and was within the control boundaries of the Reading-based regional civil defence headquarters. From Reading, one of the twelve regional HQs in the country, the next upward link in the chain was the Home Secretary himself.

Prior to 1939, the Island's Chief Constable, Col R.G.B. Spicer, had combined his normal police duties with those of a County ARP Officer. In February of that year, acting on a recommendation from its ARP Committee, the Isle of Wight County Council decided to appoint a full-time ARPO, with an annual salary of £300. Shortly before war was declared in September, Brigadier-General H.E.C. Nepean left his Head Warden's duties at Ryde to take over the senior county role.

His County Control was linked to six area report centres on the Island. They were at Newport itself, Ryde (which also had responsibility for Bembridge), Cowes (also covering East Cowes), Shanklin (also covering Sandown), Ventnor and Freshwater (for the West Wight). Each of the report centres had its own network of boldly-marked, sandbagged posts for the ARP wardens – the front line troops of civil defence. These sparsely-furnished posts served as mini-headquarters for the groups into which each of the report centre areas was divided. Each group was further divided into sectors.

The majority of ARP personnel on the Island, as elsewhere in the country, were unpaid volunteers. reporting for duty in their 'spare time.' When war broke out, full-time wardens

Gas mask drill at East Cowes in June 1938. Presumably the unmasked man in the centre was the instructor! (Mabel Emms)

were paid a weekly wage of £3, which was below the national pay average, but considered 'easy money' (by those in more demanding work) during the eight months of the *Phoney War*, when the wardens had little else to do but watch out for blackout infringements. The public attitude changed when the bombs began to fall in 1940.

In March 1942 a break-down of full-time ARP personnel on the Island revealed 106 wardens (including two women) on the payroll; 33 members of first-aid parties (all men); two men and four women stationed at first-aid posts; three men and 45 women (mostly telephonists) in the report centres; eleven men and 20 women in the ambulance service; 38 men in rescue parties; two male messengers; and three senior male Fire Guards. The break-down (totalling 267) did not include senior administrative staff, and no record appears to have survived of the large number of volunteers in the Island's ARP services.

Ernie Jolliffe, Deputy ARP Officer in Ryde, remembers:

Of course, the sirens were always going. I remember someone telling me that, next to Dover, Ryde had the most air raid alerts in the country during the war. Jerry used Ryde Pier as his 'finger' . . . a few degrees to one side of it was Portsmouth, and a few to the other was Southampton. What often happened was that Jerry would come over Ryde and would then meet the Portsmouth AA batteries. He would lose his nerve and let his bombs go before he reached the mainland, or turn tail and drop them as he made his getaway. That's how a great many bombs ended up in Ryde — we had 290 high-explosive bombs dropped on the town, and, of course, a large number of incendiary bombs.

Ryde was, however, more fortunate than several other Island towns in the war, with Cowes, Shanklin and Ventnor all suffering a substantially greater amount of damage. Ernie Jolliffe's summing-up of his wartime civil defence work is: "Three days of real tragedy per year, about the same amount of comedy . . . and the rest of the time you were bored to death!"

Local Government

Throughout the war years the Isle of Wight's system of local government continued to operate within the same basic framework as in peacetime. However, the first war in British history to truly involve the whole of the population was bound to radically change the emphasis of the work undertaken by officers of the Island's principal local authorities.

Beneath the level of the Isle of Wight County Council, the Island's various districts had been governed since April 1933 — when a series of amalgamations had taken place — by six second-tier authorities: the two borough councils at Newport and Ryde; the three urban district councils of Cowes, Sandown-Shanklin and Ventnor; and, covering the sparsely-populated remainder, the Isle of Wight Rural District Council. All had been largely pre-occupied since early 1937 with civil defence preparations for the total war that, in varying degrees of pessimism, was expected.

Wartime duties devolving upon the councils and their officers included the maintenance and

Ernie Jolliffe's ARP warden's authorisation card, dated 14 December 1938 and signed by Chief Constable Spicer, who also served as County ARP Officer at that time. (Ernie Jolliffe)

safeguarding of water supplies and sewerage facilities; the fire service (regular and auxiliary) before the nationalised NFS came into being; repairs to houses damaged by enemy action (by arrangement with local builders); emergency mortuary arrangements; the recruitment and training of Fire Guards; the British Restaurants (community feeding centres); the provision of rest centres; rescue, first-aid and demolition services (on behalf of the county council); liaison with hospitals and the health authority; and the organisation of morale-boosting social and sporting programmes — the 'Holidays at Home.'

The threat of a German invasion prompted the Government to organise the setting-up of county and district invasion committees, comprising representatives of local authorities, the military, police, civil defence, Home Guard, WVS and other essential services. Their main duties included the preparation (and, should it have proved necessary, the implementation) of

An early picture of Carisbrooke's civil defence force . . . the Vicar included! (CCM)

plans designed to warn, protect and assist the civilian population in the event of an invasion. A district committee was only to act independently if communications with the County Invasion Committee were disrupted, or the district became isolated.

In the Isle of Wight, several local district committees were set up in addition to the county's. They met regularly, meticulously detailing their plans, arrangements and procedures — everything from invasion codewords to the number of wheelbarrows available at private homes; from emergency mortuary arrangements to a list of Home Guard cadet messengers — in secret books. Area sub-committees were appointed for outlying areas. (See Appendices)

When it was all over — in fact, it was a matter for earnest debate long before the formal conclusion of hostilities — the Isle of Wight councils were faced with rehabilitating their war-ravaged resorts, and resuming the business of attracting the holidaymakers who were so vital to the Island's economy. The Borough of Ryde was quick off the mark with its June 1945 purchase of the Appley Hall estate, sloping attractively down to the sea between the town itself and Puckpool. Along the east coast of the Island, the problems were more severe. The seafront at Shanklin (neighbouring Sandown suffered far less by comparsion) was a scene of utter devastation, thanks to the combination of repeated enemy damage and the paraphernalia of the PLUTO installations.

A town totally dependant on the tourist trade, Shanklin had paid a heavy price for its wartime sacrifices. It bore no grudges. When, in 1959, the pre-war cast-iron promenade lift — linking the seafront with the town above — was finally replaced by a modern successor, the opportunity was taken to remind residents and visitors alike of the town's considerable contribution to the 1939-45 war effort. In the foyer at the foot of the lift shaft a plaque was unveiled recording the PLUTO pipeline's associations with the site.

The Police Force

The Isle of Wight was policed by its own constabularly when war broke out in 1939. By the end of the conflict it had become inextricably linked to the neighbouring Hampshire force on the mainland.

Amalgamation took place in April 1943, with the creation of the Hampshire Joint Police Force — a result of legislation under the wide-ranging Defence Regulations. In common with the remainder of the joint force, several Island officers trained from that year onwards in control duties at incidents involving damage from air raids. This was an important role because Incident Control Officers had the responsibility for co-ordinating and controlling members of the organisations involved (ARP, the fire service, medical teams etc), deploying men and vehicles as required, and directing rescue work. Some officers attended courses in bomb recognition; others gave lectures to civil defence personnel on methods of immobilising vehicles and put-

Led by Ernie Jolliffe (right), the Deputy ARPO, and Rex Burton, Head Warden, Ryde's ARP Corps march past the reviewing dais in 1940. Taking the salute is Major-General Jack Seely, Lord Lieutenant of Hampshire and the Isle of Wight, who stands with the Mayor of Ryde, Alderman Henry Weeks. (Ernie Jolliffe)

Island women served alongside the men in the Auxiliary Fire Service. Miss H.L. Burton (right) was an AFS telephonist at Ryde. She is pictured with dispatch rider Rose Carter in the town's Edward Street. (D. Corney)

ting petrol pumps out of action, in the event of a German invasion.

When, inevitably, members of the police force left for service in HM Forces, their places were taken either by men of the First Police Reserve (retired regular police officers) or the newly-formed Police War Reserve, whose Island recruits came from a variety of backgrounds.

The Fire Service

The Isle of Wight operated as Division 14D of the wartime National Fire Service, set up in August 1941 through amalgamation of the town brigades and the Auxiliary Fire Service — whose members had heavily outnumbered the ranks of the regular firemen on the Island.

Until the Luftwaffe lost its punch in 1944 the locally-based firemen were often engaged in fighting the results of the most prevalent, and — because of the sheer number that were dropped in clusters — the most destructive of the weapons flung against the Island by the enemy: the small, cylindrical incendiary bomb. It was dangerous work, and, inevitably, there were casualties — but the worst day of the war for the NFS on the Island was caused by the high-explosive bombs dropped in January 1943 by 'tip and run' raiders on Shanklin. Nine firemen, one firewoman and two dispatch riders were killed

Members of the National Fire Service enjoy a cuppa at their tea van in Newport. The inscription on the van reads: "Presented by the non-British staff in the Argentine of the Buenos Aires Greater Southern, Western and Midland Railways to the National Fire Service in the Isle of Wight (Fire Force No. 14)" The photograph was probably taken in 1942. (Eddie Mosling)

Fifty years after it was painted on the wall at the top of Victoria Grove, East Cowes, this wartime indication to firemen of a nearby static water supply remained easily readable in 1989. (Author)

in the direct hit on the Landguard Road fire station.

Organisation of the Fire Guard, the title adopted in 1941 for the vital, but essentially boring, compulsory firewatching scheme, was the responsibility of the district councils, working in close co-operation with the civil defence services.

Public Transport

The clear public transport necessity on the Isle of Wight during the war was the conveyance of war-workers to the industrial sites at Cowes. With all non-essential passenger journeys discouraged, in line with national policy, it was to be the dominant feature of services on both rail and road networks.

As they performed this essential wartime task, the trains and buses continually ran the gauntlet of the Luftwaffe bombers. However, the rail system, despite many mishaps, emerged in rather better shape than much of the mainland network. Little in the way of lasting damage was caused by the enemy to track, property or rolling stock, and the Island railway managers were able to re-introduce what was virtually a pre-war service as early as VE-Day in 1945.

At the outbreak of war, all Island train services were operated by the Southern Railway. The system was at its height. Lines radiated from Newport to Cowes, Ryde, Sandown and Freshwater, the important Ryde-Ventnor line served the holiday resorts on the east coast, and branch lines connected Brading with Bembridge and the rural junction of Merstone with Ventnor West. On 1 September 1939, along with the remainder of the nation's railway system, the effective wartime control of the Island network passed to the Government under the provisions of the Emergency Powers (Defence) Act. For the next six years there would be no tourists to transport to the holiday beaches.

Workers' traffic, on the other hand, increased to a tremendous degree. Large numbers of people commuted daily to the two Cowes stations (Mill Hill and the Cowes terminus). Their evening departure, in four or more workers' trains leaving within minutes of each other, was a remarkable operating achievement on the single track railway.

Austerity ruled. The attractive sage green livery of the Island's immaculately maintained tank engine fleet gave way in 1941 to plain black, and surplus coaching stock, parked for the duration in out-of-the-way sidings, acquired a protective covering of grey paint. The staff at

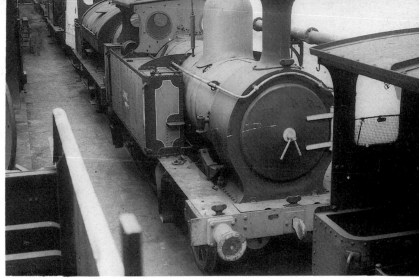

A wartime shunting mishap at Ryde St John's Road Station. Locomotive W16 Ventnor *has collided with a third class brake coach during black-out conditions in April 1940. (CCM)*

Sacrificed for the war effort . . . the former Isle of Wight Railway's tank engine Ryde. *Built in 1864, withdrawn in 1932 and shipped to the mainland in 1934, it is seen at Eastleigh Works with other veteran locomotives which had been earmarked for preservation by the Southern Railway. The nation's wartime need for metal ended all hopes of that — and* Ryde *was broken up in August 1940. (Author)*

Ryde's railway works enhanced an already widely-respected reputation for ingenuity and improvisation by converting a passenger van into a mobile gas contamination unit, and equipping a flat truck with a fire pump as a precaution against fire on Ryde Pier. Neither adaptation was, in the event, required. Nor were the rail blocks which were part of the Island's anti-invasion plan in 1941 — and the railway along Ryde Pier, threatened with being blown to smithereens if the enemy had shown his face, thankfully survived the war intact!.

Wartime train passengers on the Island stood a very good chance of being caught in an air raid. If they were, there was no excuse for not knowing the correct procedure — it was precisely set out in each compartment on boldly printed posters which had replaced the scenic views and Southern Railway advertisements of pre-war years: There was at least one occasion when an enterprising driver, approaching a town under attack, utilised one of the five tunnels on the Island network as an impromptu air raid shelter for the entire train and its passengers.

Southern Vectis, the Island's principal bus operators, had carried 6½ million passengers in 1938, the last full year before the war. The company's pre-war fleet comprised 87 buses and 25 coaches, operating a summer network of 325 route miles (230 in winter). The company performed three vital wartime functions, of which the most important, as with the railways, was the conveyance of war-workers to the yards and factories in the Cowes area. Bus convoys — more than a dozen from Ryde alone — became a familiar sight on this operationally-demanding daily task.

A second role was the provision of substitute services for sections of the rail network temporarily incapacitated by the Luftwaffe. The third was to make vehicles available — either for specific military transporation tasks on the Island or through requisitioning — to the national war effort. This began in the last few days before the war's outbreak, when Southern Vectis was called upon to deliver Territorial Army units arriving from the mainland to their allotted gun and searchlight sites on the Island.

At the end of that operation the company's vehicles were returned safely to their depot — but it was a different story when the military demanded buses and drivers at the height of the invasion scare in 1940. A vast amount of the Brittish Army's equipment had been left behind at Dunkirk, and when the 12th Infantry Brigade arrived on the Island in June it was with a conspicuous lack of motorised transport. Since the soldiers were on constant invasion standby, some means of transporting them to their

Very few photographs were taken of Isle of Wight trains during the war years. This view, showing a Brading-bound train at the Bembridge branch line terminus, dates from the immediate post-war period. Locomotive W14 Fishbourne is still in its drab wartime black livery. (Author)

Advice for bus passengers in an air raid . . . driver George Gawler and inspector Walt Dyer are pictured outside the Southern Vectis office in Newport. (Southern Vectis Museum)

defensive positions from wherever they happened to be at the time of an alert had to be found.

For the Southern Vectis drivers, automatically excluded from service in the Forces because of their reserved occupation, this was an unexpected military call-up. Reg Davies was among those who were attached, along with their vehicles, to the 6th Black Watch. He recalls:

We were on continuous 24-hour duty that summer. The only time we were allowed to leave our company of soldiers was to go into Newport to service the buses — and have a bath and a change of clothes at home. We had to go one at a time, and we weren't given much time, either! My company was camped under the trees at Fishbourne. At first the drivers slept in the buses, but, after a while, a lady who owned a large wooden hut on the opposite side of the road invited us to use that as sleeping quarters. So we took our seat cushions over there and slept a bit more comfortably.

Southern Vectis responded to the national shortage of fuel by converting a few of its buses to run on gas — some with self-contained producer units, and others with them carried in trailers. The Island's hilly terrain proved an insurmountable obstacle to the experiment; the gas-powered vehicles functioned well enough going downhill, and on the flat, but their hill ascents were quite another story. It was not uncommon for them to expire en route, and they almost always ran late.

A longer-lived venture was the decision to equip some buses with perimeter seating in

Albany Barracks, Newport, in 1940 . . . Southern Vectis bus drivers are pictured with two of the soldiers for whom they were providing round-the-clock transport. (Reg Davies)

order to provide maximum standing room, and so carry more passengers. Roy Brinton, who used the buses regularly as a wartime school-boy, well remembers the experience of travelling in what inevitably became known as the 'cattle trucks': "Officially, they were supposed to carry 60-odd people, but it has been recorded that 80 passengers crawled off them at times in Newport. You could walk up Quarr Hill (on the main Ryde-Newport road) faster than one of those buses, when fully laden!"

The war saw the recruitment of many conduc-

tresses (the wartime clippies) in a bid to ease the manpower shortage. The black-out made their job a virtual impossibility at times, with interior lighting in buses reduced to the barest mini-mum. It was as bad for the drivers, with only a pinprick of light from their vehicle's masked headlamps to guide them. Another depressing effect of wartime austerity was the grey paint which progressively replaced the green and cream pre-war bus livery.

Southern Vectis suffered limited war damage to property in Newport and Shanklin, and a number of its buses were singled out for atten-tion by Luftwaffe gunners. However, all vehi-cles retained for wartime use by the company on the Island survived the conflict.

TWENTY

War on the Wards

Fought as much on the streets of the local town as on the foreign battlefields, the people's war of 1939-45 thrust Britain's doctors and nurses into the Front Line. On the Isle of Wight, full and dramatic employment was assured for the Island's medical teams as soon as the Luftwaffe began dropping its bombs in the early summer of 1940.

Emergency medical back-up for the wartime Islanders — the resident population plus the thousands of locally-stationed servicemen and women — was dispensed in three forms. Firstly, in its pre-NHS shape, it came from the existing general hospitals. Secondly, it was available from the network of first-aid facilities set up under the aegis of ARP. Finally, for the benefit of the greatly expanded military presence, it was supplied by the medical branches of the Armed Forces. The divisions would, of necessity, become blurred as the war progressed.

With co-ordination the keyword for all things, the plans drawn up in 1941 for the defence of the Isle of Wight from enemy attack included a full break-down of the medical services available from all sources. The four hospitals equipped for the full range of emergency medical services at that time were at Ryde (Royal IW County Hospital); Shanklin (Home of Rest); and East Cowes (Frank James Hospital and the Osborne House Convalescent Home for Officers). In addition, the Army had its Parkhurst Military Hospital at Albany Barracks.

Down the list were the Army's medical reception sites and their approximate civilian equivalents, the ARP first-aid posts. In the former category were the Cochrane Block at Osborne House; 12th Field Ambulance HQ at Barton Manor, East Cowes; the regimental medical post at Albany; a receiving station at Golden Hill Fort, Freshwater; and the 23rd Casualty Clearing Station, based in the requisitioned Totland Bay Hotel.

There was one ARP first-aid post for each area of the Island, and a network of smaller first-aid points. The posts were at Northwood House, Cowes (plus three first-aid points); Frank James Hospital, East Cowes (plus two first-aid points); the County Hall clinics at Newport (plus eight first-aid points, including a dressing station at the Parkhurst Prison Officers' Sports Pavilion); the Royal IW County Hospital, Ryde (plus seven first-aid points); Scio Hospital, Shanklin (plus six first-aid points); the Royal National Hospital at Ventnor (plus six first-aid points); and 13 first-aid points in the West Wight. In addition, a mobile first-aid post was stationed at Wootton, midway between Ryde and Newport.

A Matron's Memories

The war imposed severe demands on the Florence Nightingales of the 1939-45 war. Recollections of wartime work in the Island hospitals follow from two women who were at either end of nursing's seniority scale. Firstly, Agnes Phillips recalls dramatic days as Matron at the Girls' Friendly Society's Home of Rest in Winchester Road, Shanklin — taken over by the Ministry of Health as the town's wartime emergency hospital:

We had 112 beds, in five wards, at the Home of Rest, and they had to do for general hospital work as well as for convalescent servicemen. We had a lot of wartime casualties of various types in there, particularly after the air raids on the Catholic Church and Shanklin Fire Station. I remember that on the day all those firemen were killed the Germans shot up the hospital itself with cannon fire.

I remember we had a really nasty night once. I think it was German planes going back home — we always used to get the backlog. The RAF had intercepted, as I recall, and they were battling it out over us. The noise was incredible. I was with a little

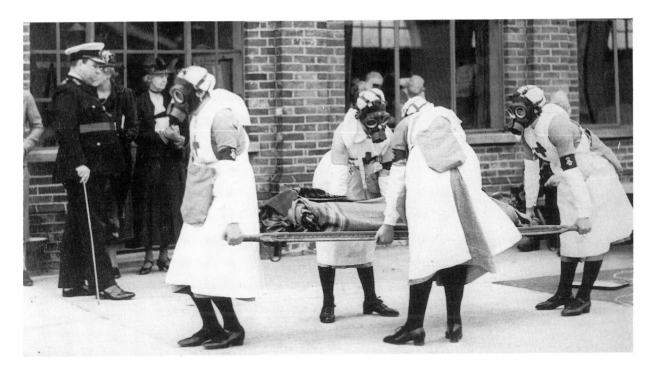

Nurses from the British Red Cross Society are pictured during anti-gas training at Cowes just before the outbreak of war. (IWCC)

boy who had been operated on that day, and he was terribly frightened. At one stage I heard a screaming noise, so I laid on top of him to protect him. It was a German aircraft, which had just skimmed over the roof of the hospital on its way to crashing into the sea.

In July 1946 the Ministry of Health relinquished the Home of Rest, and the Girls' Friendly Society returned it to its pre-war use — the role in which it survives today.

Life at the 'County'

Joan Searle — the former Nurse Matthews — spent the war years as a student nurse at the Royal IW County Hospital, Ryde, the most important of the Island hospitals:

My early memories are of the black-out. The hospital had large wooden shutters, which had also to be used during the day every time the air raid siren sounded, in order to prevent glass breaking and injuring the patients. The ensuing chaos of this operation can be imagined! The sirens always seemed to sound in the middle of blanket-bathing, the

bedpan round or some other activity, causing embarrassment to patients and utter confusion to everything and everyone.

Nurses queued at the kitchen for their weekly rations of butter, margarine and sugar, and one of the big decisions of the week was whether to eat 'all' the butter first, and enjoy it, or mix it with the margarine! Precious clothing coupons had to be used for our uniforms — these were pre-NHS days, of course. Tin hats were provided, but not many seemed to fit very well, and some almost obscured vision by falling over the forehead!

The very busy, tragic night of the Cowes Raid will always live in the memory. Victims lying on the floor, between beds and in the corridors . . . the lights failing, then the emergency generator, and the work continuing with lanterns.

Despite everything, we all found lasting friendships. When money permitted, and it was usually through a pooling of resources, we enjoyed our recreation by attending dances at the Commodore — there was no shortage of partners because of the military stationed on the Island! — and having a cup of coffee (and a bun, if we were lucky) at Beti's in Union Street. They were hectic days, but most of the memories are of a happy comradeship, and are thought of now with much nostalgia.

Medical Miscellany

In 1941 the Island was among the first areas of the country to put into operation the Ministry of Health scheme whereby women were trained for national service as nursing auxiliaries in the Civil Nursing Reserve. The Osborne House Convalescent Home for Officers was offered as a training centre, and the 24 places on the initial course were quickly filled. Thereafter, courses under the experienced guidance of Osborne's Matron were held at fortnightly intervals.

There was something of a two-way traffic in blood to and from the Island. In June 1941, for example, arrangements were being finalised for a visit to the Island of the Emergency Blood Transfusion Service; 'collections' from volunteers were fixed for Ryde, Newport and Cowes. At the same time, the local press recorded that, in the first six months of the year, 250 bottles of plasma had been sent to the Island from Oxford, for distribution among the local hospitals.

The war effort of the British Red Cross Society on the Island knew no bounds. Red Cross women worked tirelessly in an astonishing variety of roles. At one extreme, they could be seen at the wheel of many of the ambulances sent to the scenes of bombing raids. At the other, they were constantly helping the war savings movement by collecting remarkable sums for the Society's Penny-a-Week Fund.

A vital Red Cross contribution, provided in conjunction with the WVS and a number of other voluntary women's organisations, was organisation of the Central Hospital Supply Service from a headquarters depot at Totland Bay. Teams of women, working from local depots in towns and villages throughout the Island, made and dispatched thousands of garments and 'comforts' for use by hospitals and many other institutions and charities. Dressing gowns were the speciality — the ladies at Newport depot were turning them out at the rate of 15 a week early in 1941!

The efficiency of the ARP medical back-up services owed a lot to the training given by members of both the Red Cross and St John Ambulance — and to their active involvement at the air raid sites. Never was this more evident than on the night of the Cowes Raid in 1942. St John sent seven of its ambulance divisions into action to provide much-needed first-aid assistance — and another three to help out in any other way that was deemed necessary.

TWENTY-ONE

War on the Land

A two-word colloquialism dominated the farmers' war on the Isle of Wight. It was the abbreviated title by which each of the all-powerful County War Agricultural Committees throughout the land were soon known – the War Ag. This wartime institution generally served as a shot in the arm for an industry which had been seriously neglected during the inter-war years. Much of the land which had been allowed to become derelict, or had been utilised for livestock, now came under the plough.

Graham Ward farms at Stagwell, in the northwest of the Island. He lived there during the war as a young schoolboy, when the farm was run by his father, and well recalls the impact made by the Island's County War Agricultural Committee:

In order to grow wheat, people were urged to bring under cultivation land they had never ploughed before. At Stagwell, where we had previously never ploughed land at all, we ploughed up about 16 acres. Most of the farms were still in the horse-drawn era at that time; there were very few tractors – I think there were about two in this area. The War Ag had what machines there were and, of course, they made the best use of them, going round and doing work for the farmers, ploughing the land etc. They had the drills, and they helped to bring a lot of land under cultivation; a lot of good crops were grown. We grew what was called 'dredge corn,' a mixture of oats and barley, and that was for our own cows. People were expected at that time to grow as much of their own food as possible.

Farmers were paid a £2 subsidy for every new acre ploughed up. Statistics produced soon after the war by the Ministry of Agriculture show clearly the rapid, and progressive, expansion of cultivated land on the Island. In June 1939, three months before the outbreak of war, the total acreage of arable land was 17,338. A year later,

Men stationed at Nettlestone's anti-aircraft battery augmented their rations by starting up their own small farm nearby! A gunner collects the eggs for tomorrow's breakfast. (IWM)

the figure had grown to 20,745, rising by similar annual margins until it reached 33,536 in June 1944 – practically double the 1939 total. Permanently grassed land (for hay or grazing) decreased by a roughly corresponding amount during the same period – from 41,476 acres in 1939 to 25,916 five years later.

Graham Ward well recalls the visits to Stagwell of the War Ag's thresher:

It was driven by Len Downton, who always had another chap – Frank Draper – with him. You

Ministry of Food advice . . . a June 1943 advertisement from the Isle of Wight Mercury *at Ventnor. (Ron Trodd)*

always needed about seven people at least to run a thresher, and these two were in charge of the crew, who were usually Land Girls. Later, on a couple of occasions, they came instead with German prisoners-of-war. The first time this happened, I remember distinctly going with my mother up into a little bedroom in the farmhouse, from where you can look down the road towards the horse stables. Outside the stables that day were about seven German prisoners, standing in the road.

That was a heart-stopping moment for me! It was always frightening to think of Germans — and there they were, real live ones! I remember some of them had bits of their own uniforms, but mainly they were dressed in British Army khaki which had been dyed a different colour, a sort of purple which came out a dark purple-brown. On the backs of their jackets circular patches of a different colour had been inserted; they also had diamond-shaped patches on their trousers, one on the leg and another on the backside. Mother made them an apple pudding each day they were with us, to supplement their rations, and a young chap, who had served with an E-boat, called to thank her. Whether they would have been so amiable if the boot had been on the other foot, I really don't know.

The Wight Tomato Crop

When the Germans began their occupation of the Channel Islands in July 1940, a vital supply line of food was lost to the United Kingdom. Potatoes and tomatoes had formerly arrived in huge quantities from the growers on Jersey and Guernsey. The Isle of Wight did its bit in making up the shortfall in tomatoes, with the borough council at Ryde setting up an enterprising scheme in the grounds of its waterworks at Knighton. Initially advised and assisted by an expert from Jersey, the council cultivated a large tomato crop there, under the management of the aptly-named George Toms. Dozens of boxes of the fruit were dispatched almost daily in season, mainly to markets in London, providing much-needed food in the capital. At Newport, the borough council turned its recreation ground over to the production of tomatoes.

Loading the crop at the site set up by the Borough of Ryde at Knighton Waterworks for the wartime production of tomatoes. (Raymond Weeks)

Island farmer Charles Holbrook, of Atherfield Green, recalls growing 10,000 plants and sending off around 2) tons of tomatoes per week at the height of the season. "Along with most of the Island's tomatoes, they went to Cardiff for the South Wales miners, or to Newcastle for the Durham miners. This continued, in season, throughout the war."

The Beetle Bombs

The Island increased its potato yield from five tons per acre in 1939 to a 1942 peak of 8.4 tons — almost a ton above the then national average — which put it among the top four potato-growing counties in England and Wales. Perhaps German intelligence had some inkling of this. because, in 1943, the Luftwaffe threatened the entire potato crop on the Island with surely the oddest bombing incident of the entire Second World War.

It was not until 1970 that details of this hushed-up incident were first made public. Richard Ford, an eminent entomologist and zoologist, living at Yarmouth after his retirement from the British Museum, told in newspaper interviews of his involvement with the Germans' attempt to destroy the British potato crop by dropping 'bombs' filled with . . . Colorado beetles! He revealed that the first beetle bomb was dropped in 1943 about one mile north-west of the Island village of Chale:

The whole affair was hush-hush because the Government did not want to cause alarm among the public. We beat the problem with the aid of teams of evacuee schoolchildren. They were pledged not to talk, and then they helped me round up the beetles. It was my duty to destroy them immediately, so I plunged them into boiling water. I still possess a few dried-up specimens as souvenirs.

The bombs were, in fact, rather crude cardboard containers, and I believe the Germans, because of their Teutonic precision, made a big practical error in their approach. We discovered that they dropped the beetles in groups of either 100 or 50, so our beetle hunters knew how many they had to seek out and destroy to overcome any particular attack. I hate to, think what might have happened if they had scattered them indiscriminately.

Mind the Peas!

Islanders dug very seriously for victory. A good example of how seriously is provided by the visit in 1941 of a bomb disposal team to Kite Hill at Wootton to deal with a UXB in a field. The owner was insistent that the bomb squad men should contact him first before locating the bomb, because, they were told, "the fields are ploughed with green peas, which are just through the surface, and the owner is anxious the crop should not be damaged . . ."

The *Isle of Plenty*

Although subject to the same rationing restrictions as the remainder of the country, the Isle of Wight coped rather better than many parts of mainland Britain with the shortages imposed by the war. Indeed, by April 1943, it was coping so well that the national press began carrying prominent stories about "the delightful state of affairs" on what they tagged "the Isle of Plenty." Reporting from Ryde, the *Daily Mail* sought explanations for the apparently abundant supply of everything from fancy cakes to large stocks of pre-utility clothes — and razor baldes!

There were several reasons, including the fact that, when war came in September 1939, the shops had been expecting a further six weeks' holiday trade. They were left with large stocks — but none of the holidaymakers whose pre-war presence had doubled the resident population. Few visitors ventured across the Solent thereafter — and all were banned from April 1942, when the Island became a 'restricted area' in the interests of defence.

An administrative slip-up meant that, in 1943, bakers and confectioners were still allocated sugar based on peacetime holiday consumption, drapers' supplies were similarly estimated on their pre-war orders — and it was still possible to obtain any brand of tobacco or cigarettes in apparently unlimited amounts. But the abundance of food was explained by the industry of the Islanders themselves. "Everybody grows vegetables or keeps chickens or rabbits, and there are pig clubs everyhwere," reported the *Mail.*

The last words fell to the Mayor of Ryde, Alderman Henry Weeks, who told the *Mail's* incredulous reporter that he had had new-laid eggs for breakfast every day for the past two years. He kept 24 hens, nearly 50 rabbits and grew tomatoes. Commented the Mayor: "The Island certainly is an Isle of Plenty, but the people deserve to feed well. We are right in the front line here, visited by sneak raiders almost daily . . . we were determined from the beginning that we should not starve whatever happened.",

TWENTY-TWO

Children at War

Total war is no respecter of age. Several school-children lost their lives in the air raids on the Island, and many others lost their parents, other close relatives or friends. Yet, the war was as exciting as it was dangerous for the youngest members of the Island's then 80,000 resident population. The massive influx of military men and machines was a constant source of fascination, and even the air raids which almost daily threatened the lives of children provided many a boost to that most timelesss of schoolboy hobbies: collecting. Fragments from a wrecked German dive-bomber or an odd-shaped piece of shrapnel made excellent wartime souvenirs.

School, of course, carried on – but with notable variations from the peacetime norm, as Graham Ward. who attended Northwood School, recalls:

We had always to take our gas masks to school, and we had gas mask drill every day. We used to wear them while we walked round the playground, crocodile-fashion, for about five or six minutes. I remember they used to get all steamed up in the eyepiece. There were three big air raid shelters at the school, built partly in the ground and party above it. When the sirens went in the day we had to march in orderly fashion into these shelters.

The headmaster was really keen on gardening. There were already some school gardens, and the more senior boys had gardening lessons and dug their own plots as part of the school curriculum. Then came 'Dig for Victory,' and, when we started having school dinners, in about 1941, the headmaster's idea was to provide as many of the vegetables for them as possible from the school gardens. So the whole lot was turned over to vegetables, and we also had about a third of an acre along Wyatts Lane, about 100 yards from the school, which was planted out with potatoes.

With the tragic exception of Ryde's Bettesworth Road School (and the replacement classroom in St Michael's Church Hall) Island schools were not seriously disrupted by the war. Statistics produced in June 1943 showed that only one, Ventnor's St Boniface Road School, had been evacuated for civil defence use. It was used as a store – mainly by the WVS – and also as a training and recreational base for the Air Training Corps. Out of school, collecting war debris often proved a hazardous pastime – sometimes with tragic results. A seven-year-old Shanklin boy was killed in 1942 when a live missile exploded while he was looking for empty cartridge cases in Hungerberry Copse.

The Evacuees

The schools did, of course, have to absorb a number of mainland evacuees, although nothing like the number originally anticipated, and, in many cases, for only the shortest of stays. While, happily, there were exceptions, the 1939 evacuation generally imposed a great strain on the uprooted city children and, equally, their Island hosts – several of whom welcomed the youngsters into their homes without notice of any kind. Some of the problems are well illustrated in the following accounts from both 'sides' – beginning with the recollections of a Shanklin family whose small hotel was an obvious choice for accomodating the youngsters. Teresa King, a teenager herself at the time, remembers:

We had 14 evacuees – although they had threatened us with 30! Their ages ranged from six to 14, and they were all from Portsmouth. One of the first things that comes to mind is their eating habits. They didn't seem to know anything about what we considered to be good food. All they ever wanted was fish and chips! Their behaviour was a little different, too. I remember seeing two big girls fighting. Just like a couple of cats, they were, all over the floor. I had never seen anything like it in my life . . . it was quite an eye-opener! An elderly couple nearby had two boys billeted with them. They went out to play one day and came home with a bench for the garden. That was a nice gesture − unfortunately, they had taken it from the path overlooking the cliffs!

The traumas suffered by many of the Portsmouth evacuees themselves started on the day they were dispatched by ferry from Southsea's Clarence Pier to Ryde Pier Head. Several of them gave graphic accounts of their horrific experiences to a group of local history enthusiasts gathering material for booklets on wartime life in the city, *Portsmouth at War*, extracts from which are reproduced here:

Evacuee 1, on the arrival at Ryde: "We were herded into trains, and when I say 'herded' I'm not exaggerating − it was absolutely chaotic. There seemed to be no organisation at all . . . the police took charge and led us through, out on to the platform . . . they took 16 children away to fill up a train. I went to protest and tell them they couldn't do that − they were dividing a family of five children. That's as far as I got. For the first and only time in my life. I was frogmarched by two policemen and pushed into the train behind those 16 children. The door was locked behind me so I that I could not get out . . ."

Evacuee 2, on the journey to the reception centres: "We went from Ryde round on the train that goes to Sandown. It stopped at Brading and we all got off; then we all got on again − and then we got out. Then some got on and some were left at Brading. I was among those left. After quite a long time on the station we were walked to the Church of England School. There we were all examined, presumably to see if we were clean and if we had lice or something . . . if they found any with flees or nits, they put a band around their head, and said it had to stay on . . ."

Evacuee 3 (an adult helper), on arrival at temporary initial accomodation: "We arrived at Gurnard Pines Holiday Camp, which was for 240 people − there were 500 of us. The holidaymakers had only gone out

The Mayor of Ryde attends a Christmas party for evacuated children in 1940. In the background (left) is Councillor Alfred Williams, who was killed the following Easter when a German bomb scored a direct hit on his Monkton Street home. (Raymond Weeks)

that morning, and they'd gone out under protest; in fact, the police had had to get them out. They had broken bottles and thrown them into the swimming pool, they'd left half-drunk bottles of whisky and gin all over the place, and they'd smashed the toilets . . . if a child wanted to spend a penny, we had to tell them to go and use the bushes. The whole staff of the holiday camp had walked out, leaving the manageress and her husband there. The kitchens were six inches deep in water."

Evacuee 4 (another adult), on the subsequent movement around the Island: "We went to Yarmouth in a bus, and went into the school hall. Nobody knew where we were going to stay. People just came in and said: 'Well, I'll take that one.' I began to get rather angry . . . there was one poor girl and she'd got some odd complaint, but I knew she was a very good girl and very helpful. So I said: 'Right, if you want a cattle market, we'll have one.' I took this girl and said: 'Now this girl can go to the highest bidder. I know she can do housework, and she's very polite.' Immediately, she was taken . . ."

TWENTY-THREE

Of Spies and Saboteurs

Few people in Sandown knew much about Dorothy O'Grady. Her next-door neighbour in The Broadway was not even aware of her name until the police called in the summer of 1940. The 42-year-old housewife kept herself very much to herself. By the end of that year, however, her name was known throughout the Isle of Wight, and was about to be drawn to the nation's attention as a whole. Dorothy Pamela O'Grady, revealed as an enemy spy, had been sentenced to death.

The strange story of Mrs O'Grady has never been fully told. It probably never will be, since all the evidence produced at her various court appearances was given in camera, with the public excluded, and the long list of charges brought against her − under the Treachery Act, the Official Secrets Act and the Defence Regulations − added very little detail to the publicly-known facts.

Dorothy O'Grady had moved to the Isle of Wight with her husband in the mid-1930s. Mr O'Grady, some 20 years older than his wife, and a former sailor, had just retired from the London Fire Brigade. The couple lived for a time in Lake, then left the Island for a period before returning shortly before the outbreak of war in 1939 to reside at Osborne Villa, in The Broadway at Sandown. When the Luftwaffe bombs began to fall in London, Mr O'Grady responded to an appeal for the city's ex-firemen to return to the service. He was engaged in this work when Dorothy, who had remained on the Island, was first arrested in August. There was never any suggestion that Mr O'Grady knew anything of the alleged activities which were to lead to his wife's death sentence; Dorothy consistently refused to see him following her arrest.

At Sandown, Mrs O'Grady was most often seen taking her black retriever for long walks. It was her persistence in walking into areas to which public access had been banned by the military authorities that aroused suspicions of treasonable intentions. Surveillance was mounted, and sufficient evidence apparently obtained to charge her with offences under the Defence Regulations. Mrs O'Grady was summoned to appear before the County Bench at Ryde in August to answer the charges. When she failed to appear, a warrant was issued for her arrest. She was found staying under an assumed name in the West Wight. When arrested and taken to Yarmouth Police Station, she told officers: "I was too scared to attend."

All we know of the subsequent court proceedings in Ryde on 15 October is that Dorothy O'Grady was committed for trial at Hampshire Assizes. The two-day trial was held at Winchester, in camera, on 16-17 December before Mr Justice Macnaghten, when Mrs O'Grady, defended by Mr J. Scott-Henderson, pleaded not guilty to all nine charges put to her. Among general allegations that, with intent to help the enemy, she had committed acts either designed, or likely, to impede the operations of the British Forces, the charges specifically accused her of approaching a prohibited place (the foreshore); making a plan which might have been useful to the enemy; cutting a military telephone line; and possessing a document with information on defence measures. The offences were alleged to have taken place between various dates in August and September.

It took the trial jury a little over an hour to reach their verdict. Mrs O'Grady was found guilty on seven of the nine counts, including two of the capital charges brought under the Treachery Act. She had nothing to say, and the Judge ("amidst an impressive silence," according to contemporary mnewspaper reports) told her: "On evidence that admitted of no doubt, the jury have found you guilty of treachery. For that crime the law prescribes but one sentence, and it is my duty to pass that sentence upon you." Mr Justice Macnaghten then donned the black cap and sentenced Dorothy O'Grady to be hanged. She listened in silence, and was then led from the court.

Although a number of women had been sentenced to death for similar offences in England during the First World War, none had actually been executed. There was, therefore, considerable public interest throughout the country in the Dorothy O'Grady case. A few days after Christmas the national newspapers were reporting her application to appeal against the death sentence. It was at this point that the Luftwaffe bombers re-entered the story. Documents which would have been used to support the appeal were destroyed in a direct hit on the chambers of her counsel, Mr Scott-Henderson — an unhelpful move by the airmen of the nation Mrs O'Grady was supposed to have been working for.

The appeal was finally held at the Central Criminal Court in London (the Old Bailey) on Monday 10 February 1941 before Lord Caldecote, the Lord Chief Justice, Mr Justice Humphreys and Mr Justice Tucker. Although the hearing was held in camera, an application to permit Mr O'Grady (said by the *Daily Express* to have been "dismayed and astonished" when he heard of the charges against his wife) was allowed. It was the first time he had been in the presence of his wife for months, for her refusal to see him had continued throughout her period in prison on remand. Mr O'Grady heard his wife answer her name from the dock in a quiet, steady voice.

At the conclusion of the judgement, which was delivered in camera, Lord Caldecote announced in open court that the appeal had been successful. He said: "The conviction on the two capital charges under the Treachery Act has been quashed, and sentence has been passed by the Court on charges on which the appellant was convicted, but on which the Judge passed no sentence. This Court has passed a sentence of fourteen years' penal servitude on the counts other than those under the Treachery Act."

So Dorothy O'Grady, spared the hangman's noose, was sent instead to prison for 14 years. She served the full term in Holloway Jail,

O'GRADY NOT TO DIE, GETS 14 YEARS

MRS. O'GRADY, forty - two - year - old British housewife, who was sentenced to death at Hampshire Assizes for treachery, successfully appealed yesterday. The convictions on the capital charges under the Treachery Act and the death sentence were quashed, but she was sentenced to fourteen years' penal servitude on other counts.

Her husband, L.C.C. fireman and ex-sailor, who was dismayed and astonished when he heard of the charges against his wife, was present at her appeal yesterday.

He was present at the Central Criminal Court, and when it was decided to hear the appeal in camera an application for Mr. O'Grady to be admitted was granted.

While she was in prison on remand, Mrs. O'Grady had refused to see her husband.

Dorothy Pamela O'Grady, of Sandown, Isle of Wight, was present in the dock to hear the arguments in support of her appeal. She answered her name in a quiet, steady voice.

Nine Charges

At the conclusion of the judgment, which was delivered in camera, Lord Caldecote announced, in open court:

"The conviction on the two capital charges under the Treachery Act has been quashed, and sentence has been passed by the Court on charges on which the appellant was convicted, but on which the Judge passed no sentence.

"This Court has passed a sentence of fourteen years' penal servitude on the counts other than those under the Treachery Act."

It had been alleged that Mrs. O'Grady, in the Isle of Wight, made a plan likely to be of assistance to the military operations of the enemy, and that, with intent to help the enemy, she cut a military telephone wire.

She answered nine charges under the Treachery Act, the Official Secrets Act and the Defence Regulations.

The Daily Express *reports Dorothy O'Grady's successful appeal against the death penalty in February* 1941. (Daily Express/CCM)

returning to the Island in 1955. Back at Osborne Villa on the day of her return, she was interviewed by Sandown-based journalist Ted Findon for the *Daily Express*. Ted recalls:

I don't think she really wanted to come back – she had had such a good time at Holloway! She was something of a Mother Superior there, a matronly figure looking after the young women in the prison. She was probably regarded as more important than the Governor! As I recall, after her return to Sandown, she ran a sort of bed-sit business from Osborne Villa. As regards her being a spy for the Germans, I am sure she was never that . . .

That is an opinion shared by many people at Sandown. If Dorothy O'Grady was guilty of wartime treachery, she took the reasons for her inexplicable involvement to the grave.

One That Got Away

There were other arrests on the Island of people suspected of helping the enemy – notably, Rose Murphy, who was sent to prison for signalling morse coded messages to German planes from Sandown – but not all of the Island's wartime saboteurs were brought to justice. T.C. Hudson, Chief Planning Engineer at J Samuel White's Somerton Works during the war, recalls one who got away:

We were making airframes, rudder bars,, control columns and various other items for Spitfires, and, in addition to parts for other aircraft, Mosquito engine mountings. The building stood a few hundred yards from where I lived (and still live). One night, after the sirens had wailed, I was about to enter the shelter at home when I saw the door of one of the factory's shelters was open, and a light was showing. I waited, and, after some minutes, the door was closed. The following evening I saw the man in charge of the night-shift and told him what I had seen. He emphatically denied the door was open; he said he had personally shut it. Quite as emphatically, I said I was not mistaken, and, if I saw it again, I would report it to the authorities.

A few days later I was talking to the late W. Backshall, who at that time was in the Inspection Department, working at night. He told me that, although he checked the machines when going on duty, before the night ended he was getting jobs that were faulty. This made him undertake a second check, which showed the machine settings had been tampered with. From then on he checked the machines several times at different intervals. The man to whom I had spoken was responsible for the work done in the machine shop. Mr Backshall and I agreed he was a saboteur. Before we could do anything about it, he had disappeared, never to return.

Appendices

APPENDIX 1

ISLE OF WIGHT AIR RAID STATISTICS

ALERTS
First: 11.55pm – 1.30am, Wednesday 5 June 1940
Final: 7.40pm – 7.52pm, Sunday 5 November 1944
Total number officially recorded: 1,594 (Fred Kerridge: 1,603)

Yearly break-down:
1940 – 350 (351)
1941 – 499 (501)
1942 – 379 (379)
1943 – 231 (233)
1944 – 135 (139)

Day with greatest number: Tuesday 11 March 1941 (9)
Longest sequence of 'alert days': Tuesday 18 March – Sunday 11 May 1941 (55)

RAIDS
First: Sunday 16 June 1940
Final: Friday 14 July 1944
Total number producing attacks on Island: 125

BOMBS (etc)
Number dropped: 1,748 (exploded and unexploded)

Break-down by type:
High-explosive – 1,392
Oil bombs – 20
Parachute mines – 10
V1 flying bombs – 6
Phosphorous bombs – 5
'G' mines – 3
Unexploded bombs – 371
Unexploded 'G' mines – 1

Note: Countless thousands of incendiary bombs were also dropped.

CASUALTIES
Deaths: 214 (92 men, 90 women, 32 children)
Serious injuries: 274
Note: Not including the many people treated at first-aid posts.

DAMAGE
Total number of buildings damaged: 10,873

Break-down by district:
Cowes UDC – 4,821
Borough of Newport – 1,868
Sandown-Shanklin UDC – 1,809
Ventnor UDC – 1,413
Borough of Ryde – 742
Isle of Wight RDC – 220

Destroyed/damaged beyond repair: 552

Break-down by district:
Cowes UDC – 234
Ventnor UDC – 120
Sandown-Shanklin UDC – 83 (almost all at Shanklin)
Borough of Ryde – 60
Borough of Newport – 37
Isle of Wight RDC – 18

APPENDIX 2

TYPICAL ARP AREA ORGANISATION
SANDOWN-SHANKLIN AREA

Area covered: Sandown, Shanklin, Lake, Brading, Newchurch, Alverstone, Godshill.

Report centre: Town Hall, Shanklin.
Alternative: Savoy Hotel, Sandown.

Full-time staff:
Shanklin — LARPO/Sub Controller (Fred Yelf)
           Secretary (1)
           Telephonists (6)
           Drivers (3)
           Wardens (4)
           Caretakers (2)
           Equipment Officer (1)
           M/cycle messengers (2)
Lake —   Wardens (3)
Sandown — Wardens (5)

Rescue parties: 4

Decontamination squad: Shanklin (Hildyards)

Ambulances: Shanklin — 2. Sandown — 1. Brading — 1 (on call)

Sitting case cars: Shanklin — 2.

Rendezvous points:
1. Arthurs Hill/Wilton Park Road, Shanklin
2. Victoria Avenue/Westhill Road, Shanklin
3. Church Road/Popham Road, Shanklin
4. Stag Inn, Lake
5. Wackden's Garage, Sandown

Equipment stores: Shanklin WVS and Hildyards, Shanklin.

Warden's posts:
Shanklin — Town Hall/Napier Garage/Merle Lodge
Lake — opposite Post Office
Sandown — Hawkesworth Road/Savoy Hotel/Tower House
Brading — Town Hall
Newchurch — Church Hall
Godshill — Parish Hall

First-aid post: Home of Rest, Shanklin

Hospital: Home of Rest, Shanklin

First-aid points:
Shanklin — Town Hall
Lake — Church Hall
Sandown — Town Hall
Brading — Church Hall
Newchurch — Church Hall
Godshill — Parish Hall

Gas cleansing stations:
Shanklin — Wilton Park Laundry and Hildyards (Personnel)
Sandown — Grafton Lane

Clothing decontamination: Wilton Park Laundry, Shanklin

Start-up: February 1938

Stand-down: 2 May 1945

APPENDIX 3

COUNTY INVASION COMMITTEE

COMPOSITION (*as at May* 1943):
Lord Mottistone (Major-General Jack Seely), Lord Lieutenant of Hampshire and the Isle of Wight; Sir Godfrey Baring, Chairman of the Isle of Wight County Council; The Senior Military Commander, Isle of Wight; R.G.B. Spicer, Chief Constable, Isle of Wight; Mrs S.C. Needham, County Organiser, Women's Voluntary Service; P.E. White, Clerk to the IW County Council / County ARP Controller.

Special representatives for the rural areas:
Lieutenant-Colonel W.A. Murray (East Wight); Lieutenant-Colonel A. de Lande Long (Wootton and Central); A.A.H. Wykeham (West Wight).

Other emergency officers:
Brigadier-General H.E.C. Nepean, Emergency Communications Officer; S.G. Ball, County Leader, Works and Planning Emergency Organisation; R. Preston, Food Command Liaison Officer; J. Selwyn Jackson, District Transport Officer, Ministry of War Transport; D.A. Marshall, Assistance Board Officer, Isle of Wight.

WARNINGS — *of invasion:*
1. Preliminary Warning: The enemy has made preparations which suggest an intention to invade in the near future. (For personal attention; no overt action).
2. Stand To: The enemy's preparations are completed, and conditions are particularly favourable for invasion. (For action within Army Commands specified in the message — the Isle of Wight was in Southern Command. Key officers recalled from leave; district invasion committees mobilised in readiness).
3. Action Stations: Invasion of England. (County and district invasion committees in continuous session; emergency procedures in force; liaison with military authorities).

WARNINGS — *of enemy airborne/seaborne raids:*
1. Expect Bugbear: The codeword Bugbear may be issued shortly. (Home Guard will not be mobilised).
2. Bugbear: Raid is imminent. (Home Guard may be mobilised).
3. Bugbear — Stand Down: Revert to normal state of readiness.

APPENDIX 4

TYPICAL DISTRICT INVASION COMMITTEE

Extracts from the Ryde Invasion Committee War Book (as at May 1943**):**

DISTRICT COVERED:
Borough of Ryde and certain areas outside borough boundaries (HQ: Ryde Town Hall. Alternative HQ: Basement, Ryde Police Station).

COMPOSITION:
The committee, chaired by the Mayor (with the Deputy Mayor serving as Deputy Chairman), also comprised the following office-holders: Chairman, Ryde Food Control Committee (and Communal Feeding Sub-Committee); O/C 'A' (Ryde) Company, Home Guard; O/C Troops in Ryde; Police Inspector; ARP Officer; Medical Officer of Health; Company Officer, Ryde National Fire Service; Town Clerk and Food Executive Officer; Chairman, Ryde Public Health and Evacuation Committee; Fire Guard Staff Officer; Emergency Information Officer; Sub-Committee Chairmen (4); Ryde Centre Organiser, WVS. A further 31 names of officers or organisations – including public utility undertakings – were listed as being "concerned with the Ryde Invasion Committee." Mr Edwin Sheppard, the Assistant Town Clerk, served as Clerk to the Committee.

AREA SUB-COMMITTEES:
1. Havenstreet (HQ: School House).
2. Fishbourne and Kite Hill (HQ: Alteens, Wootton Bridge).
3. St Helens (HQ: ARP Post).
4. Seaview and Nettlestone (HQ: Watson's Estate Agency, Seaview / ARP Post, Seaview).
Note: There was also an Information and Publicity Committee, with an After-Raid Sub-Committee.

EMERGENCY FEEDING:
1. British Restaurants (2, accomodating 400 people at each).

2. Rest Centres (accomodating 1,370 in total; at Commodore Cinema, Star Street (with adjoining Unity Hall); Congregational Hall, Melville Street; Methodist Schoolroom, Well Street; St John's Parish Hall, Oakfield; Horsenden, Corbett Road; Weston Hut, Oakfield; Ryde Town Hall; The Cedars, West Hill Road; East Hill, Ashey Road; Methodist Schoolroom, Binstead; Methodist Schoolroom, Havenstreet; Church Hall, Seaview; Mission Hall, St Helens).

3. Emergency Feeding Centres (accommodating 2,200 in total; at Squadron Hotel, Union Street; Royal Victoria Yacht Club, St Thomas's Street; Young's Cafe, Union Street; Central School, St John's Road; London Hotel, Swanmore Road; Haylands Manor Stables, Corbett Road; Weston Cafe (British Restaurant), St John's Hill; Gassiott School, Oakfield; Ryde School, Queen's Road).

4. Mobile Canteens (5 – 2 WVS; 3 IW County Council, stationed at Newport).

AIR RAID SHELTERS:
1. Public shelters (with accommodation) were listed at: Atlantic Hotel (92); Lion Hotel (55); Hanover House, George Street (50); London Hotel (50); Ashey Road (50); Barfield House (100); 3, 8, 9 Brigstocke Terrace (150); Barton's Yard, High Street (50); Elephant & Castle (105); Star Inn (50); 1, 2 Sydney Terrace (100); 3, 4 Sydney Terrace (100); Western Esplanade (50); Quay Road (50); Lind Place (50); Victoria Street (50); Winton Street (50); Dover Street (50); Royal Spithead Hotel, Bembridge (100).

2. School shelters: Bettesworth Road (180); St John's Road Junior (240); CE Junior, Player Street, and RC Warwick Street (270); St John's Road Central (300); CE Senior, Green Street (100); Oakfield CE Boys (120); Oakfield CE Girls (100); Oakfield CE Infants (110); Havenstreet Council (80); Binstead CE Junior (90); Nettlestone Council (90); St Helens CE, Nettlestone (120); St Helens Council (100); Bembridge CE (150); School of Art, George Street (100).

DISPOSAL OF DEAD:
1. Mortuaries (with accommodation) were listed at: Ryde Cemetery (20); Madeira, Somerset Road (25); Royal IW County Hospital (5).

2. Emergency mortuaries: Congregational Chapel schoolroom, Marlborough Road (30); Congregational Church schoolroom, George Street (50); Congregational Chapel schoolroom, Haylands (25); Chapel schoolroom, junction of High Street and Well Street (100); Parish Hall, St John's Hill, Oakfield (50); Lower Green Methodist Chapel schoolroom, St Helens (40); St Peter's Church Hall, Seaview (100); Methodist Chapel schoolroom, Binstead (30); Methodist Chapel vestry and store, Havenstreet (20).

ANTI-GAS:
Public Cleansing Stations were listed at Milligan Road and the Town Hall, with a third, for Civil Defence personnel, at the Town Yard, Monkton Street. Clothing and equipment decontamination would be undertaken at St Helens Laundry, Carpenters Road, while Carter's stables at East Upton had been earmarked for use as a Food Treatment Centre (there was a fully-trained and equipped six-strong volunteer Food Decontamination Squad). The Town Yard would handle the decontamination of both roads and vehicles.

APPENDIX 5

SEARCHLIGHT BATTERIES IN THE ISLAND
(Showing complement as at August 1941)

WEST: 392 Battery / 48 Searchlight Regiment RA:
(Battery HQ, Northwood: 80 personnel)

Cowes (F Troop): 38
Gunville (F Troop): 30
Sainham (G Troop): 48
Mottistone (G Troop): 40
Hamstead (H Troop): 48
Little Thorness (H Troop): 9
Middleton (I Troop): 50

EAST: 391 Battery / 48 Searchlight Regiment RA:
(Two troops only on Isle of Wight)

Ashey (B Troop): 41
Foreland (B Troop): 41
Wootton (C Troop): 28
Ryde Golf Course (C Troop): 9

Notes: All sites equipped with Lewis guns and rifles. Other searchlights were operated by Coast Artillery − notably on the sea forts.

APPENDIX 6

WARSHIPS BUILT AT COWES 1939-45

Names and completion dates of all vessels constructed in wartime for Royal Navy by J. Samuel White's shipyard at Cowes:

HMS *Shearwater* (Patrol Vessel) 7/9/39
HMS *Jersey* (Destroyer) 28/4/39 *
HMS *Kingston* (Destroyer) 18/9/39 *
HMS *Havant* (Destroyer) 4/1/40 *
HMS *Havelock* (Destroyer) 22/2/40
HMS *Quorn* (Escort Vessel) 20/9/40 *
HMS *Southdown* (Escort Vessel) 8/11/40
HMS *Abdiel* (Minelayer) 15/4/41
HMS *Krakowiak* (Escort Vessel) 28/5/41 ø
HMS *Puckridge* (Escort Vessel) 30/7/41 *
HMS *Southwold* (Escort Vessel) 9/10/41 *
HMS *Tetcott* (Escort Vessel) 11/12/41
HMS *Grey Goose* (Steam Gunboat) 4/7/42
HMS *Quentin* (Destroyer) 15/4/42 *
HMS *Quiberon* (Destroyer) 22/7/42 ‡
HMS *Quickmatch* (Destroyer) 30/9/42 ‡
HMS *Easton* (Destroyer) 7/12/42
HMS *Eggesford* (Destroyer) 21/1/43 ☆
HMS *Stevenstone* (Destroyer) 8/3/43
HMS *Talybont* (Destroyer) 19/5/43
HMS *Stord* (Destroyer) 6/9/43 □

HMS *Swift* (Destroyer) 6/12/43 *
HMS *Sioux* (Destroyer) 5/3/44 ¢
HMS *Volage* (Destroyer) 26/5/44 ‡
LCT 3 (Tank Landing Craft) 1/4/44
HMS *Cavalier* (Destroyer) 22/11/44 ƒ
HMS *Carysfort* (Destroyer) 20/2/45
HMS *Contest* (Destroyer) 9/11/45 †

KEY:
* vessels sunk during war years
ƒ Royal Navy's fastest ship as late as 1971
† world's first all-welded destroyer
ø Polish-operated in war; later HMS *Silverton*
□ *Norwegian-operated in war; later sold to Norway*
¢ *Canadian-operated in war*
‡ *later converted to A/S frigate*
☆ *later sold to Federal German Navy; renamed Bronmy*

Note: A total of 21 submarine 'kills' (16 German U-Boat and 5 Italian) were credited to Cowes-built warships during the war − some with assistance from other vessels.

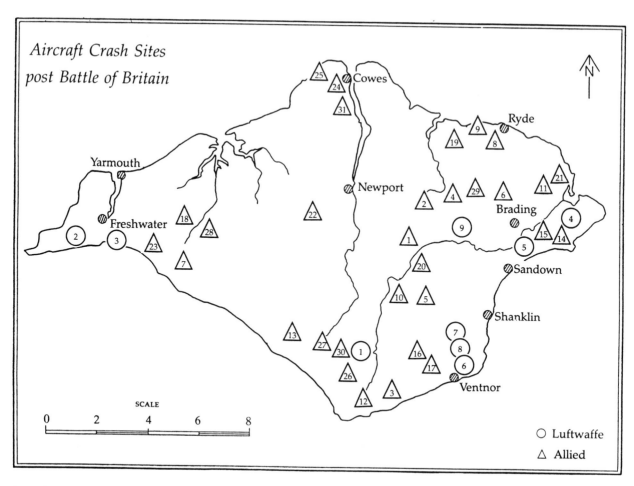

Map showing location of post-Battle of Britain aircraft crash sites on the Island.

Allied crash sites: 1 Hurricane V6627 – Near Haseley; 6 November 1940. 2 Hurricane R4177 – Duxmore; 6 November 1940. 3 Hurricane P2924 – St Lawrence; 7 November 1940. 4 Hurricane P2683 – Ashey Down; 7 November 1940. 5 Spitfire N3242 – Rill Farm; 28 November 1940. 6 Blenheim V5396 – Brading Down; 22 December 1940. 7 Blenheim V5396 – Brook; 22 March 1941. 8 Hurricane BD940 – Haylands; 22 November 1941. 9 Hurricane Z3899 – Binstead; 22 November 1941. 10. Swordfish DK691 – Near Godshill; 20 April 1942. 11 Spitfire AR377 – Rowborough Farm; 10 June 1942. 12 Spitfire AD504 – St Lawrence; 10 June 1942. 13 Spitfire EN965 – Atherfield; 17 June 1942. 14 Gladiator K7985 – Culver; 28 July 1942. 15 Gladiator L8030 – Culver; 28 July 1942. 16. Spitfire BR186 – Stenbury Down; 1 November 1942. 17. Spitfire BR174 – Stenbury Down; 1 November 1942. 18. Halifax W7768 – Eades Farm, Newbridge; 20 December 1942. 19 Ventura (u/i) – Eleonor's Grove, Binstead; 21 January 1943. 20 Spitfire (u/i) – Near Newchurch; 5 May 1943. 21. Typhoon DN303 – St Helens; 29 May 1943. 22 Typhoon JP844 – Garstons Farm, Newport;

5 November 1943. 23 P38 Lightning (u/i) – Compton Down; 27 November 1943. 24. P51 Mustang FD508 – Somerton Aerodrome; 2 December 1943. 25 P38 Lightning (u/i) – Near Gurnard; 31 December 1943. 26 Albermarle V1711 – St Catherine's Down; 13 March 1944. 27 B26 Marauder (u/i) – Near Kingston; 12 May 1944. 28 Typhoon N735 – Near Calbourne; 7 June 1944. 29 A20 Havoc (u/i) – Ashey; 7 June 1944. 30 Spitfire MJ219 – Near Chale Green; 11 June 1944. 31 Tiger Moth – Somerton Aerodrome; 14 September 1944

Luftwaffe crash sites: 1 He 111 6N+HL – The Hermitage, Whitwell; 10 April 1941. 2 He 111 1G+CC – Farringford, Freshwater; 8 May 1941. 3 Ju 88 7T+JH – Wellow Down; 30 May 1941. 4 Ju 88 4D+CH – Bembridge Down; 24 July 1941. 5 Bf 109 Blue 4+ – Yaverland; 27 May 1942. 6 Ju 88 M2+FH – Wroxall Copse; 19 August 1942. 7 Ju 88 4U+GH – St Martin's Down; 25 August 1942. 8 Do 217 U5+GP – St Martin's Down; 7 February 1943. 9 BF 109 (u/i) – Newchurch Brading area; 16 August 1943

Note: u/i denotes unidentified aircraft

APPENDIX 7

THE CRASHES

Total Allied crashes on the Isle of Wight − 47

Yearly break-down:
1940 − 22
1941 − 3
1942 − 9
1943 − 7
1944 − 6

Break-down by type:
Albermarle − 1
Anson − 1
Battle − 1
Blenheim − 2
Gladiator − 2
Halifax − 1
A20 Havoc − 1
Hurricane − 14
P38 Lightning − 2
B26 Marauder − 1
P51 Mustang − 1
Spitfire − 13
Swordfish − 1
Tiger Moth − 1
Typhoon − 3
Ventura − 1
Unidentified − 1

Total Luftwaffe crashes on the Isle of Wight − 19

Yearly break-down:
1940 − 10
1941 − 4
1942 − 3
1943 − 2

Break-down by type:
Dornier Do 217 − 1
Heinkel He 111 − 2
Junkers Ju87 − 1
Junkers Ju88 − 5
Messerschmitt Bf 109 − 7
Messerschmitt Bf 110 − 3

Note: These lists do not include the large number of German planes lost in the sea surrounding the Island. (See map for crash sites).

APPENDIX 8

OPERATION PLUTO

The strategic importance of the Isle of Wight to the war effort was prominently underlined by its role in Operation PLUTO (Pipeline Under the Ocean) during the build-up to D-Day in 1944. It was the ultimate link this side of the Channel in the network of pipelines and pumping stations, originating at the tanker ports on the Mersey and Bristol Channel, through which the oil to fuel the Allied advance flowed − and the departure point for its subsequent journey to France.

Construction work on the buried link across the Island from the cross-Solent (SOLO) pipeline terminal at Thorness to Shanklin was hidden from the public view by large camouflage netting, while, at Shanklin Lift and Sandown Granite Fort, the seafront pumping stations for dispatching the precious fuel to Cherbourg were well-guarded and cleverly concealed from both the Luftwaffe and inquisitive locals, who might have forgotten that careless talk really could cost lives at that vital juncture of the war.

Those residents who had not already been forced out of their Shanklin Esplande homes by the Luftwaffe found they were now required to vacate their premises in the interests of national security. The bomb-scarred appearance of the seafront certainly helped to conceal the PLUTO installations, but the pipeline's route to the sea via Shanklin Pier − passing over the anti-invasion gap which still existed in the neck − was more difficult to hide.

In the event, PLUTO did not prove an immediate success. Sea-to-shore connections presented problems, and it was not until late September that fuel pumping from Sandown Bay was able to start. Thereafter, some 56,000 gallons were pumped daily under the Channel. To service the Allied advance as it moved along the French coast, PLUTO was later extended by the laying of pipelines to Boulogne − and, eventually, as far as the Rhine − from Dungeness, in Kent, enabling the amount of fuel passing daily across the Channel to rise to one million gallons. By VE-Day in 1945, PLUTO had delivered 72 million gallons to the Allied forces. The hardware was later salvaged, with virtually all the 23,000 tons of lead in the pipes recovered for peacetime uses.

A 65-yard section of pipeline that was left alone can still be seen today in its original position within the grounds of Shanklin Chine − on the last part of the wartime route from the TOTO reservoir in Hungerberry Copse to the seafront pumping stations.

Bibliography

Books and Pamphlets

Adams, R.B.: *Red Funnel . . . and Before* (Kingfisher Railway Productions, 1986).

Air Ministry (Air Historical Branch): *The Second World War — Royal Air Force: Signals Volume Four* (1950).

Allen, Wing Cdr H.R.: *Who Won the Battle of Britain?* (Arthur Baker, 1974).

Allen, P.C./MacLeod, A.B.: *Rails in the Isle of Wight* (George Allen & Unwin, 1967).

Bray, Peter/Brown, Fay: *The Ventnor Area at War 1939-45* (Ventnor Local History Society, 1989).

Britton, Andrew: *Once Upon a Line — Volume Two* (Oxford Publishing Company, 1984).

Cantwell, Anthony: *Fort Victoria 1852-1969* (IW County Council Cultural Services, 1985).

Cantwell, Anthony/Sprack, Peter: *The Needles Defences* (The Redoubt Consultancy, 1986); *The Needles Batteries* (Cantwell & Sprack, 1982). *Puckpool Battery* (The Redoubt Consultancy).

Chamberlin, E.R.: *Life in Wartime Britain* (B.T. Batsford, 1972)

Colvin, Ian: *The Chamberlain Cabinet* (Victor Gollancz, 1971)

Cotton, Geoffrey: *Fifty Years of Yarmouth (IW) Lifeboats* (IW County Press, 1974)

Cox, Richard: *Operation Sea Lion* (Thornton Cox)

Darwin, Bernard: *War on the Line* (First published 1946; Reissued by Middleton Press, 1984).

Davies, Ken: *Solent Passages and their Steamers* (IW County Press, 1982).

Dear, Ian: *The Royal Yacht Squadron 1815-1985* (Stanley Paul & Co., 1985)

Devine, A.D.: *Dunkirk* (Faber & Faber, 1944)

Dixon, June: *Uffa Fox: A Personal Biography* (Angus & Robertson, 1978).

Fleming, Nicholas: *August 1939 — The Last Days of Peace* (Peter Davies, 1979)

Fox, Uffa: *More Joys of Living* (Nautical Publishing Company, 1972)

Hyland, Paul: *Wight: Biography of an Island* (Victor Gollancz, 1984).

Jones, Jack and Johanna: *The Isle of Wight — An Illustrated History* (The Dovecote Press, 1987)

Ladd, J.D.: *Assault at Sea 1939-45* (David & Charles, 1976).

Lampe, David: *The Last Ditch* (Cassell, 1968).

London, Peter: *Saunders and Saro Aircraft Since 1917* (Putnam, 1988)

Messenger, Charles: *The Commandos* (William Kimber, 1985).

Mitchell, Garry/Cantwell, Anthony/Cobb, Peter/Sprack, Peter: *Spit Bank and the Spithead Forts* (G.H. Mitchell, 1988)

Morris, Eric: *Churchill's Private Armies — British Special Forces in Europe 1939-42* (Hutchinson, 1986)

Newman, Richard: *Southern Vectis — The First 60 Years* (Ensign Publications, 1989).

Parker, Alan: *Shanklin between the Wars* (A.G. Parker, 1986).

Philpott, Bryan: *German Bombers Over England* (Patrick Stephens, 1978)

Porter, D.R. 'Jack': *I Remember . . . Looking Back 80 Years* (D.R. Porter, 1983).

Price, Alfred: *Luftwaffe Handbook 1939-45* (Ian Allan, 1977)

Quigley, D.J.: *Princess Beatrice's Isle of Wight Rifles — A Regimental History* (D.J. Quigley, 1976).

Roskill, Captain S.W.: *History of the Second World War — The War at Sea Volumes One & Two* (HMSO).

Sandown-Shanklin UDC: *Sandown-Shanklin Urban District Council 1933-1974* (1974)

Shores, Christopher: *Duel for the Sky* (Blandford Press, 1985)

Tute, Warren/Costello, John/Hughes, Terry: *D-Day* (Sidgwick & Jackson, 1974).

Watson, Captain R.C.: *Annals of a Bembridge Lifeboatman* (R.C. Watson, 1951)

Watt, Ian A: *A History of the Hampshire and Isle of Wight Constabulary 1839-1966* (Hants & IW

Constabulary, 1967)
WEA (Portsmouth Branch) Local History Group: *Portsmouth at War Volumes One and Two* (WEA).
White, J. Samuel Ltd: *White's of Cowes* (1953).
Winter, C.W.R.: *The Manor Houses of the Isle of Wight* (The Dovecote Press, 1984)

Newspapers and Periodicals

Daily Express.
Daily Mail.
Daily Mirror.
Isle of Wight Chronicle.
Isle of Wight County Press.
Isle of Wight Guardian.
Isle of Wight Mercury.
Isle of Wight Times.
Southern (Daily) Evening Echo.
The (Evening) News Portsmouth.
British Legion Journal (November 1938)
FlyPast (July 1989).
War in the Air (August 1989)
Yesterday in Hampshire, Sussex & Isle of Wight (June 1989).

Original Sources

Public Record Office (Kew): War Diaries — WO 166/917, 1067, 3236, 4145, 11209. Fort Record Books — WO 192/129, 130, 131, 133, 134, 281, 282, 283, 284, 285, 286, 287, 288, 289, 290.
Isle of Wight County Record Office: ARP (Isle of Wight) Log Books 1939-1944 Volumes 1 to 13 (6 and 12 missing). Sandown Home Guard records.
Carisbrooke Castle Museum: *Notes for The Island at War exhibition* (A.L. Hutchinson, 1974) and associated documents (including war production records of J. Samuel White's and Saunders-Roe; Sandown-Shanklin ARP records; Ministry of Defence Naval Historical Branch records; and Ministry of Agriculture statistics for World War 2).
Nunwell House Home Guard Museum: Original documents — 20th (Nunwell) Battalion HG.
Tangmere Military Aviation Museum, West Sussex: Display material relating to Battle of Britain.
Royal Air Force Museum, Hendon: Documents, plans etc relating to World War 2 radar installations on Isle of Wight.
Imperial War Museum: Various World War 2 material.
Others: Borough of Ryde Invasion Committee *War Book*. Fred Kerridge air raid log books 1940-1944. Mary Watson diaries 1938-45.

Selected Index

to people and places